MONROE COLLEGE LIBRARY

WIT   D0327179   LIBRARY

Demystifying the
GLOBAL
ECONOMY

Demystifying the
GLOBAL
ECONOMY

A Guide for Students

David E. O'Connor

GREENWOOD PRESS
Westport, Connecticut • London

HC
54
.O26
2002

Library of Congress Cataloging-in-Publication Data

O'Connor, David E. (David Edward)
  Demystifying the global economy : a guide for students / David E.
O'Connor.
    p.   cm.
  Includes bibliographical references and index.
  ISBN 0–313–31863–8 (alk. paper)
  1. Economic history—20th century. 2. Globalization. I. Title.
HC54.O26   2002
337—dc21   2001054709

British Library Cataloguing in Publication Data is available.

Copyright © 2002 by David E. O'Connor

All rights reserved. No portion of this book may be
reproduced, by any process or technique, without the
express written consent of the publisher.

Library of Congress Catalog Card Number: 2001054709
ISBN: 0–313–31863–8

First published in 2002

Greenwood Press, 88 Post Road West, Westport, CT 06881
An imprint of Greenwood Publishing Group, Inc.
www.greenwood.com

Printed in the United States of America

The paper used in this book complies with the
Permanent Paper Standard issued by the National
Information Standards Organization (Z39.48–1984).

10 9 8 7 6 5 4 3 2 1

Copyright Acknowledgments

The author and publisher gratefully acknowledge permission for the use of the following material:

"The Global Sullivan Principles of Corporate Social Responsibility," by Reverend Leon H. Sullivan. Reprinted by permission of the International Foundation for Education and Self-Help (IFESH).

"The Case for Globalisation," *The Economist*, September 23, 2000, pp. 19–20. © 2000 The Economist Newspaper Group, Inc. Reprinted with permission. Further reproduction prohibited. www.economist.com.

"NGOs: Searching for Solid Ground," by Candido Grzybowski, *The UNESCO Courier*, September 2000, pp. 35–36. Reprinted by permission of *The UNESCO Courier*.

"Lessons from East Asia and Eastern Europe," *Entering the 21st Century: World Development Report 1999/2000* (New York: Published for the World Bank, Oxford University Press, 2000), p. 17. Reprinted with permission of the World Bank.

"Freedom and Economic Growth," *Freedom in the World: The Annual Survey of Political Rights and Civil Liberties, 2000–2001* (New York: Freedom House, 2000). Reprinted by permission of Freedom House, Inc.

"Trade, Poverty, and the Human Face of Globalization," speech by Mike Moore at the London School of Economics, June 16, 2000. Reprinted by permission of the World Trade Organization.

"Terms and Conditions of Work," from the Summary of *ILO Tripartite Declaration of Principles Concerning Multinational Enterprises*. Copyright © International Labour Organization. Reprinted by permission of the International Labour Organization.

"Platform Summary," *50 Years Is Enough* (www.50years.org). Reprinted by permission of 50 Years Is Enough: US Network for Global Economic Justice.

"On the Threshold: Projects for Accelerating Human Development in the 21st Century," by Ruth Kagia, *UN Chronicle* 4 (2000–2001), pp. 21–22. Reprinted by permission of the United Nations Department of Public Information.

"A Necessary Choice," *The State of the World's Children: 2001* (New York: UNICEF, 2001), pp. 31–32. Reprinted by permission of UNICEF.

"Report of the United Nations Conference on Environment and Development" (Rio de Janeiro, June 3–14, 1999). Posted online by the United Nations Department of Economic and Social Affairs (DESA). Copyright © 1999 United Nations.

"Adopting a Human Perspective" and "What Is an Ecosystem Approach?" *World Resources 2000–2001: People and Ecosystems, the Fraying Web of Life* (Washington, DC: World Resources Institute, 2000), pp. 10–11, 226. Reprinted by permission of the World Resources Institute.

"Is the 'Population Explosion' Over?" by Lori Ashford, *Population Bulletin* 56, 1 (March 2001). Reprinted with permission of the Population Reference Bureau.

"A World Together," by Erla Zwingle, *National Geographic* 196, 2 (August 1999), pp. 12–13, 16. Reprinted by permission of the National Geographic Society.

Editorial cartoons are reprinted by permission of syndicated cartoonist Bob Englehart and the *Hartford Courant*.

Contents

Preface   ix

Acknowledgments   xiii

Common Abbreviations in the Global Economy   xv

Timeline of Key Events in the Global Economy: 1900–2002
and Beyond   xix

The Global Economy Explained   1

1   The Global Economy: An Introduction   3

2   International Trade: Spinning the Web, Part 1   29

3   Multinational Corporations: Spinning the Web, Part 2   55

4   Gaps in the Global Web: The "Have" and "Have Not"
Countries   83

5   A Planet at Risk: Global Challenges for the
Twenty-First Century   113

Primary Documents on the Global Economy   139

Glossary of Selected Terms   185

Annotated Resource Guide   199

Index   215

Preface

The global economy is an abstract term, but at its core is the existence of the vast network of economic relationships among over 200 countries. The global economy deals with how goods and services are produced, consumed, and exchanged in domestic and international markets. It is also concerned with financial transactions in capital markets, cross-border mergers and acquisitions of companies, greenfield investments, and currency trading in foreign exchange markets. Over the past 150 years, the conduct of business in the global economy has swung like a pendulum between two poles—from highly integrated global markets on the one hand to fragmented and disjointed markets on the other. This book explores these shifts between integration and isolation, the functioning of global economy today, and globalization's effects on the quality of life for billions of people in the contemporary world.

This work provides a variety of material for student researchers and interested readers. A list of "Common Abbreviations in the Global Economy" is included to help untangle the web of organizations, groups, institutions, and economic vocabulary from the ADB (Asian Development Bank) to the WTO (World Trade Organization). The "Timeline of Key Events in the Global Economy: 1900–2002 and Beyond" traces major economic, scientific, cultural, and political factors that have influenced the fits and starts of the globalization pendulum. This timeline gives a yearly account of forces that have often fueled, and sometimes derailed, the globalization juggernaut over the past century.

Five focused chapters follow the frontmatter. These chapters use current examples and cases, statistical data organized into tables and graphs, and editorial cartoons to connect each topic to the real world. The first chapter, "The Global Economy: An Introduction," establishes a foundation for the book. It examines how government policies and technology nurtured a more integrated world economy during the first great age of globalization during the nineteenth and early twentieth centuries, and again during the second great age of globalization during the post–World War II era. The second chapter, "International Trade: Spinning the Web, Part 1," focuses on the role of trade in linking the global community. It highlights the roles of regional trade organizations such as the European Union, international organizations such as the WTO, and foreign exchange markets in deepening global interdependence. It also presents controversies related to trade, including claims of unfair trade practices, the reality of trade imbalances, and protectionism. The third chapter, "Multinational Corporations: Spinning the Web, Part 2," concentrates on the role of foreign direct investment (FDI) as an agent for economic integration. This chapter contrasts the two types of FDI—mergers and acquisitions and greenfield investments—and examines the main reasons for the phenomenal growth of FDI in recent years. It also discusses controversial business practices of multinationals in the global economy and the changing perception of corporate social responsibility in terms of workers' rights, environmental protection, and relationships with indigenous peoples. The fourth chapter, "Gaps in the Global Web: The 'Have' and 'Have Not' Countries," explores the deep economic rifts between the developed (the global North) and the developing (the global South) countries. Glaring disparities between the nations of the North and South exist in virtually all realms of the global economy—production and consumption, trade and investment, financial investments in capital markets, technology, and so on. The chapter stresses the importance of sustainable economic development and explains how this goal is supported by international organizations, investments in nations' productive resources, and good governance. The fifth chapter, "A Planet at Risk: Global Challenges for the Twenty-First Century," more closely examines the main stresses on the global economy, including those related to the environment, energy, overpopulation and poverty, the global financial architecture, the North-South digital divide, cultural homogenization, and international terrorism. It also ponders the question of economic equity in global markets.

The "Primary Documents on the Global Economy" is a collection of fifteen source readings that represent the views of scholars, international organizations, nongovernment organizations (NGOs), and governments. The introduction to each document provides important background information about the document's author or sponsoring institution and the topic. Most of the documents present and defend a point of view. For instance, "The Case for Globalisation" (*The Economist*) argues persuasively that the benefits of highly integrated global markets far outweigh the costs. "Freedom and Economic Growth" (Freedom House) makes a compelling case for expanding political freedoms and liberties as a way to promote economic growth and development. And "50 Years Is Enough: Platform Summary" (50 Years Is Enough) makes an impassioned plea for meaningful reform of the global financial architecture to promote economic justice throughout the world. These documents also examine critical issues and problems in the global economy. For example, "NGOs: Searching for Solid Ground" (*UNESCO Courier*) focuses on the growing role of NGOs in the global economy. Other documents deal with financial crises ("Lessons from East Asia and Eastern Europe," World Bank), workers' rights ("Terms and Conditions of Work," International Labor Organization), corporate social responsibility (*The Global Compact. The 9 Principles*, United Nations), children's rights ("A Necessary Choice," UNICEF), the environment (The World Resources Institute Adopts an Ecosystem Approach to Managing the World's Resources), overpopulation ("Is the 'Population Explosion' Over?" Population Reference Bureau), and cultural homogenization ("A World Together," *National Geographic*).

Finally, the book includes two handy reference tools. The first is an extensive "Glossary of Selected Terms." This usable glossary explains important economic terms and organizations associated with the global economy. An "Annotated Resource Guide" of recommended books and pamphlets and audiovisual and electronic resources will steer readers toward other timely resources in the realm of global economics. The brief annotations focus readers' attention on how each source might be used to research selected topics.

Readers of this book will likely be awed by the progress of the globalization juggernaut, which is traveling at a pace and on a scope unparalleled in human history. Yet, readers will also wonder whether its pillars—freer trade, FDI, and capital market flows—are built on bedrock or sand. The supportive technological footings on which these pillars rest seem solid. After all, what has been discovered cannot suddenly be undiscovered. But the policies governing the use of modern technologies—and the conduct of business in global markets—are ever shifting. The globalization process, which has moved in fits and starts for the past 150 years, is evidence enough that changes in government policies can change the direction of the global economy.

How far will the globalization pendulum swing in the twenty-first century? Alas, the crystal ball is somewhat murky on this point. However, one thing is certain: people's current decisions will influence the path of globalization. Globalization is not an end in itself, but rather a means to an end, namely, a more prosperous and secure world for all people. Thus, the success of globalization cannot be measured solely by statistics on trade, investment, and capital flows. Instead, there is a growing consensus that an expanded economic pie can result in an improved quality of life for all people. By 2050, the population of the world is expected to climb by another 3 billion people, and nearly all of this growth will occur in the poorer nations. Globalization has already contributed to higher economic growth rates and economic development in some countries. But in a world polarized by wealth, technology, and other factors, the central challenge is how to invite the mass of humanity to globalization's feast.

Acknowledgments

The author would like to thank the following individuals for their assistance in preparing this book: Melissa Emero, of Copyright Clearance Center, Inc., for her help in seeking some permissions; Linda Mathes, Jane White, Donna Haddad, and Peter Salesses of the Edwin O. Smith High School Library Media Center for technical assistance; Len Hebert and Bob Viara for their help in producing the charts and graphs; the entire Government Publications research staff at the Homer Babbidge Library (University of Connecticut, Storrs, CT) for their research support; and Barbara A. Rader, Executive Editor at the Greenwood Publishing Group, for her encouragement, advice, and guidance.

Common Abbreviations in the Global Economy

ADB	Asian Development Bank
ADB Group	African Development Bank Group
APEC	Asia-Pacific Economic Cooperation (group)
ASEAN	Association of Southeast Asian Nations
BITs	bilateral investment treaties
CARICOM	Caribbean Community and Common Market
CEE	central and eastern Europe
CIS	Commonwealth of Independent States
COMECON	Council for Mutual Economic Assistance
COMESA	Common Market for Eastern and Southern Africa
CSD	Commission on Sustainable Development
DAC	Development Assistance Committee
DOE	Department of Energy (U.S.)
DOW	Dow Jones Industrial Average
DSB	Dispute Settlement Body (WTO)
EBRD	European Bank for Reconstruction and Development
EC	European Community
ECB	European Central Bank
ECOSOC	Economic and Social Council (UN)
ECOWAS	Economic Community of West African States
ECSC	European Coal and Steel Community Treaty

EEA	European Economic Area
EEC	European Economic Community
EFTA	European Free Trade Association
EMU	European Monetary Union
EPA	Environmental Protection Agency (U.S.)
EU	European Union
FAO	Food and Agriculture Organization (UN)
FDI	foreign direct investment
FSAP	financial sector assessment program
FSC	foreign sales corporation
FTAA	Free Trade Area of the Americas
G-8	Group of Eight (countries)
G-7	Group of Seven (industrialized countries)
G-20	Group of Twenty (countries)
GATT	General Agreement on Tariffs and Trade
GDP	gross domestic product
GNP	gross national product
GSP	Generalized System of Preferences
HDI	Human Development Index
HIPC	Heavily Indebted Poor Countries (Initiative)
IBRD	International Bank for Reconstruction and Development (World Bank)
ICPD	International Conference on Population and Development
ICSID	International Center for Settlement of Investment Disputes
ICT	information and communications technologies
IDA	International Development Association
IDB	Inter-American Development Bank (Group)
IFC	International Finance Corporation
IFI	international financial institution
ILO	International Labor Organization
IMD	International Institute for Management Development
IMF	International Monetary Fund
INGOs	international nongovernmental organizations
IT	information technologies
ITO	International Trade Organization
LDCs	least developed countries

M&As	mergers and acquisitions
MEA	multilateral environmental agreement
MERCOSUR	Common Market of the South
METI	Ministry of Economy, Trade and Industry
MFN	most-favored nation (status)
MIGA	Multilateral Investment Guarantee Agency
MITI	Ministry of International Trade and Industry
MNC	multinational corporation
NGO	nongovernmental organization
NAFTA	North American Free Trade Agreement
NTA	New Transatlantic Agenda
NYSE	New York Stock Exchange
ODA	official development assistance
OECD	Organization for Economic Cooperation and Development
OFC	offshore financial center
OPEC	Organization of Petroleum Exporting Countries
PPP	purchasing power parity
PRB	Population Reference Bureau
PRGF	Poverty Reduction and Growth Facility
R&D	research and development
ROSC	report on the observance of standards and codes
RTA	regional trade agreement
SAP	structural adjustment program
SAR	Special Administrative Region
SDR	Special Drawing Rights
TNC	transnational corporation
TRIPS	Trade-Related Aspects of Intellectual Property (agreement)
UN	United Nations
UNCTAD	United Nations Conference on Trade and Development
UNDP	United Nations Development Program
UNEP	United Nations Environmental Program
UNESCO	United Nations Educational, Scientific, and Cultural Organization
UNFPA	United Nations Population Fund
UNICEF	United Nations Children's Fund
USSR	Union of Soviet Socialist Republics

WEF	World Economic Forum
WHO	World Health Organization
WTO	World Trade Organization

Timeline of Key Events in the Global Economy: 1900–2002 and Beyond

1903   Orville and Wilbur Wright pioneer flight at Kitty Hawk, North Carolina

1913   Henry Ford employs the moving assembly line in automobile production

1914   World War I breaks out in Europe, paralyzing global trade and investment

1919   The League of Nations is formed

The International Labor Organization (ILO) is formed to protect workers' rights

1920   The first commercial radio station in the United States, KDKA, begins its broadcasts

1923   The Union of Soviet Socialist Republics (USSR) is formally established

1929   The Stock Market crash signals the beginning of the Great Depression in the United States

1930   Most of the industrialized world sinks into a global economic depression

The Smoot-Hawley Tariff is passed in the United States, severely restricting foreign trade and touching off trade wars

The world population hits 2 billion people

1939   World War II erupts in Europe, crippling the global economy

1941   The Freedom House is founded in the United States

1942   Research begins at the University of Pennsylvania on a large electronic computer, the Electronic Numerical Integrator and Calculator (ENIAC)

1943   IBM invents the Mark 1 computer, but has little interest in developing computers commercially

1944   The Bretton Woods Conference is held in New Hampshire, creating the International Monetary Fund (IMF) and the International Bank for Reconstruction and Development (IBRD)—the World Bank

   The fixed exchange rate system is established

1945   The United Nations (UN) is created

   The United Nations Educational, Scientific, and Cultural Organization (UNESCO) is founded

   World War II ends in Europe (May) and Asia (September)

1946   The ENIAC is completed

   The ILO joins the UN system

   The "iron curtain" divides the East from the West, and the Cold War begins

   The Electronic Control Company becomes the first U.S. computer firm

1948   The General Agreement on Tariffs and Trade (GATT) is created

   The Marshall Plan provides massive U.S. aid to war-torn Europe

   The World Health Organization (WHO) is formed

1949   The People's Republic of China is established under Mao Zedong

   The Council for Mutual Economic Assistance (COMECON) is founded

1951   The European Coal and Steel Community (ECSC) Treaty begins European economic integration

1955   The International Finance Corporation (IFC) is formed and is added to the World Bank Group

1957   The Rome treaties create the European Economic Community (EEC) and the European Atomic Energy Community (Euratom)

1959   The Inter-American Development Bank (IDB) Group begins operations

1960   The European Free Trade Association (EFTA) is formed

   The Organization of Petroleum Exporting Countries (OPEC) is founded

   The International Development Association (IDA) is formed and is added to the World Bank Group

1961   The Organization for Economic Cooperation and Development (OECD) is founded

1964   The African Development Bank (ADB) Group begins operations

1966   The Asian Development Bank (ADB) begins operations

Telstar begins the age of satellite communications

1969   The Internet is created as an "internetworking of networks"

1971   The Generalized System of Preferences (GSPs) is implemented

The World Economic Forum (WEF) is founded (originally called the European Management Forum until its name changed in 1987 to the WEF)

1972   The United Nations Environmental Program (UNEP) is formed

E-mail (electronic mail) is created

The Freedom House begins annual rankings of countries based on level of freedom

1973   A flexible exchange rate system replaces the fixed exchange rate system

The Caribbean Community and Common Market (CARICOM) is formed

1975   The Economic Community of West African States (ECOWAS) is founded

The Group of Seven (G-7), comprising the seven leading industrialized nations, is formed

The Microinstrumentation and Telemetry Systems company produces the first commercially viable personal computer

Bill Gates founds the Microsoft company

The world population climbs to 4 billion people

1977   A global consumer boycott of Nestlé products erupts over the sale of instant baby formula in developing countries

Fiber optics technology enables light-wave communications

Modems are invented to transmit computer data over telephone lines

1983   The first intercity communications route using fiber optics is established

1984   Toxic fumes released from Union Carbide's Bhopal (India) fertilizer plant kill thousands, increasing calls for more corporate social responsibility

1986   The nuclear accident at the Chernobyl (USSR) nuclear power plant kills thousands, increasing calls for more corporate social responsibility

1987   The Montreal Protocol targets ozone-depleting substances

1989   Poland becomes the first Soviet bloc nation to elect a noncommunist government

The massive oil spill by the *Exxon Valdez* off the coast of Alaska devastates local ecosystems and renews calls for corporate responsibility

The Agreement on a Global System of Trade Preferences is adopted

The Asia-Pacific Economic Cooperation (APEC) Group is founded

The World Wide Web is invented by Tim Berners-Lee

1990   A *Human Development Index* is introduced by the United Nations Development Program (UNDP) to measure progress toward sustainable economic development

1991   The USSR is dissolved

COMECON is disbanded

The Commonwealth of Independent States (CIS) is formed

The European Bank for Reconstruction and Development (EBRD) is founded

1992   The Rio Conference generates *Agenda 21*, a plan for global development

Framework Convention on Climate Change creates targets for reducing greenhouse emissions

1993   The Maastricht Treaty creates the European Union (EU)

The EU Cohesion fund devotes billions of dollars to reduce economic disparities among member nations

1994   The European Economic Area (EEA) creates a single market for EU and EFTA nations (only Switzerland votes not to join the EEA)

MERCOSUR, the Common Market of the South, is formed

The Marrakesh meeting concludes the GATT Uruguay Round, and creates the World Trade Organization (WTO) to replace GATT

The Western Hemisphere is introduced to the idea of a free trade area for the thirty-four nations of North and South America

The North American Free Trade Agreement (NAFTA) takes effect

The International Conference on Population and Development takes place in Cairo, Egypt

1995   The WTO officially replaces GATT

The New Transatlantic Agenda (NTA) creates stronger partnerships between the United States and the EU

25,000 nongovernmental organizations (NGOs) operate globally

The Trade-Related Aspects of Intellectual Property (TRIPS) agreement is implemented

1996   The Heavily Indebted Poor Countries (HIPC) Initiative is launched by the IMF and the World Bank

        The Helms-Burton Act strengthens the U.S. embargo on Cuba

1997   Hong Kong becomes a Special Administrative Region (SAR) of China

        A global consumer boycott of Nike is called to protest sweatshop working conditions in some of the company's overseas plants, mainly in Asia

        The East Asian financial crisis begins (1997–1998)

        The Kyoto Protocol targets greenhouse gases and global warming

1998   Foreign exchange trading hits $1.5 trillion per day

        The Group of Eight (G-8) is formed by including Russia along side the G-7 countries

        The ILO announces its "Declaration of Fundamental Principles and Rights at Work"

        The Russian financial crisis begins (1998–1999)

1999   The European Central Bank (ECB) begins operations

        Macao is returned by Portugal to China

        The Poverty Reduction and Growth Facility (PRGF) is established

        The Millennium Round of trade negotiations stalls at the WTO's ministerial conference in Seattle, Washington

        The Treaty of Amsterdam paves the way for an EU enlargement

        The euro is introduced as the EU's common currency

        The Global Compact is adopted by the United Nations

        The Global Sullivan Principles of Corporate Social Responsibility are introduced by the Reverend Leon H. Sullivan

        The "banana war" trade dispute erupts between the United States and EU

        The Group of Twenty (G-20) is created to promote inclusion in global decision making

2000   Foreign direct investment (FDI) in the global economy tops $1 trillion

        120 countries have democratic governments

        The volume of international trade reaches $7.6 trillion

        China moves from its low-income status to lower-middle-income status

        The U.S. merchandise trade deficit of $449 billion is a new record

        63,000 multinationals operate in the global economy

        Nearly 1,900 bilateral investment treaties (BITS) are in effect

Official development assistance (ODA) by Development Assistance Committee (DAC) nations drops from $56 billion (1999) to $53 billion in 2000

The world population hits 6 billion people

2001   The Summit of the Americas (Quebec City) gains preliminary agreement for the creation of a thirty-four-nation Free Trade Area of the Americas (FTAA)

The United States and the EU quietly settle the banana war

The Ministry of Economy, Trade, and Industry (METI) replaces the Ministry of International Trade and Industry (MITI) in Japan

Capital flight continues to drain $10 to $20 billion annually from Russia

The U.S. economy, with a nominal gross domestic product (GDP) of over $10 trillion, remains the world's dominant economy

China is selected to host the 2008 Summer Olympics

China is admitted to the WTO

Terrorist attacks on New York City and Washington, DC slow international trade and FDI

2002   The euro replaces the national currencies of the twelve EU countries that belong to the European Monetary Union (EMU)

WTO membership stands at 144 countries

THE FUTURE

2005   An EU enlargement may add six countries to this free trade area including Cyprus, the Czech Republic, Estonia, Hungary, Poland, and Slovenia

Target date for the founding of the FTAA

2009   The controversial Three Gorges Dam in China is scheduled for completion

Target date for the announced EU pledge to expand trade preferences for the world's forty-eight poorest nations

The Global Economy Explained

1

The Global Economy:
An Introduction

WHAT IS THE GLOBAL ECONOMY?

The term "*global economy*" conjures up many images. To some, it points to a future of unlimited economic opportunities and unparalleled prosperity. This view touts the benefits of an interdependent world—a world bound together by free trade, responsible foreign investment, enlightened transnational organizations, advanced technologies, and democratic governments. To others, the global economy is equated with an inexorable spread of unregulated capitalism that has run amuck. This view warns of a future of inescapable dependencies—a world where people and countries are subservient to the will of powerful multinational corporations (MNCs) and global institutions, where the exploitation of human and natural resources is the norm, and where cultural homogenization replaces the planet's rich diversity.

So how then should we define the global economy? The most objective approach is to focus on the features, rather than on the anticipated consequences, of the global economy. Here, there is greater consensus. Broadly speaking, the "global economy" is defined as an international web of individuals, firms, transnational organizations, and governments that make production and consumption decisions. Let's explore the most important factors that spin the web called the global economy.

Technology is one key factor that has revolutionized the way business is done in the global economy. In particular, innovative information and communications technologies (ICTs) have created a more integrated world, linked by computers, the Internet, communications satellites, telephones, and so on. ICTs permit people to store, process, and transmit enormous quantities of information to a global audience. In fact, the blinding speed of technological advances in ICTs is such that in 2001 more information could "be sent over a single cable in a second than in 1997 was sent over the entire Internet in a month."[1] Similarly, transportation technologies such as supersonic airlines, supertankers, automobiles, and high-speed rail transport have linked people and places as never before. In short, new ICTs have provided individuals and businesses with instance access to markets across town or across the world.

Multinational corporations (MNCs or multinationals) are a second important feature of today's global economy. *MNCs* are firms that own and operate production facilities in more than one country. They connect the world's economies in two main ways. First, they invest heavily in foreign countries, a process called foreign direct investment (FDI). By the 1999, the value of assets owned by multinationals in foreign countries was nearly $18 trillion according the United Nations Conference on Trade and Development (UNCTAD). In the late 1990s and early 2000s, much of investment by multinationals involved cross-border mergers or acquisitions of existing firms. Second, by the close of the twentieth century multinationals produced and sold $13.5 trillion dollars worth of products and employed over 40 million workers through their foreign affiliates.[2] Thus, multinationals play a major role in both production and consumption decisions on a global level.

Transnational organizations, a third essential ingredient in the global economy, are formal groups that are designed to deal with global issues or problems through collective action. Most transnational organizations are composed of representatives selected by member governments. Transnational organizations have grown in size and power, especially since World War II. Today, for example, the "Big Three" transnational economic organizations—the *International Monetary Fund* (IMF), the *World Bank* (IBRD), and the *World Trade Organization* (WTO)—have tremendous influence on economic relations between countries. The IMF helps countries stabilize the value of their currencies and promotes macroeconomic stability. The World Bank extends loans, mainly to poorer countries, to fund development projects. The WTO oversees trade relations among countries and supports freer trade in the global economy. Other important transnational organizations that deal with global or regional economic issues include the United Nations (UN), regional development banks, and regional trade organizations. On a more grassroots level, nongovernmental organizations (NGOs) coordinate the actions of people across national borders to achieve common goals.

Governments, which have generally supported global integration of markets, represent a fourth important force in today's global economy. Governments have strengthened the economic web of cross-border business activity in three important ways. First, most governments have accelerated trade liberalization—the movement toward freer trade—in global markets. This is accomplished by reducing or eliminating trade barriers (such as import tariffs and quotas), granting universal access to the Internet (e-commerce), and pledging to adhere to international rules governing fair cross-border exchanges. Most countries have also become willing partners in multilateral trade organizations such as the WTO, or regional trade blocs such as the European Union (EU) or the North American Free Trade Agreement (NAFTA). Second, governments have supported FDI, which increased fivefold between 1990 and 2000. Incentives such as tax breaks serve to attract cross-border investments by multinationals, as do bilateral investment treaties (BITs)—which have grown by 400% over the past twenty years. Third, governments have supported freer capital market flows. Capital markets deal in financial assets such as stocks, bonds, or other financial securities. Many restrictions on cross-border financial investments in capital markets have been dropped in recent years, and new communications technologies in global capital markets have made these investments both profitable and volatile. (For more on capital market volatility, see the discussion on the East Asian crisis later in this chapter.)

GLOBALIZATION AND THE GLOBAL ECONOMY

The term "global economy" refers to the international web of individuals, firms, transnational organizations, and governments that make production and consumption decisions. A closely related term is "*globalization*," which is often used to describe the process by which the global economy becomes more integrated and interdependent. In this economic context, globalization stresses the expansion of the three main types of cross-border business activity—international trade, FDI, and capital market flows. It also extols the virtues of modern capitalism such as private ownership and control of resources and production facilities, high-tech methods of production, and the mass consumption of goods and services.

Yet globalization, in its broadest sense, also integrates people's political and cultural identities with those of the larger global community. In this broad context, globalization has taken on a distinctly Western orientation. That is, many of the most basic features of a more globalized world are taken from American and European traditions. This reality is not particularly surprising since the United States and west European countries are among the most highly industrialized and prosperous nations of the world. Politically, globalization favors the protection of human rights and democracy over totalitarianism. Culturally, globalization affects people's tastes in the arts and encourages lifestyles that are fast-paced, urban, and comfortable with the latest technologies. The mass media, which includes television, radio, print sources, and now the Internet, tends to reenforce the globalization process through program content, advertising, and the limitless access to information over the Internet.

At the heart of the global economy today is *economic globalization*. Most economists and philosophers view globalization primarily through an economic lens. Even with this common lens, there is no universally accepted definition of economic globalization. Economist Richard C. Longworth writes:

I define globalization as the creation of a global economy. More specifically, it is a revolution that enables any entrepreneur to raise money anywhere in the world and, with that money, to use technology, communications, management, and labor located anywhere the entrepreneur finds them to make things anywhere he or she wants and sell them anywhere there are customers.[3]

Edward Luttwak offers an even more colorful definition of globalization. According to Luttwak, "globalization [is] the much-celebrated unification of the puddles, ponds, lakes and seas of village, provincial, regional and national markets into a single economic ocean."[4]

For our purposes, "economic globalization" refers to a deliberate movement by individuals, MNCs, transnational organizations, and governments to increase the flow of goods, services, people, real capital, and money across national borders, in order to create a more integrated and interdependent world economy. In fact, because economic globalization is so intertwined with the global economy some economists use these terms almost interchangeably. Let's briefly examine the history of globalization to see what's new about the new global economy.

HOW *NEW* IS THE NEW GLOBAL ECONOMY?

The term "globalization" came into common usage during the 1990s, but most economists today concede that many of the basic elements of a global economy were present much earlier in history. For example, economic globalization during the nineteenth and early twentieth centuries created a highly integrated world economy. At the center of this effort to globalize the world economy was Great Britain, which aggressively sought trade and investment opportunities in the Americas, Africa, Asia (particularly India and China), Australia, and New Zealand. Pivotal in establishing Great Britain's leadership role in the emerging global economy was the repeal of the Corn Laws in 1846—an action that removed trade restrictions on the import of foreign grains. In reality, the repeal of the Corn Laws gave birth to Britain's free trade policies. Britain was also successful in industrializing its economy and in maintaining enormous commercial and military fleets to facilitate an orderly exchange of resources and finished products in global markets.

From the mid-1800s to the outbreak of World War I in 1914, Great Britain and other major European powers such as France and Germany created webs of economic and political alliances within and between their respective empires. In a very real sense, modern globalization was born during this period. At times, these economic relationships were mutually beneficial. For example, massive British investments in the American railroad industry during the late 1800s enabled the United States to build this critical feature of its economic infrastructure. At other times, Britain and other major powers forced trade or foreign investments on unwilling partners. Such was the case in China during the 1840s and 1850s when Britain's superior military power compelled China to open its doors to trade, cede Hong Kong to Britain, and accept a British military presence in the country.

EARLY TECHNOLOGIES OF THE GLOBAL ECONOMY

The development of new technologies during the eighteenth and nineteenth centuries—particularly advances in transportation and communications—stimulated the globalization process. Revolutionizing transportation was the application of the steam engine—a technology that was pioneered by James Watt and John Wilkinson in the 1760s to 1780s—to transport by land and sea. The steam-powered railroad locomotive, which was invented by George Stephenson in 1825, increased the mobility of people, resources, and products in Great Britain. Rail lines were laid to link the commercial centers of the country, and the relatively inexpensive rail transportation quickly replaced slow and more costly transport by cart and draft animals. Other industrializing nations, including the United States, quickly followed Britain's lead. By 1867, the United States had completed a transcontinental railroad that spanned North America.

The steam engine was also applied to water transportation during the late eighteenth and early nineteenth centuries. As early as 1783, French inventor Claude Jouffroy d'Abbans successfully tested steam-powered paddle wheels on steamboats. Americans John Fitch (1790) and Robert Fulton (1807) pioneered the commercial use of steamboats to transport passengers and freight on rivers—most notably on the Mississippi River. This paddle wheel technology was useful in linking local economies, but was impractical for rougher sea travel. In the late 1860s, however, more powerful and seaworthy screw propellers—again powered by the steam engine—were installed on larger commercial ships. By the 1870s, these steamships had made wind-powered sailing ships obsolete. Steam powered locomotives and ships had made the movement of goods and people faster and cheaper and, in doing so, strengthened the global economic web that the Europeans were weaving.

At about the same time in history, technological advances in the realm of communications were linking people and places that had long been separated by geography. One key innovation of the early nineteenth century was the telegraph, a device capable of sending a message over a wire using electrical current. The first commercial use of the telegraph occurred in 1837 when William F. Cooke and Charles Wheatstone installed a functional telegraph in England. In 1838, Samuel F. B. Morse developed a sophisticated electromagnetic receiver and a signaling code—called Morse code—to facilitate long-distance communication. Combined, these inventions gave birth to modern long-distance communications. In fact, in 1858 the first transatlantic telegraph cable had been installed, connecting Newfoundland with Ireland. And while this first attempt to connect North America and Europe failed soon after the cable was laid, a functional transatlantic cable was in place by 1866. Other developments in communications quickly followed, including Alexander Graham Bell's invention of the telephone (1876) and Guglielmo Marconi's successful experiments in wireless communication—and the birth of radio (1895)—as we entered the twentieth century.

THE NEW GLOBAL ECONOMY STALLS

The political upheavals and economic chaos of the 1914–1945 period temporarily slowed the globalization juggernaut to a snail's pace. The twentieth century's global wars—World War I (1914–1918) and World War II (1939–1945)—struck directly at the foundations of the emerging global economy. These wars disrupted international trade, discouraged FDI, and diverted resources from the production of consumer and investment goods to the production of military hardware. Ultimately, these global wars caused the deaths of millions of people, destroyed much of the infrastructure of the warring countries, and contributed to the collapse of countries and empires. Furthermore, the most important global institution of the 1920s and 1930s—the League of Nations—faltered as international tensions mounted. Founded in 1920 to promote international peace and prosperity on a global level, the League was all but abandoned by its sixty-three member nations as the clouds of war gathered over Europe and Asia by the late 1930s. In effect, World War I and World War II focused people's attention on conflict rather than on international cooperation.

A further erosion of the global economy resulted from the severe global depression of the 1930s. An economic *depression* is a prolonged economic downturn characterized by a reduction in the country's gross domestic product (GDP), low domestic and international investment, a high rate of unemployment, massive business failures, and a generalized despair by both consumers and producers. This global downturn, which was called the Great Depression in the United States, caused countries to limit the movement of people, goods and services, and money across national borders. For example, countries erected high trade barriers, such as import tariffs and import quotas, to protect domestic producers from lower-priced foreign imports. The Smoot-Hawley Tariff (1930), which increased U.S. tariffs by 60% on average, was designed to protect domestic firms and jobs. The results were devastating for the American economy, however, as the volume of U.S. trade promptly dipped by one-half. The Smoot-Hawley Tariff had also touched off a trade war, as other nations retaliated with higher tariffs and quotas of their own. Today, many economists agree that the severity of the global depression of the 1930s resulted, in large measure, from the misguided trade restrictions imposed by countries.

THE BRETTON WOODS CONFERENCE: THINKING GLOBALLY (THE CREATION OF THE IMF AND THE WORLD BANK)

The Bretton Woods Conference was convened in July 1944 in Bretton Woods, New Hampshire. While representatives from forty-four countries participated in the conference, it was clear from the start that the dominant players would be the United States and the United Kingdom. The delegates to the conference were keenly aware of the destructive effects of trade wars on the global economy, as evidenced by the collapse of international trade in the early 1930s. Still reeling from the ravages of the global depression of the 1930s and the ongoing destruction of World War II, the delegates laid the foundation for a more stable postwar international monetary system. Two major global institutions were created at the conference: the IMF and the World Bank.

The IMF officially came into existence in December 1945 and began operations in the spring of the following year. The overriding goals of the IMF, in 1946 and today, are to stabilize the global economy and to promote economic development. Over the past half-century, the IMF has worked to accomplish these goals through a set of three policies: surveillance, technical assistance, and financial assistance. Surveillance involves active monitoring of countries' policies to promote stable currencies. Technical assistance refers to the expert advice that is provided in the realms of tax policies, the creation of financial institutions, and currency stabilization. The IMF's financial assistance takes the form of loans to help nations pay for their imports, to make payments on foreign debts, or to stabilize currencies that are losing value. In recent years, some IMF policies have been controversial—especially those related to the IMF's structural adjustment programs (SAPs), which list the conditions for receiving IMF assistance.

The World Bank provides loans for development projects throughout the world. In the 1940s, its work focused on providing loans and other assistance to reconstruct war-torn Europe. Since the 1950s, however, it has been most concerned with promoting economic development in the developing countries. To achieve this overriding goal, the World Bank has been joined by four affiliated institutions. Collectively, the World Bank and its affiliates are called the *World Bank Group*. These affiliates include the *International Development Association* (IDA), which makes long-term low-interest loans called "credits" to the poorest countries; the *International Finance Corporation* (IFC), which loans money to private firms in developing countries; the *Multilateral Investment Guarantee Agency* (MIGA), which encourages foreign investment in developing countries; and the *International Center for Settlement of Investment Disputes* (ICSID), which mediates financial disputes between foreign investors and host countries.

FROM THE GATT TO THE WTO

Shortly after the successful Bretton Woods Conference concluded, delegates from eighteen nations met in Geneva, Switzerland (1947), to negotiate another international agreement—this time to promote freer and fairer international trade. The result of these negotiations was the General Agreement on Tariffs and Trade (GATT) which was formally approved by the United States and twenty-two other countries in 1948. Dropped from the original plans, however, was a proposal to create a new international organization—the International Trade Organization (ITO)—to administer and enforce the principles of GATT. Opposition to the creation of the ITO stemmed from some countries' unwillingness to compromise on sovereignty issues. That is, opponents feared that a powerful international organization to monitor and enforce trade rules among nations would impinge on the authority of national governments. Despite this setback, the GATT provided a forum for open multilateral discussions of trade issues and established trade principles that laid the foundation for freer and fairer trade among countries.

So how did GATT's four main principles promote freer international trade? First, it required that *most-favored-nation* (MFN) status be granted to all member countries. Under the MFN principle, any trade concession granted by one member to another would automatically apply to all GATT members. Second, GATT members were expected to reduce or eliminate most nontariff trade barriers. Third, reporting of tariffs or other trade barriers was required. That is, GATT members that imposed temporary tariffs or other trade barriers were required to admit that barriers existed. Fourth, the equal treatment principle guaranteed that countries would treat imported goods in the same way as domestically produced goods.

By the early 1990s, many countries believed that a stronger institution was needed to expand on and enforce the negotiated rules of international trade. In 1994, at a GATT meeting in Marrakesh, Morocco, 125 GATT members signed an agreement that established a new and stronger institution called the World Trade Organization (WTO).

When the WTO began operations in 1995 it, unlike the GATT, had clear procedures for hearing and ruling on trade disputes. The WTO was also given authority to expand on GATT's central mission, which had traditionally supported trade in manufactured goods, by also supporting freer and fairer trade in services (banking, securities, telecommunications, insurance, and so on), agricultural products, and intellectual properties (books, computer software, recordings, and so on). By January 2002, the WTO had 144 members and a waiting list of about two dozen countries.

INTERNATIONAL TRADE: STRENGTHENING THE GLOBAL MARKETPLACE

International trade is another force that strengthens the economic ties among countries in the global economy. *International trade* occurs when individuals, firms, or governments import or export goods or services. Imports are the products that are purchased from other nations, while exports are the products sold to other nations. In 2000, the WTO reported, the volume of international trade had grown to $7.6 trillion.

Why do nations trade? In part, international trade is desirable because it increases the availability of goods and services to consumers. Without much effort you could probably identify many goods in your home that were produced abroad. For instance, where was your television, VCR, and discman produced? Have you ever checked the labels on your clothing? How many articles of clothing do you own that were manufactured in a different country? And did you have time for a cup of cocoa, tea, or coffee for breakfast this morning? These goods are also imported from countries such as Ghana (cocoa), India (tea), and Brazil (coffee). Without question, consumers would have fewer choices if trade did not exist.

So why don't nations simply produce all of the goods and services that they need in their own economies? The most direct answer to this question is that the distribution of resources in the world is uneven. Hence, to produce efficiently nations must specialize in the production of goods best matched to their available resources. For example, we know that the economy of Saudi Arabia is based on the production of petroleum and that it does not produce large quantities of wheat, corn, or other foods. Why? The answer is self-evident. Saudi Arabia's available resources include the world's largest underground reserves of crude oil. It lacks sufficient arable land for large-scale agriculture, however. As a result, it has chosen to specialize in the production of oil, and not the production of corn. Other nations, such as the United States, have bountiful fertile soil, a favorable climate, and a highly skilled agricultural workforce capable of producing enough corn for domestic needs and for export to other countries. Not surprisingly, the United States is the world's leading producer of corn.

Specialization has promoted the efficient use of resources, international trade, and a level of economic interdependence unparalleled in human history. The meteoric rise in the volume of international trade since World War II has been assisted by international agreements, such as the GATT; international organizations, such as the IMF and the WTO; the end of the Cold War and the rise of democratic governments; and advanced ICTs.

REGIONAL TRADE ORGANIZATIONS

Regional trade organizations, sometimes called trade blocs, also contribute to a more integrated global economy. A *regional trade organization* is an economic alliance that promotes freer trade among member countries. To achieve the goal of freer trade, regional trade organizations typically reduce or eliminate tariff and nontariff trade barriers and encourage FDI within the economic region.

The largest, most powerful, and most integrated regional trade organization in the world today is the European Union (EU). Founded in 1993 by the Maastricht Treaty, the EU replaced the twelve-member European Community (EC)—a regional trade organization that had focused mainly on eliminating trade barriers among its member nations. In 2002, the EU comprised fifteen countries, including Austria, Belgium, Denmark, Finland, France, Germany, Greece, Ireland, Italy, Luxembourg, the Netherlands, Portugal, Spain, Sweden, and the United Kingdom. Six additional countries—Cyprus, the Czech Republic, Estonia, Hungary, Poland and Slovenia—are currently on the fast track to join the EU by 2005 or 2006. Other regional trade organizations were also at work to integrate the economies of member countries, including NAFTA, the Common Market of the South (MERCOSUR) in South America, the Association of Southeast Asian Nations (ASEAN), and the Economic Community of West African States (ECOWAS).

Regional trade organizations have, at times, been accused of restricting trade with nonmember countries, however. In one highly celebrated case in 1999, the United States accused the EU of restricting banana imports by U.S. firms operating in Central America. While the

WTO agreed that the EU restrictions on banana imports were illegal and ordered the EU to drop the restrictions, the EU staunchly refused. It wasn't until the spring of 2001 that the so-called banana war between the EU and the United States was resolved. In 1999, the EU also banned the import of hormone-treated beef from the United States and Canada, claiming that the beef constituted a health hazard to European consumers. Again, the WTO sided with the United States and again the EU refused to drop the ban. While regional trade organizations promote regional integration and prosperity in member countries, the danger of excluding others from the international feast is a very real challenge to the new global economy.

MNCs: SEEKING PROFITS IN THE GLOBAL ECONOMY

For centuries, MNCs have woven an intricate economic web to produce, transport, and sell their output in the global economy. MNCs, by definition, operate production facilities in more than one country. To operate in foreign countries, MNCs have built new production facilities, merged with existing firms in the host country, or acquired foreign firms. Thus, through construction, mergers, and acquisitions, they supply some of the glue that binds the global economy together. And this type of investment, usually called FDI, has accelerated in recent years—topping $1 trillion in 2000.[5]

There are a number of reasons why corporations choose to invest in other countries, but all have the same bottom line—profit. MNCs, like other businesses, exist to earn profits. How does investing in other countries help them increase their profits? The answer is by decreasing the costs of production or by increasing total revenues, or by doing both. Multinationals can cut production costs in four main ways:

- Controlling essential resources: Multinationals, like other firms, need a reliable supply of resources to produce goods or services. During the early twentieth century, the Aluminum Company of America (Alcoa) invested heavily in foreign countries to gain control of bauxite, the essential ingredient in its product line (aluminum). More recently, the DeBeers company of South Africa has invested in other countries to solidify its control over raw diamonds.

- Using less expensive resources: MNCs' investments in some countries is based on the availability of low-cost resources, particularly labor resources and natural resources. FDI by Nike and its subcontractors, for example, has created production facilities in Indonesia, the Philippines, Thailand, Vietnam, and in other low-wage nations to lower production costs.

- Avoiding costly business regulations: MNCs sometimes reduce production costs by locating in developing countries, which typically have fewer regulations on business activities. For example, there are relatively few environmental laws regulating mining operations in Indonesia, oil drilling in Nigeria, logging in Southeast Asia, or plantation agriculture in Brazil (coffee).

- Circumventing trade barriers: Trade barriers are meant to discourage foreign imports either by raising the price of the imported good (tariffs) or by limiting the quantity of the imported good (import quotas). MNCs can avoid trade barriers by locating foreign affiliates inside these countries or inside countries that have duty-free access to these countries. Japanese investments in Mexican *maquiladoras* (duty-free assembly plants), for example, permit free access to American markets. This is because Mexico, the United States, and Canada are all members of NAFTA and, as a result, many goods and services travel freely across their national borders.

Multinationals can also increase profits by increasing their revenues. Two common approaches to raising revenues are by tapping new markets and by expanding the firm's product line.

- Tapping new markets: MNCs, like other firms, seek new markets to increase sales. The story of McDonald's illustrates this process. In 1955, the first McDonald's restaurant opened in Des Plaines, Illinois. By 2000, over 28,000 McDonald's restaurants were located in 119 countries around the world. And on an average day, McDonald's serves 43 million customers.[6] Other major MNCs—particularly those that produce consumer goods—have also aggressively sought out new markets by expanding abroad, including PepsiCo and Coca-Cola, IBM, and General Motors.

- Expanding the product line: Another common method used to increase sales—and ultimately profits—is to expand the MNC's product line. The Swiss MNC, Nestlé, illustrates this process. Since World War II, Nestlé has expanded on its traditional coffee and chocolate markets by acquiring firms in other industries such as pet food (Spillers Petfood, United Kingdom), processed foods (Carnation, United States), mineral water (Perrier, France), candy (Victor Schmidt & Sohne, Austria), and nutrition (PowerBar, United States). By 2000, Nestlé was the world's largest food manufacturer with over 500 factories in 77 countries.[7]

NEW TECHNOLOGIES OF THE NEW GLOBAL ECONOMY

The rate of technological changes accelerated during the twentieth century and, thus, contributed significantly to the ease with which people, goods, and ideas could travel across a city or continent. For example, the invention of the internal combustion engine by German inventor Nikolaus Otto (1876) and the application of this type of engine to automobiles by Karl Benz and Gottlieb Daimler (1885) set the stage for the commercial application of these technologies. American entrepreneur Henry Ford took auto production to the next level—the mass production of cars on a moving assembly line (1913). Over the next decade, Ford Motor Company's passenger-car output increased ninefold, from about 200,000 (1913) to over 1.8 million (1923). The mass production and consumption of automobiles, in turn, set in motion additional needs for paved roads, highways, and bridges. The use of the internal combustion engine was soon expanded to power trucks, buses, and other vehicles. Air flight, pioneered by Orville and Wilbur Wright in 1903, also revolutionized transportation first by propeller propulsion and later by jet propulsion. In the realm of communications, the invention of the telephone by American Alexander Graham Bell (1876) opened the door to a host of related communications technologies, including satellite communications (Telstar, 1966), fiber optics (1977), modems (1979), and facsimile (fax) machines.

The computer revolution began in earnest during World War II. Research on the world's first large electronic computer—the Electronic Numerical Integrator and Calculator (ENIAC)—was successfully completed in 1946. This project, headed by John W. Mauchly and John P. Eckert Jr., opened the doors for a profitable postwar computer industry. Since the 1940s, technological advances have brought the highly competitive computer industry from the use of vacuum tubes, to transistors, to integrated circuits, to the microprocessor. New technology also enabled computers to become more compact, more powerful, and less expensive. In 1975, Microinstrumentation and Telemetry Systems produced a commercially viable personal computer. Soon, a number of competitors, including Apple and IBM, were vying for larger shares of the fast-growing personal computer market. The rise of software companies, including Bill Gates's Microsoft (1975), further stimulated the use of computers in the workplace, schools, and homes. Today, the computer is firmly woven into the fabric of most people's daily lives in the industrialized countries—and particularly in the United States.

But what's really *new* about the technologies of the *new* global economy? The answer to this question centers on the melding of communications and information technologies. That is, the integration of computers, satellite communications, the Internet, fiber optics, mobile phones, and other devices "has broken the bounds of cost, time and distance, launching an era of global information networking."[8] Consider that in 1988, only 100,000 people in the world owned a computer with a direct connection to the Internet (an Internet host). A decade later, the number of Internet hosts had jumped to 36 million. By 1998, the United Nations Development Program (UNDP) estimated that 143 million people used the Internet—a figure that was expected to increase to 700 million people by 2001, and 1 billion people by 2005.[9] To illustrate the advantages of this merging of communications and information technologies, consider the following scenario.

Its [the Internet's] speed and cost advantages are clear. A 40-page document can be sent from Madagascar to Côte d'Ivoire, for example, by five-day courier for $75, by 30-minute fax for $45 or by two-minute email for less than 20 cents—and the email can go to hundreds of people at no extra cost. The choice is easy, if the choice is there.[10]

A Brief History of the Internet

The Internet is an international web of computer networks. This web connects business, educational, and government computer networks. In the early stages of its development, it was described simply as "the internetworking of networks"—or Internet, for short.

The Internet was created in 1969. At this time, the U.S. Department of Defense created the Internet—then called ARPANET—as a means of communication in the event of a nuclear attack. The benefit of the Internet was that it had no central location that could be destroyed by a single nuclear blast. It wasn't long before people in the scientific community, in both the public and private sectors, were using the Internet as a speedy and reliable method of communicating with one another. In the 1970s, the basic Internet infrastructure was established, and conveniences such as e-mail (1972) were developed to broaden its appeal. Most Internet users during the 1970s and 1980s were Americans and Europeans.

The invention of the World Wide Web by Tim Berners-Lee in 1989 brought the benefits of the Internet to a mass audience. What Berners-Lee developed was a user-friendly and nearly cost-free vehicle to locate information anywhere on this network of networks. In an interview granted to the *UNESCO Courier* in 2000, Berners-Lee commented that "[t]he basic idea of the Web is that it is an information space through which people can communicate, but communicate in a special way, by sharing their knowledge in a pool. . . . Advantages of the Web range from enhanced collaboration between people in different countries to reading a newspaper sitting in a remote village."[11]

THE RISE OF DEMOCRACY AND THE TRIUMPH OF GLOBAL CAPITALISM

The new global economy is also supported by the rise of democratic governments and by the freedoms that typically accompany democratic systems. Why is this so? Political freedoms and democratic institutions, by their nature, rely on individual choices and decision making. In the political realm, individuals in democratic systems are free to express their personal views as well as their preferences for candidates in the voting booth. These same types of freedoms are also inherent in a capitalist economic system. Capitalism encourages people to pursue their own self-interest and to profit from their talents and initiative. Global capitalism has expanded opportunities for people to seek out the most profitable business activities through trade and FDI. In doing so, they contribute to a more highly integrated and interdependent world that values the free flows of ideas, goods and services, people, and capital across national borders.

The direct relationship between the rise of democracy and the expansion of the global economy was illustrated in dramatic fashion with the collapse of communism in the former Soviet Union and in central eastern Europe during the late 1980s and early 1990s. Under communism, the USSR (1922–1991) and the nations of central and eastern Europe (mid-1940s to the late 1980s and early 1990s) were mainly isolated from the expanding trade, FDI, and other economic and political connections with the Western countries. This isolation was a result of the Cold War mentality, which created two distinctly different ideological camps—one favoring democratic political institutions and market-oriented economies (the West) and the other favoring totalitarian political institutions and communist economies (the East). The inherent weaknesses of communism, such as weak incentives to work or produce efficiently, bloated and stifling government bureaucracies, and the mismanagement of scarce resources by central planners, eventually resulted in the collapse of these centrally planned economies and the repressive dictatorships that supported them. Since the late 1980s and early 1990s, most of these "transition countries" have made strides to develop market economies and to institute democratic political systems.[12]

The movement toward political freedoms and democracy during the twentieth century has been dramatic. At the beginning of the century, for example, there wasn't a single country in the world that based its government on the principle of universal adult suffrage. Even countries with long democratic traditions, such as the United States and the United Kingdom, barred women and some minorities from full participation in their political systems. By 2000, however, democratic governments based on universal adult suffrage had become the world's dominant political system. The Freedom House counted 120 electoral democracies in the world by 2000—62.5% of all countries. The *Freedom House*, which was founded as a nonprofit organization in 1941, is dedicated to promoting democracy and freedom worldwide.[13]

In an even broader measure of freedom, which includes people's political rights and civil liberties, the countries of the world score even higher, according to the Freedom House. Political rights are defined as the rights of the people to "participate freely in the political process." These rights include the right for all adults to vote and run for elected office. They also include guarantees that these elected officials will make the important decisions for the country. Civil liberties include people's rights to "develop views, institutions, and personal autonomy apart from the state." According to the Freedom House's *Freedom in the World: The Annual Survey of Political Rights and Civil Liberties, 2000–2001*, three-quarters of all nations were either free (eighty-six countries) or partly free (fifty-nine countries), as opposed to not free (forty-seven countries), depending on how well they met the standards for political rights and civil liberties, as shown in Figure 1.1.[14]

ECONOMIC FREEDOM AND THE GLOBAL ECONOMY

Expanded political and economic freedoms have strengthened economic ties among countries in today's global economy. In essence, a symbiotic relationship exists between political freedom, on the one hand, and economic freedom on the other. This is because the centerpiece of each kind of freedom is individual decision making. American economist Milton Friedman, who was awarded the Nobel Prize in Economic Science in 1976, recognized this relationship nearly a generation ago when he wrote:

Economic Freedom is an essential requisite for political freedom. By enabling people to cooperate with one another without coercion or central direction, it reduces the area over which political power is exercised. In addition, by dispersing power, the free market provides an offset to whatever concentration of political power may arise. The combination of economic and political power in the same hands is a sure recipe for tyranny.[15]

Figure 1.1
Freedom in the World Survey of Political Rights and Civil Liberties, 2000

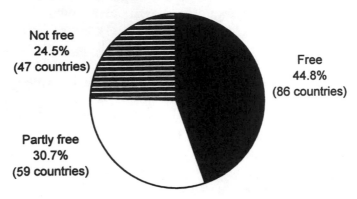

Not free
24.5%
(47 countries)

Free
44.8%
(86 countries)

Partly free
30.7%
(59 countries)

Source: Data from Freedom House, *Freedom in the World: The Annual Survey of Political Rights and Civil Liberties, 2000–2001.*

Recent research suggests that economic freedoms contribute substantially to the economic prosperity of individual countries and the global economy. Perhaps the most recognized and objective measure of economic freedom is the annually updated *Economic Freedom of the World* (*EFW*), which is published by the Hong Kong Centre for Economic Research, the Fraser Institute (Canada), and the Cato Institute (United States).[16] The *Economic Freedom of the World: 2001 Annual Report* used 23 criteria to measure economic freedom in 123 countries. These criteria focused on qualities such as private property rights, the rule of law, enforcement of contracts, level of government control or regulation, existence of trade barriers, and the overall stability of the economy. What conclusions were drawn from these and earlier *EFW* reports? The *Economist* reported that "[t]he conclusion is abundantly clear: the freer the economy, the higher the growth and the richer the people. Countries that have maintained a fairly free economy for many years did especially well."[17] A sampling of the most free and least free economies of the world is shown in Table 1.1.

RESISTANCE TO GLOBALIZATION: THE ROLE OF NGOs

In spite of the deliberate steps that many individuals, firms, organizations, and governments are currently taking toward a globalized economy, resistance to the process—and to the institutions that sup-

Table 1.1
Economic Freedom Rankings, 1999

Most Free Economies	Position	Least Free Economies	Position
Hong Kong SAR	1	Myanmar	119
Singapore	2	Algeria	120
New Zealand	3	Congo (Dem. Rep.)	121
United Kingdom	4	Guinea-Bissau	122
United States	5	Sierra Leone	123

Source: Fraser Institute, *Economic Freedom of the World: 2001 Annual Report.*

port it—is growing. Those who oppose globalization reject the notion that it is inevitable and, instead, believe that people should choose a different path toward global prosperity. This opposition gained international attention in 1999 with massive grassroots protests against globalization at the WTO ministerial conference in Seattle, Washington. Some labor organizations, for example, blamed globalization for the flight of businesses from industrialized countries to low-wage developing countries. Environmentalists opposed the degradation of the natural environment by powerful MNCs. Human rights activists decried the exploitation of low-skilled foreign workers by MNCs or by the power elite within their own countries. Similar protests at the annual World Bank and IMF meetings in Washington, DC, in the spring of 2000 also raised questions about the desirability of the present race toward globalization, and signaled the birth of a new global powerhouse—NGOs.

Nongovernmental organizations (NGOs) are formal organizations created to share information about issues with people and to instigate reforms by governments, businesses, or international organizations. NGOs tend to share certain traits. First, most have branches or affiliates in at least three countries. Hence, most are international organizations. Second, NGOs tend to be organized along democratic lines. Thus, the leadership of NGOs must consider the views of members, particularly when an NGO represents a number of different constituencies or affiliated organizations. Third, NGOs have clearly established goals that are articulated in a mission statement. Many NGOs are concerned with promoting sustainable economic development in the less developed countries, preserving the environment, supporting social programs, caring for refugees and the poor, and protecting human rights. Finally, NGOs are activist organizations. That is, they work to create needed changes or reforms in the political, economic, and cultural realms. This activism sometimes boils over into street protests, global consumer boycotts, letter-writing campaigns, and involvement with educational programs.

The phenomenal growth in the number of NGOs since the 1970s has made them major players in the new global economy. By some estimates, the number of NGOs operating in the world by the mid-1990s had topped 25,000—5,000 with operations based solely in one country and 20,000 international NGOs (sometimes referred to as INGOs) with operations in at least three countries.[18] There are a number of reasons for the impressive growth in NGOs. First, the rise of democracies worldwide over the last quarter of the twentieth century created new opportunities for people to express their views—individually and in grassroots organizations such as NGOs. Second, modern information technologies (ITs), telecommunications networks, and transportation systems have made it easier for people to communicate and organize into effective groups, even across national borders. Third, as NGOs grow in number and strength they are better able to achieve their goals and, thus, increase their credibility as agents for change in the global arena. Today, governments, international organizations (e.g., WTO, World Bank, and IMF), and the UN have pledged to cooperate more closely with selected NGOs. In fact, in a 1999 report, Secretary-General Kofi A. Annan of the UN referred to NGOs as "indispensable partners" of the UN and as vital in "the process of deliberation and policy formation."[19]

GLOBALIZATION AND FINANCIAL CONTAGION: THE CASE OF THE EAST ASIAN CRISIS OF 1997–1998

While much of the world embraces globalization, critics contend that global economic stability is jeopardized. This conclusion rests mainly on the danger of financial contagion in a highly integrated and interdependent global economy. *Financial contagion*, as the term implies, refers to the rapid spread of a financial crisis from one country or region to other countries or regions. In the late 1990s, financial crises in East Asia, Brazil, and Russia had far-reaching effects on other economies around the world.

The East Asian crisis of 1997–1998 began in Thailand, rapidly spread across East Asia, and eventually reached most of the industrialized world. While there are many interpretations about how the crisis started, several underlying causes of the financial contagion seem clear. First, some of the East Asian economies, including Thailand, Malaysia, Indonesia, South Korea, and even Japan, were in the midst of an overexuberant and speculative investment boom during much of the 1990s. This meant that billions of dollars—much of it derived from foreign investors—was being invested in the capital markets (securities markets), real estate, corporations, and other assets in these East Asian nations. Second, as investors' demand for these assets increased, their prices were "bid up" to artificially high levels. Investor optimism continued to fuel this speculative boom during the mid-1990s. Third, it was inevitable that this speculative boom peaked. Optimism faded quickly and speculators rushed to sell off their stocks, properties, businesses, or other assets hoping to cash in before the bottom dropped out of the market. And what was the impact of this rush to sell off these assets? The ensuing stampede to sell—a process that some economists refer to as the *herd mentality*—caused the value of assets to collapse. As stock prices fell, property values dipped, and the entire financial system quaked. Macroeconomic problems soon kicked in such as unemployment (loss of jobs as firms declare bankruptcy), inflation (as the currency loses its value), and negative growth (decline in GDP).

So how does this national problem become an international crisis? In an interdependent global economy, it is often said that when one economy sneezes other countries catch the flu. In the East Asian crisis, for example, the weaknesses associated with unwise, short-term, speculative investments had weakened most of the economies of East Asia. But each crisis needs a spark to ignite it. The spark for this crisis was the collapse of the Thai currency, the baht, in July 1997. This collapse triggered a serious crisis in investor confidence not only in Thailand's economy, but also in the economies of Thailand's neighbors. Within just a few months, nervous investors in Malaysia, Indonesia, and South Korea were also jumping ship by selling off assets—an action that caused the same kinds of macroeconomic instabilities that Thailand was already experiencing.

In time, the contagion spread worldwide. Japan, which had long relied heavily on its export markets in East Asia, faced hardships when its traditional East Asian markets soured. Similarly, American farmers, high-tech industries, and other businesses that had exported heavily to crisis stricken East Asia saw their markets shrink. The contagion also af-

Bob Englehart, *The Hartford Courant* (13 January 1998). Reprinted with permission.

fected capital markets worldwide. As the Asian crisis deepened in the fall of 1997, stock exchanges from Hong Kong to New York City recorded record-breaking declines. In fact, on October 27, 1997, the New York Stock Exchange (NYSE) plunged 544 points—the largest drop in the Dow Jones Industrial Average in history. Even massive aid by the IMF, other multilateral aid from the Asian Development Bank (ADB) and the World Bank, and bilateral aid from other countries was insufficient to shore up these economies. In total, $125 billion was committed to the rescue of Indonesia, Korea, and Thailand from their economic free-fall, as shown in Table 1.2.[20]

What the East Asian crisis demonstrated was that the world's economies, which were connected by international agreements, organizations, and technology, were also connected by unpredictable financial speculation and herd behavior. Author and economist Robert Gilpin states: "[T]he immense scale and velocity of international financial flows and the equal swiftness of information flows today have resulted in a situation where, with the push of a button, billions of dollars can be shifted from one country to another, and the whole globe can quickly be drawn into the maelstrom."[21] This lesson has been ingrained into

Table 1.2
The Asian Crisis: Financial Bailout, 1977–1998 (in billions of $US)

Aid Commitments	Indonesia	Korea	Thailand	Totals
IMF Aid	$15.0	$21.1	$4.0	$40.1
Multilateral Aid*	$10.0	$14.2	$2.7	$26.9
Bilateral Aid	$24.7	$23.1	$10.5	$58.3
Total Aid	$49.7	$58.4	$17.2	$125.3

*Includes the ADB and the Work Bank.
Source: IMF, "Recovery from the Asian Crisis and the Role of the IMF" (An IMF Issues Brief, 2000).

the minds of world leaders since the East Asian crisis of the late 1990s. What is less clear is how countries will reform the global financial architecture to address these glitches in the global economy.

THE GLOBALIZATION JUGGERNAUT

The process of globalization is an established fact as the world enters the uncertain waters of the twenty-first century. Today, many economists view globalization in all of its realms—economic, political, and cultural—as a fait accompli. That is, they believe that the global economy is so thoroughly integrated that a change in direction is not only undesirable, but even unthinkable. Consider the elements that are already in place to support global economic integration:

- major transnational organizations such as the IMF, World Bank, and the WTO that oversee economic relations among nations and have the authority to enforce their rules and policies;
- powerful MNCs that have invested trillions of dollars in business operations worldwide and sell trillions of dollars worth of goods and services through foreign affiliates;
- regional trade organizations such as the EU and NAFTA that have opened their borders to freer trade, FDI and other flows of money, people, and resources;
- major international agreements that set global standards to protect human rights, the environment, and other areas of global concern;

- a high-tech infrastructure in IT, telecommunications, and transportation that has facilitated the speed and ease of international flows of goods, people, and capital;
- regulatory reforms that have encouraged the opening of new markets around the world, megamergers among some of the world's largest corporations, and twenty-four-hour-per-day networking among global financial institutions;
- democratic political institutions that have generally been supportive of a freer global marketplace and have encouraged the proliferation of grassroots groups such as NGOs; and
- prevailing beliefs that assume that globalization is inevitable and that the benefits of integrated markets far outweigh the costs.

There can be little question that the globalization juggernaut is pushing toward even greater integration of the global economy as we enter the twenty-first century. And while some economists would claim that today's globalization is little more than an old theme revisited, there is compelling evidence to the contrary. Thomas L. Friedman summarizes the unique nature of today's globalization best when he defines globalization as:

the inexorable integration of markets, nation-states and technologies to a degree never witnessed before—in a way that is enabling individuals, corporations and nation-states to reach around the world farther, faster, deeper and cheaper than ever before, and in a way that is enabling the world to reach into individuals, corporations and nation-states farther, faster, deeper, cheaper than ever before.[22]

NOTES

1. United Nations Development Program (UNDP), *Human Development Report: 2001* (New York: Oxford University Press, 2001), 30.

2. United Nations Conference on Trade and Development (UNCTAD), *World Investment Report 2000: Cross-Border Mergers and Acquisitions and Development* (New York: United Nations Publications, 2000), 2.

3. Richard C. Longworth, *The Global Squeeze: The Coming Crisis for First World Nations* (Chicago: Contemporary, 1998), 7.

4. Edward Luttwak, *Turbo-Capitalism: Winners and Losers in the Global Economy* (New York: HarperCollins, 1999), 39.

5. UNCTAD, "World FDI Flows Exceed US$ 1.1 Trillion in 2000" (UNCTAD press release, 7 December 2000), 1–2 (*www.unctad. org.en/press/pr2875en.htm*).

6. "McDo   orporation Reaffirms EPS Growth Targets and Clarifies Potential I.   .f Foreign Currency Translation on Reported Earnings" (McDonal.   .orporation, financial press release, 13 September 2000), 1.

7. "Nestlé SA (Switzerland): Profile" (*www.mind_advertising.com/ch/nestle_ch_w.htm*); and "Nestle at a Glance" (*www.nestle.com/all_about/at_a_glance/aag-home.html*), 1.

8. UNDP, *Human Development Report: 1999* (New York: Oxford University Press, 1999), 57.

9. Ibid., 58; and UNDP, *Human Development Report: 2001*, 32.

10. UNDP, *Human Development Report: 1999*, 57.

11. Quoted in "Tim Berners-Lee: The Web's Brainchild [Interview]," *UNESCO Courier*, September 2000, 47; and *Economic Report of the President: 2000* (Washington, DC: U.S. Government Printing Office, 2000), 124.

12. International Monetary Fund (IMF), *World Economic Outlook: 1999* (Washington, DC: IMF Publications, 1999), 16; and Adrian Karatnychy, "Freedom in the World: 2000–2001" (*www.freedomhouse.org/research/freeworld/2001/essay1.htm*).

13. Freedom House, "Democracy's Challenge: A Survey of Global Political Changes in the 20th Century" (*www.freedomhouse.org/reports/century.html*); and Freedom House, "Freedom in the World, 1999–2000: Electoral Democracies," 1–10 (*www.freedomhouse.org/survey/2000/tables/electdem.html*); and Freedom House, "End of Century Survey Finds Dramatic Gains for Democracy," 1 (*www.freedomhouse.org/news/pr/120799.html*).

14. Freedom House, "Freedom in the World: The Annual Survey of Political Rights and Civil Liberties, 2000–2001" (New York: Freedom House, 2000) (*www.freedomhouse.org/research/freeworld/2001/tracking.htm*); and Freedom House, "Freedom in the World, Combined Table of Countries" (*www.freedomhouse.org/research/freeworld/2001/table5.htm*).

15. Milton Friedman and Rose Friedman, *Free to Choose: A Personal Statement* (New York: Avon, 1979), xvi-xvii.

16. Fraser Institute, *Economic Freedom of the World: 2000 Annual Report*, (*www.fraserinstitute.ca/media/media_release/2000/20000111a.html*).

17. "Survey of the 20th Century: How Free is Your Country?" *The Economist*, 11 September 1999, 28.

18. Jagdish Bhagwati, "Globalization: A Moral Imperative," *UNESCO Courier*, September 2000, 20.

19. Quoted in "NGOs and the United Nations" (New York: Global Policy Forum, June 1999), 2 (*www.globalpolicy.org/ngos/docs99/gpfrep.htm*).

20. IMF, "Recovery from the Asian Crisis and the Role of the IMF" (An IMF Issues Brief, 2000) (*www.imf.org/external/np/exr/ib/2000/062300.htm*).

21. Robert Gilpin, *The Challenge of Global Capitalism: The World Economy in the 21st Century* (Princeton, NJ: Princeton University Press, 2000), 134.

22. Thomas L. Friedman, *The Lexus and the Oliver Tree: Understanding Globalization,* rev. ed. (New York: Anchor, 2000), 9.

2

International Trade: Spinning the Web, Part I

WHY NATIONS TRADE

International trade is one of the main engines driving the global economy. It occurs when people import or export goods or services. Through these voluntary exchanges of products in global markets, international trade creates a more interdependent and integrated global economy. It is important to emphasize that cross-border trade relationships are voluntary in nature. That is, the import or export of goods or services only occurs when people from different countries believe that both the buyer and the seller can benefit from the exchange. Economists often refer to this reality as the *principle of mutual benefit*, which describes the primary motivation for voluntary exchanges in all marketplaces—international and domestic. The noted Scottish economist Adam Smith observed this principle over 200 years ago when, in *An Inquiry into the Nature and Causes of the Wealth of Nations,* he wrote: "It is not from the benevolence of the butcher, the brewer, or the baker, that we expect our dinner, but from their regard to their own interest. We address ourselves, not to their humanity but to their self-love, and never talk to them of our necessities but of their advantages."[1]

The benefits of trade can be viewed from the perspective of consumers, businesses, and societies. Consumers benefit from international trade in two important ways. First, international trade increases the variety and availability goods and services for people to buy and, thus, expands people's freedom of choice in the global economy. Second, international trade creates more competitive markets, which reduces consumer prices as firms compete for consumers' dollar votes in the marketplace. Businesses benefit from international trade mainly because foreign competition provides the incentive for firms to become more efficient. Efficiency is a broad term that reflects two main ideas: that businesses use their scarce resources effectively and that they produce goods or services that people want to buy. Efficient firms thrive in competitive markets, while inefficient firms are free to fail in a market economy.

Finally, international trade benefits society by encouraging people to specialize in the production of goods or services in which they have a competitive advantage. One kind of competitive advantage that a nation or region may have is called an absolute advantage when it can produce a good more efficiently than a second region or nation. For example, the United States is the world's leading producer of corn, while Honduras is among the world's top banana producers. Why does the United States choose to produce corn rather than bananas, and why does Honduras choose to produce bananas rather than corn? The simple answer is that each nation has a different mix of resources—type of soil, amount of rainfall, skill level of workers, supply of machinery and equipment, and so on. When nations specialize in the production of goods that they produce most efficiently, fewer resources are wasted, total output increases, and surpluses of the good are available for trade with other nations.

When two nations each have an absolute advantage in the production of a good—such as corn in the United States and bananas in Honduras—the benefits of trade are readily apparent. But what if a nation has an absolute advantage over a second nation in the production of two products? Should trade take place? The answer is most likely yes. Consider the following situation. Suppose Taiwan has an absolute advantage over Mexico in the production of both microwave ovens and toaster ovens. Taiwan can produce four times as many microwave ovens as Mexico, using the same amount of resources. Taiwan can also produce twice as many toaster ovens as Mexico with a given amount of resources. Where is Taiwan's greatest advantage? Obviously, while Taiwan can produce both products more efficiently than Mexico, its greatest advantage is in the production of microwave ovens where it enjoys a 4 to 1 advantage. Economists would say that Taiwan has a *comparative advantage* in the production of microwave ovens because its production advantage over Mexico is greater in microwave ovens (4 to 1) than it is in toaster ovens (2 to 1). Similarly, economists would say that Mexico has a comparative advantage in the production of toaster ovens because this is the product in which Mexico has the lesser disadvantage. But why wouldn't Taiwan simply produce unlimited quantities of each product? The basic reason is that Taiwan, like all countries in the world, has limited resources. When nations specialize in the production of products in which they have a comparative advantage, they are able to increase efficiency and expand global output.

INTERNATIONAL TRADE: DISPARITIES BASED ON COUNTRIES' INCOME

International trade, which grew dramatically over the past several decades, has been uneven depending on the income level of countries. By 2000, the volume of international trade had reached $7.6 trillion in merchandise and commercial services. Among the most important categories of merchandise imports and exports were capital goods, such as machinery and equipment; industrial supplies and materials; automobiles and auto parts; agricultural products, including animal feeds; and petroleum. In 2000, the most robust trade was in information and telecommunications equipment. Key commercial services in international markets included travel, passenger fares, the transport of goods, financial services and insurance, and business and professional services such as accounting, engineering, data processing, and advertising.[2] In its *World Development Report 2000/2001: Attacking Poverty*, the World Bank compared the volume of international trade in goods and services for low-income, middle-income, and high-income countries from 1990 to 1998, as shown in Table 2.1.[3]

The World Bank also reported that by 2000, sixty-four countries were classified as low income (40.5% of the world's population), ninety-three countries were classified as middle income (45% of the world's population), and fifty countries were classified as high income (15% of the world's population).[4] To put this data another way, by 2000 about one-seventh of the world's population controlled over three-quarters of the world's trade.

INTERNATIONAL TRADE: DEEPENING THE GLOBAL ECONOMY

There are many reasons why trade in merchandise and services expanded so rapidly in the final quarter of the twentieth century. Most of these reasons revolve around two factors: trade liberalization and new

Table 2.1
Trade in Goods and Services: A Comparison, 1990 and 1998
(value of global exports in billions of $US)

Income Level of Nation	Per Capita GNP (1999)	Exports (1990)	Exports (1998)	Percent of Total Exports (1998)
Low income	$755 or less	$131	$209	3%
Middle income	$756–9,265	$700	$1,374	20%
High income	$9,266 or more	$3,418	$5,183	77%
World		$4,252	$6,767	100%

Source: World Bank, *World Development Report 2000/2001*.

technology. The first factor, trade liberalization, refers to conscious actions or policies by countries to reduce trade barriers such as tariffs and import quotas. The goal of trade liberalization is to increase international trade and, in doing so, to promote global prosperity. The creation of the World Trade Organization (WTO), the strengthening of regional trade organizations and agreements, and the emergence of transition countries have all supported trade liberalization in recent years.

- The WTO: By January 2002, 144 countries had demonstrated their commitment to trade liberalization by joining the WTO, the only international organization that creates and monitors global rules of trade among countries. Its primary function "is to ensure that trade flows smoothly, predictably, and freely as possible."[5]
- Regional trade organizations and agreements: Many countries had also joined regional trade organizations to promote the free flow of goods and services across member countries' borders by reducing or eliminating trade barriers. The most integrated regional trade organization is the fifteen-member European Union (EU). In North America, the dominant regional trade organization is the North American Free Trade Agreement (NAFTA). In South America, it is the Common Market of the South (MERCOSUR). In Europe, the dominant EU is joined by the smaller European Free Trade Association (EFTA). In Asia, there is the Asia-Pacific Economic Cooperation (APEC) group and the Association of Southeast Asian Nations (ASEAN). In Africa, there is the Economic Community of West African States (ECOWAS) and the Common Market for Eastern and Southern Africa (COMESA). And for Australia, there is the Australia–New

Zealand Closer Economic Relations Agreement. The spirit of trade liberalization is also reflected in the creation of new regional trade agreements (RTAs) since World War II. During the 1950s, just three RTAs were negotiated compared to nineteen in the 1960s, thirty-nine in the 1970s, fourteen in the 1980s, and eighty-two in the 1990s.[6]

- Transition countries: The *transition countries* are nations that are transforming their economies from communism to capitalism. There are twenty-eight transition countries located in eastern and central Europe and central Asia. An important feature in this market-oriented transformation is freer trade. Under communism, trade was severely restricted. For example, in Europe and central Asia most trade was limited to exchanges between the former Soviet Union (composed of Russia and fourteen other republics) and the Eastern bloc nations. The Soviet-dominated Council for Mutual Economic Assistance (COMECON), which was founded in 1949, served as a supranational planning organization responsible for integrating the economies of the region. In doing so, these countries became increasingly isolated from most economic contacts with the Western countries. With the collapse of the Soviet Union in 1991, COMECON was disbanded, freeing the former republics (now independent countries) and the Eastern bloc countries to pursue freer trade policies. In fact, many of these countries have joined the WTO, and a number of former Eastern bloc countries are negotiating for admission into the EU (Czech Republic, Estonia, Hungary, Poland, and Slovenia). In East Asia, several developing countries are also transition*ing* including China, which has achieved massive trade surpluses with the United States ($84 billion) and Japan ($25 billion), and has attracted more foreign direct investment (FDI) than any other country in the developing world.[7]

In addition to trade liberalization, a second factor has promoted trade among nations: new technology. What distinguishes recent technological advances from those of the past is the degree of integration among transportation, communications, and information technologies (IT). Consider how easy it is for businesses to communicate with one another today—to make contracts, negotiate terms for the purchase or sale of products, explore investment opportunities, and so on. The integration of computers, satellites, the Internet, and other IT offers instant access to clients, business partners, and others. Technological advances favor the wealthy industrialized countries that have greater access to these costly devices. For example, the rapid growth in exported commercial services from the industrialized countries reflects these countries' superiority in computers and IT. Commercial services exported from the industrialized countries jumped from $288 billion in 1983 to over $1,043 billion in 1997. This represented about 80% of all exported services in the global economy. The World Bank did predict that much of expanded trade in services during the twenty-first century will come from developing countries in Asia and Latin America, in part because "the rise of electronic commerce has created new possibilities for trade in services."[8] In short, technology has improved the infrastructure for global trade and, thus, has encouraged international exchanges that are faster, cheaper, and more convenient than at any other time in history.

THE WTO

The most significant recent development in the global trading system was the creation of the WTO in 1994. The WTO replaced the General Agreement on Tariffs and Trade (GATT), which had guided the global trading system from 1947–1994. The WTO adopted the main principles of the GATT, including:

- Most-favored nation (MFN) status: MFN status is based on the principle of non-discrimination in trade relations. That is, a trade concession granted to one country automatically applies to all other WTO members.

- National treatment of products: Under national treatment, imported and domestically produced goods must be treated equally.

- Trade liberalization: Trade liberalization involves the dismantling of most trade barriers. Under the GATT, eight rounds of formal negotiations among member countries took place to liberalize trade. In this same tradition, the WTO is currently trying to jump-start the ninth round of negotiations, which has already been dubbed the Millennium Round.

While there was fundamental agreement on the main principles inherited from the GATT, the WTO's organizational structure is far different from that of the GATT. The WTO is a formal international organization, rather than just an "agreement" among countries. As an international organization, the WTO has greater authority—and clearer procedures—to hear and rule on trade disputes among nations. It also exercises greater authority in forming and enforcing policies to promote freer and fairer trade. Membership in the WTO occurs only when countries, through a formal vote in their national legislatures, accept the agreed upon rules of trade—rules that were established by the 125 GATT countries that participated in the Marrakesh (Morocco) meeting in 1994. In the words of the WTO:

At the heart of the system—known as the multilateral trading system—are the WTO's agreements, negotiated and signed by a large majority of the world's trading nations, and ratified in their parliaments. These agreements are the legal ground-rules for international commerce. Essentially, they are contracts, guaranteeing member countries important trade rights. They also bind governments to keep their trade policies within agreed limits to everybody's benefit.[9]

The WTO also provides a forum for trade negotiations, offers technical assistance in trade-related matters to developing countries, and cooperates with other international organizations. The work of the WTO is coordinated by a director-general (Mike Moore) and a staff of 500 employees from its headquarters in Geneva, Switzerland.

Since the WTO started operations on January 1, 1995, its record has been dotted with successes and failures. Successes are measured by respect for the legal proceedings and compliance with WTO rulings on disputed trade practices. In the mid-1990s, the United States abided by a WTO decision to stop discriminating against gasoline imported from Venezuela and, a couple years later, also agreed to remove trade restrictions against underwear imported from Costa Rica. In the late 1990s, a WTO ruling obliged Japan to change its policy of taxing foreign alcohol, thus satisfying complaints brought against Japan by the United States, Canada, and the EU. By 2000, the WTO's Dispute Settlement Understanding (DSU) had recorded 200 complaints, about three-quarters of which were settled through quiet consultations among countries involved in the disputes.[10] Furthermore, it is generally acknowledged that even when disputes go beyond consultations, the high degree of compliance with WTO decisions, as rendered by its Dispute Settlement Body (DSB), has created a sound legal foundation on which to base future judgments.

The WTO's implementation of the Trade-Related Aspects of Intellectual Property (TRIPS) agreement, which was negotiated during the final GATT round (the Uruguay Round) and took effect in 1995, is another example of the organization's work to bring order to the global trading system. TRIPS set uniform, global standards to protect a wide variety of intellectual properties such as computer software, medicines, music, books, and a host of other processes and products. Under TRIPS, businesses that produced intellectual property were guaranteed international compliance with patent, copyright, and trademark laws. The industrialized countries supported the TRIPS agreement because it protected their advanced technology and other innovations from being pirated. Some of the poorer countries, however, resented TRIPS. They argued that TRIPS was just another way for the richer countries of the world to maintain their technological and economic dominance in the global economy.

The WTO has also had its share of growing pains since 1995. The most visible show of discontent with the WTO, and with the globalization process itself, occurred at the WTO's ministerial conference in Seattle, Washington (1999). At this four-day meeting, tens of thousands of people—many connected to nongovernmental organizations (NGOs)—took to the streets in protest against the WTO and the negative consequences of globalization. Some protesters criticized multinational corporations (MNCs) for valuing profits ahead of decent working conditions for their laborers and reasonable safeguards for the natural environment. Others focused on abuses of human rights, the loss of jobs to low-wage countries, respect for indigenous cultures, and other issues. Even within the conference halls there was discord, as representatives from some poorer countries bitterly complained that they had been systematically excluded from the WTO's decision-making process. In the end, little was accomplished at the WTO's ministerial conference in Seattle, thus stalling the Millennium Round of trade negotiations. Similar protests at the annual meetings of the IMF and World Bank in 2000 signaled that NGOs had become another voice in the debates that would shape the global economy.

The WTO has also experienced some failures in resolving trade disputes between countries. In 1999–2000, for example, the EU repeatedly rejected WTO rulings that called for an end to the EU's trade restrictions on bananas from Latin America and a repeal of its ban on hormone-treated beef from the United States and Canada. Because of the EU's refusal to abide by the WTO's rulings, the WTO's DSB allowed the United States and Canada to retaliate against EU countries with trade sanctions of their own. These U.S. sanctions included heavy tariffs on certain goods from EU nations, including Louis Vuitton handbags from France, cashmere sweaters from the United Kingdom, and pecorino cheese from Italy. In the spring of 2001, the EU and the United States came to terms on the banana dispute.

An even more serious trade dispute between the United States and the EU erupted in 2000. At the heart of this dispute was an EU complaint that certain U.S. tax policies gave U.S. firms an unfair advantage in international trade. Specifically, the EU charged that U.S. firms frequently channeled foreign revenues through foreign sales corporations (FSCs) to avoid paying taxes on these revenues. While legal under U.S.

Bob Englehart, *The Hartford Courant* (2 December 1999). Reprinted with permission.

law, FSCs create a tax savings for some U.S. firms and, in the opinion of the EU, constitute an unfair trade practice. In early 2000, the WTO sided with the EU in this dispute, noting that tax avoidance by U.S. firms was, in reality, just another type of government subsidy to these firms—a subsidy that totaled about $3.5 billion annually. According to the *Economist*, about 6,000 American firms benefited from FSCs by the late 1990s. In 1998, some U.S. firms achieved substantial tax savings, including General Electric ($150 million) and Boeing ($130 million).[11] In the early 2000s, the issue of tax havens for U.S. firms promised to dwarf U.S.-EU squabbles over bananas or beef.

OFFSHORE FINANCIAL CENTERS

Offshore financial centers (OFCs) represent many different types of financial institutions such as banks, insurance companies, securities firms, and a variety of international business companies. These "offshore" financial institutions are typically located on islands. The single largest concentration of OFCs is in the Cayman Islands. Many other OFCs can be found in the Bahamas, Bermuda, Barbados, Aruba, the

Virgin Islands, the Isle of Man, and Cyprus. Pockets of OFCs can sometimes be found "onshore" in places such as Luxembourg and Liechtenstein.

In recent years, OFCs, sometimes called the "offshore financial services sector," have come under increasing scrutiny by governments and law enforcement officials. This concern is based on two factors. First, it was estimated that about $4.8 trillion in assets (corporate revenues, securities, cash, and so on) had passed through OFCs in 1997 alone. Second, the potential for criminal activity—including money laundering and tax evasion—threatened the stability of the global economy.

Why are OFCs more susceptible to criminal activity than more traditional "onshore" financial institutions? First, OFCs are mainly unregulated by the government. This is especially true for the nonbank OFCs. This means that OFCs do not have to report suspicious transactions and do not have to submit to the types of regulation and supervision that guide business practices for onshore financial institutions. Second, OFCs have few, if any, disclosure requirements. That is, their business dealings are done anonymously. It is this secrecy, and the lack of accountability by OFCs, that open the doors to criminal activity.

At the G-7 meeting in Okinawa in the summer of 2000, the G-7 finance ministers addressed the issues of weak regulatory systems, excessive bank secrecy, and tax avoidance in the fast-paced global economy. The G-7 is made up of the seven major industrialized countries: Canada, France, Germany, Italy, Japan, the United Kingdom, and the United States. The finance ministers' main concern was the danger of financial crimes that might destabilize the global financial system. Specifically, they proposed that more uniform international standards be applied to all financial centers—including OFCs—and that appropriate supervision procedures be developed to ensure compliance with these standards. They also proposed a greater degree of cooperation among individual countries—and their law enforcement agencies—to "combat cross-border financial crime, tax evasion and regulatory abuse," including changes in laws to ensure transparency in OFCs' business dealings.[12]

THE UNITED STATES IN THE GLOBAL TRADING SYSTEM

The economy of the United States is the largest in the world with a nominal gross domestic product (GDP; not adjusted for inflation) that had topped $10 trillion in 2001. Thus, it stands to reason that the

United States has a dominant role in the global trading system. In fact, the United States has consistently been the world's leading importer and exporter of goods and services. In 2000, for example, it ranked first in the world in total trade, followed by Germany, Japan, the United Kingdom, and France.[13]

The United States exported about $1,068 billion worth of goods and services in 2000. The value of exported goods totaled $773 billion (72% of all exports) and the value of exported services totaled $295 billion (28% of all exports). Not surprisingly, the U.S. export of goods—usually called merchandise exports by economists—concentrated on products that a highly industrialized economy is capable of producing, namely capital goods (46%) and industrial supplies (22%). Other major categories of U.S. exports included consumer goods (11%), automotive vehicles and auto parts (10%), agricultural products (6%), and other (5%). The U.S. services exported in 2000 included productive activities performed by workers in fields such as financial services (banking and investing), insurance, telecommunications and transportation, and retail and wholesale trade.[14]

The Top 10 exporters of high-tech products in 1998–99, measured in billions of U.S. dollars, were:

 1. United States, $206
 2. Japan, $126
 3. Germany, $95
 4. United Kingdom, $77
 5. Singapore, $66
 6. France, $65
 7. Korea, $48
 8. Netherlands, $45
 9. Malaysia, $44
10. China, $40

Source: United Nations Development Program, Human Development Report: 2001, p. 42.

The United States imported over $1.4 trillion worth of goods and services in 2000. The value of U.S. imported merchandise totaled $1,223 billion (85% of all imports) and the value of imported services totaled $215 billion (15% of all imports). Among the most important categories of imports to American shores were capital goods (29%), consumer goods (23%), industrial supplies and petroleum (24.5%), automotive vehicles and auto parts (16%), and other (7.5%). Note that about two-fifths of all U.S. merchandise imports fell into the categories of consumer goods and automotive, reflecting a hefty American appetite for these types of goods.[15]

With whom does the United States trade? The answer is just about every country in the world. Yet, there are a number of countries that have become America's dominant trading partners, as shown in Table 2.2.[16] Note that for each of these major U.S. trading partners the dollar value of trade increased during the 1990s. The largest increase in the purchase of U.S. exports occurred in Mexico (an increase of over 200% from 1991–2000) and Canada (an increase of over 100%). The largest increases in the supply of imports to the United States came from China (an increase of over 400%), Mexico (an increase of over 300%), and Canada (an increase of over 100%).

THE UNITED STATES AND TRADE IMBALANCES

A closer examination of U.S. exports and imports over the past few decades reveals regular trade imbalances during the period. One type of trade imbalance is between the value of U.S. merchandise exports and imports. In 2000, for example, Americans exported $773 billion worth of goods, but imported merchandise valued at $1,223 billion. Thus, the U.S. imported about $449 billion ($1,222.7 – $773.3) more merchandise than it was able to export. A nation is said to have a *merchandise trade deficit* when the value of its merchandise imports is greater

Table 2.2
Top Five U.S. Trading Partners, 1991–2000 (in billions of $US)

Top Purchasers of U.S. Exports	1991	2000	Top Suppliers of U.S. Imports	1991	2000
Canada	$85	$179	Canada	$91	$229
Mexico	$36	$112	Japan	$92	$146
Japan	$48	$65	Mexico	$31	$135
United Kingdom	$22	$42	China	$19	$100
Germany	$21	$29	Germany	$26	$59

Source: International Trade Administration, U.S. Department of Commerce, Bureau of Economic Analysis.

than the value of its merchandise exports. Merchandise trade deficits have been the norm for the United States over the past quarter century, averaging about $10 billion per year in the 1970s, $94 billion per year in the 1980s, and $173 billion per year in the 1990s. In 2000, the largest U.S. merchandise trade deficits were with China ($84 billion), Japan ($81 billion), Canada ($50 billion), Germany ($29 billion), and Mexico ($24 billion).[17] Conversely, a *merchandise trade surplus* occurs when the value of a nation's merchandise exports is greater than the value of its merchandise imports. Historically, the last U.S. merchandise trade surplus occurred in 1975 when the value of U.S. exports outweighed imports by about $9 billion. Figure 2.1 shows U.S. merchandise trade deficits from 1990 to 2000.[18]

A second type of trade imbalance involves the export and import of commercial services. In 2000, for example, the United States was able to export $295 billion in services, but imported just $215 billion in services. This resulted in a *trade surplus in services* totaling $80 billion, which occurs when the value of a nation's exports of services is greater than the value of its import of services. The United States has achieved a trade surplus in services from 1970 to the present. In fact, from 1990 to 2000 the U.S. trade surplus in services averaged $69 billion per year.

Figure 2.1
U.S. Merchandise Trade Deficits, 1990–2000 (in billions of $US)

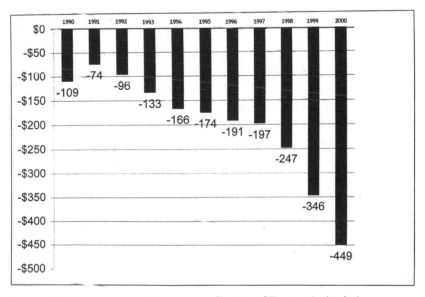

Source: U.S. Department of Commerce, Bureau of Economic Analysis.

Conversely, a *trade deficit in services* occurs when a nation imports more services than it is able to export. Despite the consistent trade surpluses in services, the overall trade deficits in merchandise and services climbed steadily during the 1990s, from a $31 billion deficit in 1991 to a $369 billion deficit in 2000.[19]

One of the most often asked questions about the performance of the U.S. economy is why the most powerful economy in the world consistently faces merchandise trade deficits. The answer to this question is not a simple one. Instead, many factors have contributed to the persistent U.S. merchandise trade deficits since the mid-1970s. First, the United States—like other countries—is subject to radical changes in the prices of essential imported products. The rapid price hikes for imported oil in 1973–1979, and again in 1999–2001, illustrate this point. Second, American consumers have acquired tastes for foreign consumer goods, especially for foreign automobiles, motorcycles, and trucks. By 2000, consumer goods and automotive goods accounted for nearly 40% of all U.S. imports. Third, the United States has enjoyed record breaking prosperity since 1991. In fact, as the nation entered 2001 it was riding the longest period of uninterrupted growth in its history. This prosperity increased the confidence of Americans, which translated into freer spending for both domestic and foreign goods and services. Fourth, confidence and consumption in some other nations suffered during the 1990s, thus reducing foreign demand for U.S. exports. International economic crises, such as the Japanese recessions in the late 1990s, the East Asian crisis (1997–1998), and the Russian crisis (1998–1999) had negative effects on U.S. exports to these regions. Finally, some experts have lamented that the United States lacks a national strategy for promoting its exports. Many of the successful advanced economies of East Asia, including Japan, have created quasi-public institutions to nurture export industries. For example, Japan's *Ministry of International Trade and Industry* (MITI) traditionally offered a variety of incentives to export industries, including tax breaks, low-interest bank loans, and grants for research and development. In 2001, many of MITI's functions were absorbed into a new institution called the *Ministry of Economy, Trade and Industry* (METI).

THE ROLE OF FOREIGN EXCHANGE MARKETS IN THE GLOBAL TRADING SYSTEM

By 2000, global trade in goods and services had hit $7.6 trillion dollars per year. But how does a firm in one country actually sell a product in a second country? After all, if an American firm sells auto parts to auto repair shops in Japan, the American firm wants payment in U.S. dollars, not Japanese yen. Similarly, Japanese exporters of goods to the United States expect payment in their own national currency. *Foreign exchange markets* provide a mechanism to convert one currency into an equivalent amount of another. Foreign exchange markets are a network of international financial institutions such as commercial banks and investment banks, and are not controlled or regulated by any government or international organization.

During the immediate post–World War II period, foreign exchange markets had one main function: to convert one currency into an equal amount of a second currency. In this way, foreign exchange markets assisted importers and exporters in the conduct of their business, the business of international trade. From the mid-1940s to 1973, the process of converting currencies was a fairly simple one since the Bretton Woods agreement of 1944 created a *fixed exchange rate system*, which tied the values of most national currencies to the U.S. dollar or to gold. In the United States, for example, the value of the dollar was equated with $\frac{1}{35}$ th of an ounce of gold. Under this system, the value of a national currency was not permitted to fluctuate beyond a very narrow band.

During the presidency of Richard M. Nixon (1969–1974), the United States and other nations abandoned the fixed exchange rate system, however, and adopted instead a *flexible exchange rate system*. Under this system, the forces of supply and demand determine the value of a currency. The focus of foreign exchange markets soon shifted to the buying or selling of national currencies for profit. In fact, since the mid-1970s national currencies have been bought and sold daily in foreign exchange markets much like stocks or commodities are traded on stock or commodity exchanges. When the demand for a currency is high, its value tends to rise or gain strength against other currencies. Generally, this occurs when an economy is experiencing robust economic growth and low rates of inflation and unemployment. When the demand for a currency falls, however, its value likewise falls. This typically occurs when an economy slips into a recession or faces some other serious economic problem. As investors in foreign exchange markets lose confidence in an economy, they scurry to sell off their holdings of that country's currency. As a result, the currency becomes weaker relative to other currencies.

There are dozens of major foreign exchange markets operating in today's global economy, and the volume of *foreign exchange trading* (the buying and selling of currencies) is staggering. In 1998, foreign exchange trading peaked at $1.5 trillion per day. By comparison, consider that the total amount of foreign trade for 1998 was just $6.6 trillion for the entire year—about $25 billion per day. In other words, on a normal business day in 1998 the value of foreign exchange trading was roughly sixty times greater than the value of foreign trade. In 2001, foreign exchange trading had fallen to $1.2 trillion per day. This decline was primarily the result of the expanded use of the euro and consolidation in the banking industry. By the late 1990s, the three dominant foreign exchange markets accounted for more than one-half of all foreign exchange trading. Each of these dominant markets is located in a different eight-hour time zone. They include London, with an average daily volume of $637 billion (32% of the world's total); New York, with an average daily volume of $351 billion (18%); and Tokyo, with an average daily volume of $149 billion (8%). The remaining 42% of foreign exchange trading was conducted in smaller markets throughout the world.[20]

In today's global economy, the governments of major countries, through their central banks, sometimes intervene to buy their own currencies (to prevent rapid depreciation) or sell their own currencies (to prevent rapid appreciation). Governments also intervene, at times, to buy or sell the currency of another country to stabilize its value, as was the case in 1998 when the United States purchased billions of dollars worth of Japanese yen to halt the yen's free-fall in international markets. Some economists use the term "*managed exchange rate system*" to describe the reality of today's exchange rate system to account for periodic government intervention in foreign exchange markets. Because sophisticated global communications systems link foreign exchange markets, the trading of currencies is a twenty-four-hour-per-day activity and there are constant fluctuations in exchange rates.

EXCHANGE RATES AND INTERNATIONAL TRADE: STRONG AND WEAK CURRENCIES

An *exchange rate* is a precise statement of the value of one currency relative to a second currency. Exchange rates are published daily in major newspapers such as the *Wall Street Journal* and the *New York Times*. Typically, four pieces of information are included: the country, the name of the currency, the U.S. equivalent, and the currency per U.S. dollar. The "U.S. equivalent" expresses the value of a foreign currency in terms of the U.S. dollar. For instance, on July 11, 2001, the Canadian dollar was worth about 66 cents and the Mexican peso about 11 cents, as shown in Table 2.3.[21] The "currency per U.S. dollar" states how many units of a foreign currency it would take to equal $1. Again, using the exchange rates shown in Table 2.3 it would take about 8 Chinese renminbi or 124 Japanese yen to equal $1.

Strong currencies? Weak currencies? Does the strength of a currency have any impact international trade? The answer is an emphatic yes. Consider the following example. In 1993, the average exchange rate between the Mexican peso and U.S. dollar was 3.12. This meant that in 1993 it took 3.12 pesos to equal $1. If an American manufacturer could produce sandals for $10 in the United States, these sandals would sell for about 31.2 pesos in Mexico (3.12 pesos per dollar × $10 = 31.2 pesos). Since 1993, however, the Mexican peso has depreciated compared to the U.S. dollar. By March 6, 2001, it took 9.65 pesos to equal $1. How does this affect the American sandal producer? Let's assume that this U.S. firm can still produce sandals for $10. Consider the impact of the weaker Mexican peso on the American sandal producers. The price of the $10 sandals in March 2001 will necessarily jump to 96.55 pesos (9.655 pesos per dollar × $10 = 96.55 pesos). Hence, because of the weaker peso the price of American-made sandals jumped to over three times the 1993 price. In other words, the weaker Mexican peso made exported U.S. sandals—and virtually all other U.S. exports to Mexico—more expensive and, therefore, less attractive to Mexican consumers.

Table 2.3
Exchange Rates, July 11, 2001

Country (currency)	U.S. Equivalent	Currency per U.S. Dollar
Canada (dollar)	.6555	1.5255
China (renminbi)	.1208	8.2769
Germany (mark)	.4393	2.2762
Japan (yen)	.008041	123.9600
Mexico (peso)	.1082	9.2450
Poland (zloty)	.2265	4.4150

Source: "Exchange Rates," Wall Street Journal.

At the same time, the weaker peso stimulated exports from Mexico to the United States. Why does this occur? Suppose a shoe manufacturer in Mexico produced shoes in 1993 for 100 pesos per pair and exported some of these shoes to the United States. What price would the Mexican firm charge for the shoes? Using the 1993 exchange rate once again, the shoe producer would likely sell the shoes for about $32 (100 pesos divided by 3.12 = $32.05). Let's assume that the Mexican shoe producer could still produce shoes for 100 pesos per pair in March 2001. How does the weaker Mexican peso affect shoe sales in the United States by 2001? Predictably, the weaker peso lowers the price of shoes—and other Mexican products that are exported to the United States. Using the March 6, 2001, exchange rate, the price of these Mexican-made shoes would be just $10.36 (100 pesos divided by 9.655 = $10.36). In effect, the relatively weak Mexican peso—and the relatively strong U.S. dollar—serves to encourage higher exports from Mexico to the United States. The strong U.S. dollar during the 1990s contributed to America's rising trade deficit with Mexico. In 1991, the United States enjoyed a trade surplus with Mexico of about $2 billion. By 2000, the U.S. merchandise trade deficit with Mexico totaled nearly $24 billion.[22] Other factors have also contributed to the U.S. trade deficit with Mexico, including U.S. participation in NAFTA—a topic that will be more fully explored later in this chapter.

REGIONAL INTEGRATION: THE EUROPEAN UNION LEADS THE WAY

Regional trade organizations, also called trade blocs, have worked to promote a freer flow of goods and services, people, money, and real capital across national borders. The world's dominant trade bloc is the fifteen-member EU. The EU is concerned not only with economic integration, but also with political and social integration among member countries. Even though the Maastricht Treaty on European Union formally established the EU in 1993, the EU's origins date back to the 1950s when six European countries—Belgium, the Federal Republic of Germany, France, Italy, Luxembourg, and the Netherlands—began the process of integration. "The Six," as these countries were sometimes called, first signed the European Coal and Steel Community (ECSC) Treaty (1951). Six years later "the Six" approved the two Rome treaties (1957), which created the European Economic Community (EEC) and the European Atomic Energy Community (Euratom). Since the 1950s, four enlargements have occurred, each expanding the trade bloc. Denmark, Ireland, and the United Kingdom joined "the Six" in 1973. Other enlargements added Greece (1981), Portugal and Spain (1986), and then Austria, Finland, and Sweden (1995) to the organization. The EU's unanimous approval of the Treaty of Amsterdam in 1999 laid the groundwork for yet another enlargement, perhaps by 2005, for six additional countries: Cyprus, the Czech Republic, Estonia, Hungary, Poland, and Slovenia. The EU insists that "Union membership is open to any European country with stable democratic government, a good human rights record, a properly functioning market economy, and the macroeconomic fitness to fulfill the obligations of membership."[23]

Today, the depth of EU economic, political, and social integration rests on its "Three Pillars." The first pillar focuses on the economic integration of the fifteen member countries. To this end, the EU created a single market where goods and services, laborers, capital, and money flow freely across national borders. In addition, the EU has created a common currency—the euro—that was introduced on January 1, 1999. The euro replaced the national currencies of twelve EU countries in 2002. The twelve EU countries that have accepted the euro as their common currency are also a part of the European Monetary Union (EMU), sometimes called the "euro-zone." An independent European Central Bank (ECB), which is located in Frankfurt, Germany, has coordinated the EU's broad stabilization policies with the central banks of EU member countries since 1999. The EU's second and third pillars have integrated some of the political, social, and legal institutions and policies of member countries. For instance, EU members coordinate their foreign and defense policies and their law enforcement efforts.[24]

NAFTA: A STEPPING STONE TO A FREE TRADE AREA OF THE AMERICAS?

NAFTA, which took effect on January 1, 1994, is the leading trade bloc in North America that comprises Canada, Mexico, and the United States. As a comprehensive trade agreement, NAFTA sought to expand trade in goods and services among the three member countries by reducing tariffs, quotas, and other trade barriers. Furthermore, the agreement included specific protections for intellectual property rights, including enforcement of patent and copyright laws for computer software, music recordings, books, designs, movies, and other information sources. NAFTA institutions have also been set up to protect workers, the environment, and fair trade within the trade bloc and between NAFTA and other countries or trade blocs.

NAFTA has been controversial since it began operations in 1994. Supporters of NAFTA argue that the agreement has succeeded in expanding trilateral trade within the trade bloc from $289 billion in 1993 to $507 billion in 1999. Furthermore, supporters note that all three member countries have experienced low rates of unemployment and high rates of foreign investment and economic growth since it was instituted. Supporters also note that NAFTA institutions protect workers' rights (the North American Commission on Labor Cooperation) and the environment (the North American Commission on Environmental Cooperation).[25] Finally, supporters believe NAFTA successes will add momentum to current negotiations to create a free trade area of the Americas (FTAA) by 2005.

Bold Steps toward a Free Trade Area of the Americas (FTAA)

The idea of a free trade area of the Americas (FTAA) has been discussed by governments in the Western Hemisphere since the mid-1990s. In the spring of 2001, leaders of the thirty-four democracies of the hemisphere, stretching from Canada to Chile, met at the Summit of the Americas in Quebec City to discuss the creation of the world's largest free trade zone. At this summit, leaders signed an agreement to open their markets by December 2005. Furthermore, the agreement pledged to cooperate in solving hemispheric problems such as poverty, drug trafficking, the Acquired Immune Deficiency Syndrome (AIDS), environmental degradation, and issues related to worker rights and human rights. While some experts viewed the creation of an FTAA as a logical extension of NAFTA, others were doubtful that the thirty-four countries could iron out the details necessary to create a hemispheric free trade zone by 2005.

Opponents of NAFTA challenge the rosy picture painted by NAFTA supporters by noting that the U.S. merchandise trade surpluses with Mexico during the early 1990s have been replaced by high trade deficits—a $24 billion trade deficit in 2000 alone. Furthermore, they point to the flight of American firms—and jobs—to Mexico. Examples of firms exiting the United States in favor of Mexico include Zenith, Nintendo of America, Mattel, Sara Lee Knit Products, Purina, Nabisco, and others. Finally, opponents argue that underfunded NAFTA commissions, committees, and working groups lack the financial resources to protect workers or the environment—mainly in regions of Mexico dominated by maquiladoras (duty-free assembly plants).[26]

Customs Unions vs. Free Trade Areas

Regional trade blocs are organized in different ways. Two of the most common types of organization include customs unions and free trade areas. A *customs union* reduces trade barriers among member nations and creates a uniform set of customs duties or other trade restrictions on imports from nonmember countries. The EU is an example of a customs union.

A *free trade area* also promotes freer trade among member nations by reducing or eliminating trade barriers. Member countries in free trade areas, however, are free to negotiate their own import quotas, tariffs, or other trade arrangements with nonmember countries. NAFTA and ASEAN are examples of free trade areas.

THE GLOBAL TRADING SYSTEM: OLD ISSUES AND NEW CHALLENGES

As the global economy moves into the twenty-first century, there are numerous challenges to the global trading system. Since the early 1990s, few have challenged the basic premise that freer trade brings with it the potential for sustained economic growth and development throughout the world. Yet, there are forces at work in the global economy presenting challenges to global trade and the spread of global capitalism.

Protectionism is one obstacle to the global trading system. It refers to the government's use of trade barriers or other restrictions to limit foreign imports. The most recognized trade barriers include tariffs, import quotas, voluntary restrictions, and embargoes. A *tariff* is a federal tax on an imported good. An *import quota* sets a specific limit on the amount of an imported good. *Voluntary restrictions* are informal agreements between countries to limit imports (a voluntary restraint agreement) or to boost exports to another country to a certain level (voluntary export expansion). An *embargo* cuts off some or all trade with another nation. Why would anyone want to limit freer trade? Those who favor protectionism—typically called protectionists—defend limits on trade using four main arguments. First, protectionists argue that trade barriers are necessary to protect infant industries in the domestic economy from more established foreign competitors. Second, protectionists believe that trade barriers protect domestic jobs by limiting the import of inexpensive foreign products—products that could drive domestic producers into bankruptcy. Third, protectionists say that trade barriers and other restrictions on trade are necessary to deter other nations from using unfair trade practices. For example, the United States slapped a stiff tariff on Russian steel in 1999 because Russian firms were dumping steel in to U.S. markets. *Dumping* refers to the sale of a foreign good at a price below the cost of producing the good. Fourth, protectionists argue that excessive specialization and trade weaken the national economy by making a nation overdependent on foreign goods, services, or resources.

A second challenge to the global trading system is the *relocalization* of economies, which is the process of "fostering community-oriented production."[27] That is, it encourages smaller, local businesses to meet most of society's economic needs. To accomplish this goal, local economies would diversify, rather than specialize. Relocalization would also mean greater restrictions on investment by MNCs and less dependence on foreign trade. The relatively small, but growing movement toward relocalization is supported by another movement—sometimes called the *new protectionism*—that advocates greater government control on trade and foreign investment and a greater voice for local peoples in the economic decisions that affect their lives.[28]

A third challenge to the global trading system is the use of economic sanctions as a foreign policy tool. *Economic sanctions* are any restrictions on trade, investments, or foreign aid that are designed to pressure a country to change a policy or an action. Typically, they are used to promote human rights and individual freedoms or to stop aggression. For example, the United States imposed economic sanctions on Cuba in 1959 to weaken the communist dictator Fidel Castro. In this case, the trade sanctions took the form of a full trade embargo, whereby the United States stopped all trade and investment in Cuba. In 1996, the United States strengthened its sanctions against Cuba by instituting the Cuban Liberty and Democratic Solidarity Act, also known as "Helms-Burton." Under this act, the United States extended its embargo to any individual or company that was caught trafficking (buying or selling) U.S. property that was confiscated by the communists in the late 1950s. The United States had imposed economic sanctions on over two dozen countries by the mid-1990s including Iran, Iraq, Sudan, and North Korea. Others, particularly human rights activists, opposed expanded trade with China until that country's human rights abuses were addressed. Economic sanctions remain controversial because some people believe the unintended costs of sanctions—especially the economic hardships inflicted on civilian populations—outweigh the benefits.

A fourth challenge to the global trading system is anticompetitive behavior by countries. For example, the Organization of Petroleum Exporting Countries (OPEC), which is a producer cartel, expects members to comply with strict guidelines concerning the amount of a

Bob Englehart, *The Hartford Courant* (24 May 2000). Reprinted with permission.

product each will produce (the production quota) and the price that each will charge for the product. A *cartel* is a formal agreement or organization among firms or nations that produce an identical product, such as oil. Today, OPEC comprises 11 member countries from Africa (Algeria, Libya, and Nigeria), Asia (Indonesia), the Middle East (Iran, Iraq, Kuwait, Qatar, Saudi Arabia, and United Arab Emirates), and South America (Venezuela). The challenge to the global trading system stems from the power of OPEC to restrict the world's supply of oil and, thus, influence its price. This power was first demonstrated in 1973–1974 when the OPEC nations were able quintuple oil prices. In 1973 the Arab members of OPEC also launched an oil embargo on the United States to protest U.S. support for Israel in the 1973 Yom Kippur War. More recently, renewed solidarity among OPEC members caused the price for oil to more than triple between early 1999 ($11 per barrel) and the fall of 2000 ($35 per barrel). Why is this a problem? Among the most important features of a freer and fairer global trading system is competitive markets. Producer cartels, especially cartels that produce an essential product such as oil, can promote global stability or contribute to economic instability through their production and pricing decisions.

Oil is the world's leading source of energy. By the close of 1999:

- global oil reserves totaled 1 trillion barrels, 78% of which were located in OPEC member countries

- the five largest oil producers in the world were Saudi Arabia, the former Soviet Union, the United States, Iran, and China

- the largest oil reserves were located in Saudi Arabia, Iraq, the United Arab Emirates, Kuwait, and Iran

Source: *Organization of Petroleum Exporting Countries, Annual Statistical Bulletin,* 1999.

A fifth challenge to the global trading system is warfare, civil strife, terrorism, or other action capable of severing commercial ties between countries. For example, Iraq's invasion of neighboring Kuwait on August 2, 1990 disrupted oil exports from the Persian Gulf region during the early 1990s. In response to the invasion, the United Nations imposed economic sanctions on Iraq and by January 1991 approved military action—called the Gulf War—to liberate Kuwait. Even after Iraq was expelled from Kuwait in February 1991, the oil exports from the Gulf region were disrupted. Iraq's oil exports were restricted by continued UN economic sanctions, while Kuwait's oil exports were slowed by fires that the departing Iraqis had set in the Kuwaiti oil fields—an action widely viewed as a type of ecoterrorism. More recently the September 11, 2001 terrorist attacks on the World Trade Center in New York City and on the Pentagon in Washington, DC, also dampened international trade. (The global impact of the September 11 attacks on the international economy are more fully examined in Chapter 5.)

NOTES

1. Adam Smith, *An Inquiry into the Nature and Causes of the Wealth of Nations* (Chicago: Henry Regnery, 1953), 25.

2. World Trade Organization (WTO), *Annual Report 2001* (Geneva: World Trade Organization, 2001), 9.

3. World Bank, *World Development Report, 2000/2001: Attacking Poverty* (New York: Oxford University Press, 2000), 274–275.

4. Ibid., 274–75.

5. "The WTO in Brief," 1 (*www.wto.org*).

6. World Bank, *Entering the 21st Century: World Development Report, 1999/2000* (New York: Oxford University Press, 2000), 54.

7. Japan External Trade Organization, "Sino-Japanese Trade Reaches Record Level in 2000" (press release, 8 February 2001) (*www.jetro.go.*

jp/it/e/press/2001/feb8_1.html); and Bureau of Economic Analysis (BEA), "Exports, Imports and Balance of Goods by Selected Countries and Geographic Areas, 2000" (Exhibit 14) (*www.census.gov/foreign-trade/press-release/current_press_release/exh14.txt*).

8. World Bank, *Entering the 21st Century*, 64; and WTO, *Annual Report 2001*, 9.

9. "The WTO in Brief," 2 (*www.wto.org*).

10. WTO, *Annual Report 2001*, 27.

11. "A Tussle over Tax," *The Economist*, 4 March 2000, 75–76; and "Another Trade War?" *The Economist*, 26 February 2000, 88.

12. Bureau of International Narcotics and Law Enforcement Affairs (U.S. Department of State), "Money Laundering and Financial Crimes," *International Narcotics Control Strategy Report, 1999* (Washington, DC: U.S. Department of State, 1999) (*www.state.gov/global/narcotics_law/1999_narc_report*); and U.S. Department of State, "Actions against Abuse of the Global Financial System: Report for G7 Finance Ministers to the Heads of State and Government" (Okinawa, 21 July, 2000) (Washington, DC: U.S. Department of State, 2000) (*www.usinfo.state.gov/topical/econ/g8okin/wwwhabuse.html*).

13. WTO, *Annual Report 2001*, 14, 16.

14. BEA, "Trade in Goods and Services: Tables," U.S. Department of Commerce and the BEA (International Accounts Data) (*www.bea.gov/boa/di/tradgs-d.htm*); and BEA, "BEA News Release," 18–19 (*www.bea.doc.gov/bea/newsrel/trad1200.htm*).

15. BEA, "BEA News Release," 18–19.

16. BEA, "Exports, Imports and Balance of Goods" (Exhibit 14), 1; "Top 50 Purchasers of U.S. Exports in 1999" (Table 10), International Trade Administration (ITA) and the U.S. Department of Commerce (DOC) (*www. ita.doc.gov/td/industry/otea/usfth/aggregate/H99t10.txt*); and "Top 50 Suppliers of U.S. Imports in 1999" (Table 11) ITA/DOC (*www. ita.doc.gov/td/industry/otea/usfth/aggregate/H99t11.txt*)

17. BEA, "Exports, Imports and Balance of Goods" (Exhibit 14), 1.

18. BEA, "U.S. International Trade in Goods and Services" (News Release, 21 February 2001) (*www.bea.doc.gov/bea/di/tradgs-d.htm*); and BEA, "BEA News Release," 15–17 (*www.bea.doc.gov/bea/newsrel/trad1200.htm*).

19. Ibid.

20. "The Explosive Growth of Foreign Exchange Trading," *Economic Report of the President: 1999* (Washington, DC: U.S. Government Printing Office, 1999), 224; and Bank for International Settlements, "Central bank survey of foreign exchange and derivatives market activity in April 2001: preliminary global data" (press release, 9 October 2001), 1–4.

21. "Exchange Rates," *The Wall Street Journal*, 11 July 2001, C11.

22. BEA, "Exports, Imports and Balance of Goods" (Exhibit 14), 1.

23. Bill Burros, Jonathon Davidson, and Maeve O'Beirne, *The European Union: A Guide for Americans, 2000* (Washington, DC: Delegation of the European Commission in the United States, 1999), 3.

24. Ibid., 3–5, 10–14, 30–33.

25. NAFTA Commission (Joint Statement of Ministers), "Five Years of Achievement," 23 April 1999 (*www.mac.doc.gov/nafta/joint.htm*).

26. "A Greener, or Browner, Mexico?" *The Economist*, 7 August 1999, 26–27; and "If Not for NAFTA, When?" *The Economist* (Mexico survey), 28 October 2000, 8.

27. Ralph Nader and Lori Wallach, "GATT, NAFTA, and the Subversion of the Democratic Process," in *The Case against the Global Economy: And a Turn toward the Local*, ed. by Jerry Mander and Edward Goldsmith (San Francisco, CA: Sierra Club, 1996), 107.

28. Colin Hines and Tim Lang, "In Favor of a New Protectionism," in *The Case against the Global Economy: And a Turn toward the Local*, ed. Jerry Mander and Edward Goldsmith (San Francisco, CA: Sierra Club, 1996), 490–491.

3

Multinational Corporations: Spinning the Web, Part 2

WHAT IS A MULTINATIONAL CORPORATION?

A *multinational corporation* (MNC) is a company that is based in one country, but owns or controls other companies— called affiliates—in one or more additional countries. From its headquarters in one country, the parent company exercises direct control over the policies of its affiliates, including policies related to the production and distribution of goods. Furthermore, the ownership of MNCs might be private, public, or some mixture of the two. MNCs, which are also called multinationals or transnational corporations (TNCs), have strengthened the economic web that ties the global economy together.

Ranked by total revenues, Exxon Mobil is the world's largest multinational, with 2000 sales receipts of $210 billion according to *Fortune*'s Global 5 Hundred ranking of the world's largest corporations.[1] Exxon Mobil is a privately owned U.S. company, with its headquarters located in Irving, Texas. The corporation's primary business is energy, including exploration, production, transportation, and sale of crude oil and natural gas. Exxon Mobil is also involved in the production and sale of petroleum products and petrochemicals, and participates in the mining of coal and other minerals. Interestingly, it was a megamerger between two oil giants—Exxon and Mobil—in November 1999 that created this corporation. Today, Exxon Mobil's production facilities are located throughout the world.

In 2000, the 10 largest corporations in the world, based on revenues, were:

Exxon Mobil, $210 billion

Wal-Mart Stores, $193 billion

General Motors, $185 billion

Ford Motor, $181 billion

DaimlerChrysler, $150 billion

Royal Dutch/Shell Group, $149 billion

BP, $148 billion

General Electric, $130 billion

Mitsubishi, $127 billion

Toyota Motor, $121 billion

Source: *Fortune*, "Global 5 Hundred: The World's Largest Corporations, 2000," 23 July 2001, F-1.

Figure 3.1 illustrates the revenues of several of the world's largest privately owned multinationals compared to the gross national product (GNP) of selected nations in 1999.[2] In 1999, General Motors (GM) was the largest corporation in the world with revenues of $177 billion—a sum greater than the GNPs of all but twenty-two countries of the world.

Another way to rank corporations is by number of employees. Using this criterion, four of the top five corporations in 2000 had a workforce of over one million workers: China National Petrolum (1,292,558), Wal-Mart Stores (1,244,000), Sinopec (1,173,901 employees), and State Power (1,137,025 employees). The fifth largest corporate employer in the global economy was the U.S. Postal Service (901,238 employees). In this ranking Wal-Mart (United States) was the only privately owned corporation, while China National Petroleum (China), Sinopec (China), State Power (China), and the U.S. Postal Service (United States) were government corporations.[3]

What Is a Conglomerate? A Case Study of Procter & Gamble

A *conglomerate* is a highly diversified corporation. Many multinationals are conglomerates. One of the most widely recognized conglomerates in today's global economy is Procter & Gamble (P&G), which, in 2000, had total revenues of about $40 billion and production facilities in seventy countries. P&G's headquarters is in Cincinnati, Ohio, and the company employs over 100,000 workers.

P&G is considered a conglomerate because of the wide variety of consumer goods and services it produces—more than 300 brands in all. Broadly speaking, these goods can be grouped under five headings, each containing brand name products

Figure 3.1
MNC Revenues and the GNP of Selected Countries, 1999 (in billions of $US)

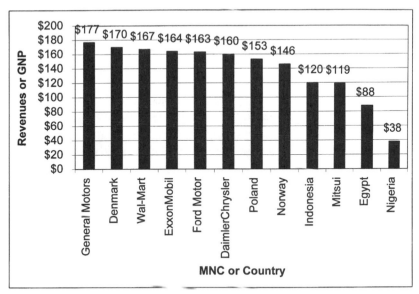

Sources: World Bank, *World Development Report 2000/2001* (New York: Oxford University Press, 2000), 274–275; and "Global 5 Hundred: The World's Largest Corporations (1999)," *Fortune* (*www.fortune.com/fortune/global 500*).

used by millions of consumers around the world. P&G's most recent acquisition was the Clairol haircare business, which was purchased in November 2001 from Bristol-Myers Squibb for $5 billion. A small sampling of the P&G product line illustrates the diversity within this conglomerate:

- Baby care: Luvs and Pampers

- Beauty care: Old Spice, Sure, Cover Girl, Head & Shoulders, Ivory, Noxzema, Herbal Essence, and Loving Care

- Health care: Pepto-Bismol, Crest, Scope, NyQuil, DayQuil, and Vicks

- Home care and paper: Febreze, Cascade, Downy, Mr. Clean, Tide, Bounty, and Charmin

- Foods and beverages: Folgers, Millstone, Jif, Crisco, and Pringles

Many conglomerates rely on production facilities located in different countries to service expanding global markets. P&G is no exception. Its recent reorganization, called Organization 2005, accelerated the pace of product development and improved delivery systems to bring new products to global markets.[4]

MNCs can also be ranked by the size of their foreign assets, such as manufacturing or assembly plants, warehouses, equipment, and so on. According to the United Nations Conference on Trade and Development's (UNCTAD) *World Investment Report 2000*, the MNC with the largest foreign assets was General Electric (U.S.), as shown in Table 3.1.[5]

There has been remarkable stability in this ranking of top MNCs, with many of the same companies occupying the top spots year after year. In fact, while there was some shuffling in the positions of several top ten MNCs from 1997 to 1998, there was just one change—the addition of BP Amoco (UK) and the deletion of Volkswagen (Germany), which fell from number 8 to number 11. Four major industries continued to dominate the top 100 list, including motor vehicles, petroleum exploration and distribution, electronics and electrical equipment, and chemicals and pharmaceuticals. Five out of the top ten MNCs have their headquarters in the United States. Furthermore, U.S. MNCs held about one-quarter of the top 100 spots, followed by Japan, France, Germany, and the United Kingdom. Not surprisingly, 99 out of the top

Table 3.1
The World's Top 10 MNCs, 1998 (ranked by foreign assets, in billions of $US)

Rank	Corporation	Country	Foreign Assets	Foreign Sales	Foreign Employees
1	General Electric	U.S.	$128.6	$28.7	130,000
2	General Motors	U.S.	$73.1	$49.9	NA
3	Shell, Royal Dutch	Neth/UK	$67.0	$50.0	61,000
4	Ford Motor	U.S.	NA	$43.8	171,276
5	Exxon Corp.	U.S.	$50.1	$92.7	NA
6	Toyota Motor	Japan	$44.9	$55.2	113,216
7	IBM	U.S.	$43.6	$46.4	149,934
8	BP Amoco	UK	$40.5	$48.6	78,950
9	Daimler-Benz	Germany	$36.7	$125.4	208,502
10	Nestlé SA	Switzerland	$35.6	$51.2	225,665

Source: United Nations Conference on Trade and Development (UNCTAD), *World Investment Report 2000*.

100 MNCs that comprised this select group had their headquarters in the industrialized nations.[6]

THE GROWTH OF MULTINATIONALS: MERGERS, ACQUISITIONS, AND GREENFIELD INVESTMENTS

There has been phenomenal growth in the number and size of MNCs during the 1990s. By 2000, approximately 63,000 MNCs with 700,000 foreign affiliates operated in the global economy. MNCs expand overseas mainly through *foreign direct investment* (FDI), a process by which MNCs gain ownership or control of production facilities or related businesses involving the distribution or marketing of goods or services. FDI takes place through mergers and acquisitions or greenfield investments.

Today, the great majority of all FDI involves cross-border *mergers and acquisitions* (M&As), which occur when two existing companies are legally joined under single ownership. In fact, cross-border M&As grew from $187 billion in 1995 to $1,144 billion in 2000, an increase of over 500%. In 2000, most of these M&As took place in the developed countries (92%), which accounted for $1,057 billion of the money spent on M&As. In addition, the megadeals—M&As worth at least $1 billion—took place in developed countries. M&A activity in the developing countries (nearly 6%) and in the economies of central and eastern Europe (less than 1%) accounted for a significantly smaller portion of global M&A activity. In addition, 175 megadeals—M&As worth at least $1 billion—were concluded in 2000, a significant jump from the 114 megadeals negotiated during 1999. The largest megadeal in 2000 occurred when the UK-based Vodafone AirTouch purchased Mannesmann of Germany for $200 billion. Predictably, the United States, which has traditionally offered a stable and profitable business climate, was the single largest target country for cross-border M&As. In 2000 alone, foreign firms purchased $324 billion worth of U.S. companies, or nearly one-third of the entire world's expenditures on cross-border M&As.[7]

The wave of corporate megamergers between U.S.-based multinationals also illustrates the global pattern of business expansion through M&As. For instance, multibillion dollar deals within U.S. borders brought Time Warner and America Online under one roof in 2001 ($112 billion, communications and media). Other recent M&As included Pfizer and Warner Lambert in 2000 ($90 billion,

" FILL IT UP, CHECK THE OIL AND BATTERY AND YOU'RE FIRED. "

Bob Englehart, *The Hartford Courant* (3 December 1998). Reprinted with permission.

pharmaceuticals), Mobil and Exxon in 1999 ($82 billion, petroleum and petrochemicals), and Sprint and MCI WorldCom in 1999 ($129 billion, communications).[8]

The second important component of FDI is *greenfield investments*, which involve the construction of entirely new production facilities such as manufacturing plants, retail outlets, oil refineries and pipelines, office buildings, warehouses, farms, or plantations. While the bulk of FDI during the 1990s resulted from M&As, some countries, including Japan, preferred greenfield investments—especially when investing in the developing world. The debate over the positive and negative impacts of FDI by MNCs, particularly in the developing world, has a long history. What are the likely short-term and long-term impacts of cross-border M&As and greenfield investments on developing economies?

In the short term, greenfield investments offer greater advantages to a host country's economic development than do cross-border M&As. This conclusion stems from one basic fact: greenfield investments result in the construction of new production facilities in the host country. Greenfield investments automatically increase the nation's capital stock (value of real capital that can be used to produce goods or services), create new jobs for construction workers and for the firm's employees, and inject new technology, management techniques, and production methods into the local economy. Greenfield investments also tend to increase competition in host countries by expanding the number of firms in an industry. GM's construction of a new production facility in Poland in 1998 illustrates the positive impacts of greenfield investments in host countries. M&As, however, typically involve the transfer of ownership or control of existing assets from a local business to a multinational. Hence, in the short term there is little or no expansion of the country's capital stock or new employment opportunities. Such was the case in the cross-border merger between German auto maker Daimler-Benz and the U.S.-based Chrysler Corporation in 1998. Furthermore, some M&As may reduce competition in the local economy by bringing smaller firms under the control of a single MNC. This is not to say that M&As offer no advantages to a country's economic development in the short term. Indeed, M&As may have an immediate impact by rescuing failing companies from bankruptcy or by strengthening a local firm's ability to market or distribute its wares in global markets.

In the long term, economists see the advantages of greenfield investments over M&As diminishing. This conclusion is based on the financial commitments that each type of FDI offers to overseas plants. After all, foreign affiliates are created to earn profits for the larger MNC. To improve corporate efficiency and, ultimately, corporate profits, cross-border M&As tend to result in improvements in or expansion of existing capital, shared technology, the transfer of vital management and technical skills, and new jobs.

The growth of FDI, particularly during the 1990s, has strengthened the economic web linking people, firms, and governments in the global economy. Table 3.2 summarizes growth trends in four key areas related to multinational investment: the total sales of MNCs' foreign affiliates, the total exports of MNCs' foreign affiliates, the total assets of MNCs' foreign affiliates, and the total number of employees of MNCs' foreign affiliates. Note that by 1999, the total exports of goods and services by foreign affiliates of MNCs totaled over $3 trillion. As impressive as this figure is, the bulk of the output produced by MNCs' affiliates—over $10 trillion worth of products—was sold in local markets. Also note the dramatic growth rate in all four areas between the early 1980s and 1999: a fivefold increase in total sales, a fivefold increase in total ex-

Table 3.2
MNCs and FDI: Selected Indicators of Growth, 1986–1999 (in
billions of $US)

Indicators	Value at Current Prices*		
	1982	1990	1999
Total sales of foreign affiliates	$2,462	$5,503	$13,564
Total exports of foreign affiliates	$637	$1,165	$3,167
Total assets of foreign affiliates	$1,886	$5,706	$17,680
Employment of foreign affiliates (in thousands)	17,433	23,605	40,536

*Current prices are not adjusted for inflation over time.
Source: UNCTAD, *World Investment Report, 2000*.

ports, more than a ninefold increase in total assets, and more than a
doubling of jobs.[9]

MNCs: FDI GROWTH AND GLOBALIZATION

The trend toward greater FDI by MNCs was well established by the
1990s. In 2000, for example, UNCTAD reported that FDI inflows had
grown to $1.1 trillion—nearly five times the recorded inflows for 1990.
FDI inflows refer to the dollar value of FDI that comes into a country.
There are many reasons for this steep climb in FDI during the final decade of the twentieth century, and evidence suggests that this dramatic
climb will continue as the global economy matures during the
twenty-first century.

One main reason for recent FDI growth is the changing business climate in the global economy. *Business climate* is a broad term used to describe factors that might encourage or discourage business activity.
Factors promoting FDI abound. First, there has been a pronounced
liberalization of investment policies in many countries. East and central
European countries, for example, have offered generous tax breaks and
fewer government regulations on MNCs to attract FDI. Profitable FDI
in this region is also enhanced by the steady progress many of these
countries have made in privatizing buinesses. Privatization opens the
doors to M&As, joint ventures between privately owned firms, and

other private-sector business activities. Second, the business climate has improved because countries have eagerly negotiated bilateral investment treaties in record numbers. Third, there has been a discernible pro-global shift in attitudes about the necessity of producing for a global market. This shift in attitude is demonstrated by greater FDI by firms in the newly industrialized countries of East Asia—Korea, Taiwan, and Singapore—that now compete successfully with MNCs from the industrialized countries of Europe and North America.

A second major reason for the rapid growth of FDI in the global economy is changing production techniques. Production techniques, broadly speaking, involve all of the ways goods or services are produced, marketed, and distributed. Technology is one key factor that has revolutionized the production, marketing, and distribution of goods. Technological advances in communications and transportation are particularly important in this regard (see Chapter 1). In a very real sense, technology is the glue that holds the ever-expanding web of MNCs—and their affiliates—together. A second production technique that has encouraged FDI in the global economy is *production sharing*, which occurs when different components of a good are produced and assembled in stages at plants in different countries. This business practice permits MNCs to consider the relative costs of resources, government regulations and tax rates, tariffs or other trade barriers, and other factors before deciding where to produce components or assemble a good. For example, many Japanese televisions are assembled in Mexican maquiladoras (duty-free assembly plants), yet most of the 1,750 components must be imported to Mexico from outside of the NAFTA region (Canada, Mexico, and the United States). A third production technique that promotes FDI is *subcontracting*, where one company hires a second company, called a subcontractor, to produce a good. Major U.S. producers of athletic shoes and sportswear such as Nike and Reebok hire foreign subcontractors to produce much of their product line. Subcontracting creates business opportunities, and the need to invest money in new plants and equipment, in the global economy. Finally, a fourth production decision that encourages FDI is market proximity. That is, MNCs locate production facilities close to buyers. It is not surprising that Ford, GM, Toyota, Volkswagen, and virtually every other major producer of automobiles located production facilities in Brazil during the 1990s. Why? The answer is simple: Brazil had the single largest market for autos in South America. UNCTAD reported that by 2000 the economically developed countries attracted 80% of all

FDI inflows, compared to 17% for developing countries and 3% for transition countries of eastern and central Europe.[10]

EXPANDING FDI WITH BITs: THE GROWTH OF BILATERAL INVESTMENT TREATIES

Bilateral investment treaties (BITs) are formal agreements between two nations designed to protect and promote foreign investments. From the late 1980s to 2000, the number of BITs grew from 385 to 1,857, nearly a 400% increase. How do BITs encourage FDI?

BITs establish the rules of investment and certain protections for firms making foreign investments. While there is some variety in specific items negotiated in BITs, a number of common features appear in most of these treaties. First, BITs clarify terms. For instance, each treaty spells out what types and how much foreign investment is covered by the BIT. Second, BITs clarify the rules of investment and sale of output. For example, most BITs guarantee equal treatment of products produced by MNCs in local markets. Third, BITs protect foreign investments. These protections usually include fair compensation for MNCs' assets if these assets are expropriated or damaged or destroyed by wars or civil unrest. Fourth, BITs guarantee the rights of MNCs to repatriate profits and capital. Repatriation refers to the freedom to return profits or assets to the parent company in a different country. Finally, BITs specify a process to settle disputes. The dispute settlement process typically creates procedures for countries and firms to come to terms if conflicts arise.

Historically, BITs were often used to protect investments made by MNCs in less stable developing countries. During the 1990s, however, BITs were routinely negotiated between countries throughout the global economy. By 2000, 173 countries had negotiated 1,857 BITs "with the dual purpose of protecting their outward investments in, and attracting inward investment from, their co-signatories."[11] The widening interest in negotiating BITs in the global economy is reflected in the regional distribution of the top thirty countries that have signed them. Ten of the top thirty countries were located in western Europe, followed by eastern and central Europe (seven), Asia (five), the Americas (four), Africa (two), and the Middle East (two).[12]

BITs are essential in promoting FDI as the global economy enters the twenty-first century. They help fill a void that currently exists in the global financial architecture. This void exists because there are few commonly accepted rules of conduct for MNC investment in the developed or developing countries, and there is no international authority to oversee FDI on a global basis. This reality can be contrasted with the specific, enforceable rules of trade that have been agreed to by members of the World Trade Organization (WTO).

FDI AND THE UNITED STATES: A DOMINANT PLAYER IN THE GLOBAL ECONOMY

The United States has the largest economy in the world. By the close of 2000, the nominal gross domestic product (GDP; not adjusted for inflation) topped $10 trillion. It makes sense, therefore, that the United States would be in a prime position to attract foreign investments (inflows) and to invest in promising business ventures in other countries (outflows). Traditionally, foreign MNCs have eagerly sought investment opportunities in the United States for a variety of reasons—stable government, sound legal system to protect private property rights, strong financial institutions, sophisticated infrastructure, skilled labor force, and, of course, a huge market in which to sell finished goods and services. By 1999, foreign MNCs had invested close to $1 trillion in the United States. About 70% of this investment came from the highly industrialized countries of Europe, followed by Asia and the Pacific (17%) and other regions (13%). The great majority of FDI from Asia and the Pacific was from one country—Japan—which accounted for nearly 90% of the region's total investment in the United States.[13]

Direct investment by U.S. firms in other countries rose to over $1 trillion by the late 1990s. In fact, U.S. FDI abroad more than doubled in the span of time between 1990 and 1999, as shown in Figure 3.2.[14] While the pace of U.S. FDI has increased in recent years, American MNCs have a long history of foreign investments. In the early twentieth century, U.S. MNCs were interested mainly in acquiring sources of natural resources, especially minerals such as nickel, copper, and oil. By the 1920s, U.S. auto manufacturers such as Ford and GM had purchased smaller European auto makers in pursuit of new products and new markets. During the mid-twentieth century, U.S. MNCs pursued many different foreign investment paths. For example, the Aluminum Company of America (Alcoa) aggressively purchased foreign resources to manufacture aluminum—a product that it had monopoly control of by the close of World War II. Other American MNCs, such as International Telephone and Telegraph (IT&T), diversified their foreign investments and, by definition, became conglomerates. Through M&As,

Figure 3.2
U.S. FDI Abroad, 1990–1999 (in billions of $US)

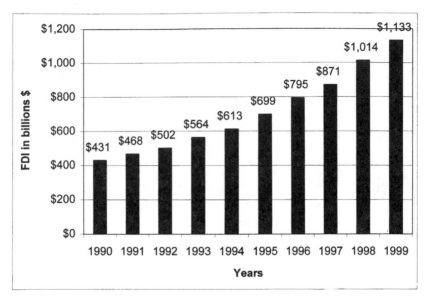

Source: U.S. Department of Commerce, Bureau of Economic Analysis, *Survey of Current Business* (September 2000).

IT&T came to own or control over 100 firms during the 1960s and 1970s in fields as diverse as food products, insurance, hotels, publishing, airlines, and rental car services. By the 1980s and 1990s, American multinationals were among the most dominant firms in the global economy. Ranked by total revenues, U.S. MNCs swept the top four places with Exxon Mobil, Wal-Mart Stores, GM, and Ford leading the pack.

Most U.S. FDI has traditionally gone to the industrialized nations. It is not surprising, therefore, that about one-half (51%) of the $1.1 trillion in U.S. FDI is invested in industrialized European countries. The remainder is spread across the globe—in Latin America and other Western Hemisphere countries (20%), in Asia and the Pacific (16%), and other regions (13%). The top five recipients of U.S. FDI by 1999 included the United Kingdom ($213 billion), Canada ($112 billion), the Netherlands ($106 billion), Switzerland ($51 billion), and Japan ($48 billion). What are the main types of investments made by U.S. firms in these countries? The largest category of FDI is finance, which includes a variety of financial services, insurance and real estate (but not depository institutions), and which accounts for 38% of U.S. FDI. Manufacturing, which includes food products, chemicals, metals, industrial machinery and equipment, electronics, and transportation equipment, accounts for another 28% of U.S. FDI. Lesser amounts are invested in areas such as petroleum and wholesale and retail trade.[15]

MNCs AND CHANGING VIEWS OF GLOBAL RESPONSIBILITY

The growth in the number, size, and power of MNCs has fueled demands for these firms to become more humane, responsible, and accountable for their actions. That is, there is greater consensus that global corporations must behave in socially responsible ways. In the vanguard of this global drive to reform business practices of MNCs are nongovernmental organizations (NGOs). NGOs are organizations designed to investigate issues or problems and to instigate reforms to correct unjust policies. MNCs, international organizations such as the WTO and the IMF, and governments are the NGOs' three main targets. NGOs apply pressure on the offending party and thereby openly challenge policies or actions of national or global concern. Among the most important global issues today are global poverty, human rights violations, environmental decay, the destruction of indigenous cultures, and workers' rights. By the late 1990s, there were over 25,000 NGOs in operation, about 80% on a global level.

The push to make corporations behave more responsibly is not a new idea. During the late nineteenth and early twentieth centuries, for example, reformers in the United States pressed for changes in the American workplace to create a safer and more humane working environment. Reform-minded journalists at the turn of the century—often called muckrakers—aggressively investigated injustices and called upon decision makers in the private and public sectors to institute needed reforms. For example, in *The Jungle* (1906), American author Upton Sinclair exposed the horrors of poverty in Chicago's slums, the lack of opportunities for immigrant laborers, and the sickening conditions that existed in the meat-packing industry. In one vivid passage, he wrote about the production of sausage from meat contaminated by dirt, sawdust, rat dung, dead rodents, and stale water.[16] Sinclair's words did not go unnoticed. *The Jungle* brought a swift response from the U.S. Congress—the creation of the Food and Drug Administration (FDA)—to monitor safety and sanitation issues in the American workplace. Other muckrakers such as Jacob Riis (*How the*

Other Half Lives, 1890), Ida Tarbell (*History of the Standard Oil Company*, 1904), Ray Stannard Baker (*Following the Color Line*, 1908), and Frank Norris (*The Octopus*, 1901) challenged major corporations—and society—to accept responsibility for rampant poverty, discrimination, predatory business practices, and other abuses. In short, muckrakers and other reformers provided a catalyst for progressive reforms in how corporate America operated nearly a century ago.

The chorus of voices demanding reforms in MNCs' business practices has grown louder over the past couple of decades. A number of tragedies in the 1980s focused the world's attention on the human and environmental damage that could result from corporate negligence. Many ordinary people, along with NGOs and other organizations, came to a similar conclusion: that corporations must be held accountable for their actions. One case involved the accidental release of toxic fumes at the Union Carbide fertilizer plant in Bhopal, India (1984), which ultimately resulted in thousands of deaths and debilitating injuries. Two years later, the meltdown of the nuclear reactor in Chernobyl, USSR, caused the deaths of additional thousands. It also resulted in radioactive contamination of air, water, and topsoil not only in the Ukraine (one of the former Soviet Republics), but also in several neighboring countries. A third corporate blunder led to a massive oil spill off the coast of Alaska. This disaster occurred when the oil freighter *Exxon Valdez* (1989) ran aground, spewing 11 million gallons of oil into Prince William Sound and the Gulf of Alaska. Exxon agreed to pay $1 billion in criminal and civil penalties for its negligence. Exxon also reported that it spent over $2 billion to spearhead the cleanup efforts that, sadly, were unable to restore the pre-spill ecological balance to the region.[17]

In recent years, demands for greater corporate responsibility have focused on three main issues: more humane treatment for workers, more concern for the natural environment, and more respect for indigenous cultures. NGOs, labor unions, religious groups, governments, international organizations, and others have participated in a broad-based movement to protect people and the planet from business exploitation. The topic of labor's fundamental rights is more fully explored in the next section of this chapter.

DEFINING WORKERS' FUNDAMENTAL RIGHTS: A CODE OF CONDUCT FOR MNCs

What fundamental rights should workers have in the global economy? Who should determine the rules to guide MNCs' behavior? How should these rules be enforced? These are some of the key questions that individuals, labor organizations, NGOs, governments, and MNCs themselves have wrestled with for over a century. Before delving into these questions, let's first distinguish between a corporate code of conduct and a code of conduct for multinational corporations. A *corporate code of conduct* is a set of rules voluntarily created by a corporation for responsible corporate behavior. Today, most major corporations have devised their own codes of conduct. For example, Nike's code of conduct guarantees a safe and healthy workplace, fair compensation, freedom of association, and limits on required work hours. Controversies surrounding Nike's adherence to its code of conduct will be examined later in this chapter.

A *code of conduct for multinationals* defines appropriate rules of behavior for all MNCs in the global economy. These rules of conduct are not devised by MNCs but instead are created by outside individuals or groups, such as labor unions, governments, or NGOs. In today's global economy, both types of codes are viewed as recommendations and do not carry penalties for noncompliance. Still, codes of conduct, particularly those that have gained the support of major industrialized countries or have been accepted by major multinationals, can pressure other governments or MNCs to abide by the code.[18]

One external group that has a great deal of clout in protecting workers' rights is the *International Labor Organization* (ILO). The ILO was founded by the Treaty of Versailles in 1919 at the conclusion of World War I, and was immediately joined by forty-two nations. In 1946, the ILO became a part of the United Nations (UN) system and, thus, solidified its position as the world's leading advocate for labor rights. Today, the ILO's membership comprises 175 member countries. It is a unique organization in that it represents the views of workers, employers, and government. Through formal collaboration among these groups, the ILO makes recommendations on international labor issues. Its broad-based mission seeks to promote workers' rights, increase employment opportunities for men and women, improve social programs, and strengthen the lines of communication between workers, employers, and government. In 1998, the ILO devised its landmark "Declaration on Fundamental Principles and Rights at Work." In this document, the ILO outlined four main principles, all of which had been named in earlier ILO labor standards called the "core conventions." These principles included:

- Freedom of association and the right to bargain collectively: This principle was derived mainly from core convention No. 87 (1948), which supported the right of workers to join labor unions, and core convention No. 98 (1949), which opposed discriminatory practices against unions or union members.

- Abolition of forced labor: This principle dates back to the earliest of the core conventions, No. 29, which opposed compulsory labor (except for military service and a narrow range of other exceptions). This principle was reinforced in core convention No. 105 (1957), which banned forced labor as a punishment for one's political views or union activity.

- Equal opportunity and treatment in the workplace: This principle stems from core convention No. 100 (1951), which demanded equal pay for equal work regardless of gender, and core convention No. 111 (1958), which demanded the end to discrimination in the workplace based on race, gender, religion, political views, or national origin.

- Elimination of child labor: This principle was established by core convention No. 138 (1973), which defined a child's legitimate working age as not less than the minimum age to complete compulsory education. Recently, core convention No. 182 (1999) was adopted to end the worst forms of child labor, including the sale of children and child prostitution.[19]

While the ILO has been a major voice in the struggle to promote and protect the rights of workers in the global economy since the 1920s, it has not been the only voice. For instance, the Organization for Economic Cooperation and Development (OECD)—a regional organization designed to promote sustained economic growth for member countries—developed its own guidelines for multinationals that operate within the thirty-country region. In many respects, these guidelines mirror the ILO's main principles including freedom of association, the right to organize and bargain collectively, nondiscriminatory treatment of workers, and so on. These guidelines are also important to the conduct of business in the global economy because the weight of many of the world's largest economies—including the United States, Japan, and most of the west European countries—has been placed behind them.

In addition to incorporating the ILO into the larger UN system in 1946, the UN has demonstrated its support for workers and workers' rights in other ways. In 1999, for example, the UN developed the *Global Compact* to further advance corporate responsibility in the global economy. Secretary-General Kofi A. Annan of the UN asked businesses throughout the world to embrace the nine principles outlined in its compact. Among the key features of this compact is its focus on world businesses to initiate, implement, and monitor their own policies in order to protect human rights, workers' rights, and the environment. The goal is enlist the support of 1,000 corporations by 2003.[20]

THE GLOBAL SULLIVAN PRINCIPLES OF CORPORATE SOCIAL RESPONSIBILITY

In the United States, another widely respected set of principles, called the "Sullivan Principles," has given direction to responsible corporate behavior since its inception in 1977. This document, authored by the Reverend Leon H. Sullivan, not only advocated for workers, rights, but also highlighted the power of the individual in the global arena. The Sullivan Principles was originally devised to guide the behaviors of firms operating in South Africa and to help the workers of South Africa speak out against the oppressive, discriminatory apartheid policies. Over time, these principles helped to mold the internal policies of MNCs and local firms alike. In 1999, the Sullivan Principles were revised. Now called "The Global Sullivan Principles of Corporate Social Responsibility," the document has garnered the support of the UN, numerous public and nonprofit organizations, and dozens of major MNCs. The text of this document follows. Included in the list of corporate signatories are British Airways, Coca-Cola, DaimlerChrysler, Ford, Hershey, Hughes Electronics, GM, Occidental Petroleum, PepsiCo, Pfizer, Procter & Gamble, Shell, and Texaco.[21]

The Global Sullivan Principles of Corporate Social Responsibility

As a company which endorses the *Global Sullivan Principles* we will respect the law, and as a responsible member of society we will apply these Principles with integrity consistent with the legitimate role of business. We will develop and implement company policies, procedures, training and internal reporting structures to ensure commitment to these Principles throughout the organization. We believe the application of these Principles will achieve greater toleration and better understanding among peoples, and advance the culture of peace.

Accordingly, we will:

- Express our support for universal human rights and, particularly, those of our employees, the communities with which we operate, and parties with whom we do business.

- Promote equal opportunity for our employees at all levels of the company with respect to issues such as color, race, gender, age, ethnicity or religious beliefs, and operate without unacceptable worker treatment such as the exploitation of children, physical punishment, female abuse, involuntary servitude, or other forms of abuse.

- Respect our employees' voluntary freedom of association.

- Compensate our employees to enable them to meet at least their basic needs and provide the opportunity to improve their skill and capability in order to raise their social and economic opportunities.

- Provide a safe and healthy workplace; protect human health and the environment; and promote sustainable development.

- Promote fair competition including respect for intellectual and other property rights, and not offer, pay or accept bribes.

- Work with governments and communities in which we do business to improve the quality of life in those communities—their educational, cultural, economic and social well-being—and seek to provide training and opportunities for workers from disadvantaged backgrounds.

- Promote the application of these Principles by those with whom we do business.

We will be transparent in our implementation of these Principles and provide information which demonstrates publicly our commitment to them.[22]

Reprinted with permission from the International Foundation for Education and Self-Help (IFESH).

RECENT CRITICISMS OF MULTINATIONALS

The growth of multinationals has strengthened the network of economic alliances, trade relationships, cross-border capital flows, and other financial transactions in today's highly integrated global economy. Critics of multinationals, and of the globalization process in general, are weary of the negative effects of this economic integration, however. Critics believe that rapid economic integration benefits the rich and powerful at the expense of everybody else. This viewpoint focuses on the destructiveness of MNCs, particularly in the less developed countries. In this argument, multinationals reap terrific benefits from freer international markets through expanded trade and FDI. In the process, however, they exploit the human and natural resources of host nations, bully local governments, market inappropriate or dangerous products, and retard the development of local economies. Some contend that MNCs have reformed their business practices and, in effect, have become good global citizens. Others argue that needed reforms have only scratched the surface of existing problems. A recent Special Report in *Business Week* concluded "only a handful of multinationals have gotten serious about cleaning up corporate practices. And even if they are well intentioned, the real test is whether the new standards and codes will mean anything in practice. In the new, wired world, there are few places a multinational can avoid scrutiny."[23] Let's briefly survey several specific criticisms of MNCs.

First, multinationals have been criticized for exploiting human and natural resources, especially in the developing world, creating what economists today call "a race to the bottom." The exploitation of local resources gives multinationals a competitive advantage over other firms by reducing production costs. Subjecting low-skilled overseas workers to sweatshop working conditions, low pay, and abusive bosses is one way to minimize production costs. For example, sweatshop conditions existed in plants run by Nike subcontractors in Asia during the 1990s. The exposure of these abuses instigated a global consumer boycott of Nike products in 1997 and prompted Nike to institute a series of reforms shortly thereafter. Included in these reforms were provisions to improve plant safety, raise wages, reduce working hours, end child labor, and provide for independent monitoring of the company's overseas production facilities—often referred to as social auditing. Some of these reforms were listed in Nike's revised code of conduct. While the Nike boycott generated significant negative publicity for this firm, many other MNCs have also been targeted by human rights activists for substandard treatment of workers including Reebok, Mattel, Liz Claiborne, Timberland, Huffy, Wal-Mart, and other familiar names.[24] The United Nations Development Program's (UNDP) *Human Development Report: 1999* comments on the inequality of opportunities in the new global economy by reporting that the "collapse of space, time and borders may be creating a global village, but not everyone can be a citizen. The global, professional elite faces low borders, but billions of others find borders as high as ever."[25]

Second, critics note that the enormous financial power and mobility of multinationals has given them the upper hand when negotiating with host countries. Multinationals negotiate for favorable tax breaks and freedom to side step or ignore environmental laws. For example, some mineral extracting multinationals operating in Papua New Guinea, the Philippines, and Indonesia have long ignored basic environmental safeguards. As a result, massive degradation of forests, rivers, and other ecosystems has occurred.[26] Closer to home, some Mexican maquiladoras have also taken advantage of weak or unenforceable environmental laws. Illegal disposal methods of hazardous wastes has not only damaged ecosystems, but has also contributed to the spread of diseases, birth defects, and other health problems in humans.[27] By 2000, about 4,000 maquiladoras—mostly foreign owned—operated in Mexico and employed over 1 million workers.[28] Commenting on the power of MNCs to pressure local governments for exemptions from environmental or other regulations, a recent *UNESCO Courier* article noted, "Foreign investors have stronger leverage than domestic companies because they can use the threat of disinvestment [pulling out of the country] more credibly and effectively."[29]

A third criticism of multinationals is that their marketing and sale of certain goods in global markets runs contrary to the public's best interest. The most publicized example of an inappropriate marketing campaign in recent history was Nestlé's marketing of instant formula in the developing world. Criticism of Nestlé stemmed from research showing that instant formula was often mixed with unsanitary water or was diluted to make the packaged mix stretch. As a result, many babies who were fed with this instant formula suffered from diseases or malnutrition. A global consumer boycott of Nestlé products was initiated in 1977 by NGOs, including the Infant Feeding Action Coalition. Soon thereafter the World Health Organization (WHO) and the United Nations Children's Fund (UNICEF) joined the campaign to stop Nestlé's marketing of instant formula in the developing world. Even after Nestlé agreed to WHO's International Code on the Marketing of Breast Milk Substitutes in the mid-1980s—which prohibited predatory marketing techniques—the company's compliance with the code was disputed and the global boycott resumed (1988).[30] Other firms have also aggressively marketed dangerous products in the developing world, including high-tar and nicotine tobacco products and pesticides that have long been banned in many countries of the developed world.

A fourth major criticism of multinationals is that their intrusion into less developed countries has retarded the development of local economies. How do MNCs damage local economies? At times local businesses are forced into bankruptcy by the so-called superstores, which offer a wide variety of products at the retail level at relatively low prices. At times, MNCs use and deplete local natural resources such as forests or arable land. For example, rain forests in Brazil and in some central African countries have been harvested at alarming rates. In the central African country of Côte d'Ivoire (Ivory Coast), about 85% of its rain forests have been destroyed through timbering. At times, MNCs establish capital-intensive production methods—production techniques that rely on sophisticated machines rather than human labor—in the manufacture of goods. Combined, these intrusions upset local economies by creating unemployment, encouraging migrations of people to already overcrowded cities, straining scarce social services, and creating greater dependence on external forces (including MNCs themselves).

A fifth criticism of MNCs hinges on their unwise or improperly executed cross-border mergers or acquisitions. In an era of megamergers, MNCs have invested hundreds of billions of dollars annually to purchase foreign firms, but the result in some cases has caused severe economic problems for the multinationals, workers, host communities, and others. One example of a cross-border "merger of equals" that has run into trouble occurred in 1998 when Daimler-Benz (Stuttgart, Germany) acquired Chrysler (Detroit, United States). This $36 billion deal, which created DaimlerChrysler, brought two profitable firms together under one roof. The goal was to create a "global powerhouse" in the automotive industry by linking the world's most recognized luxury-car producer (Daimler-Benz) with America's profitable maker of the popular Dodge Ram Pickup, Jeep Cherokee, and others. According to a special report released by DaimlerChrysler in 1998, this historic merger also sought to expand beyond traditional markets in North America and Europe by developing "new markets in Asia, South America and Eastern Europe, with Asia being a priority."[31] Soon after the so-called merger of equals was consummated, DaimlerChrysler experienced major financial problems. For instance, many of Chrysler's top executives left the firm, production costs increased, and profits dried up. Reflecting the dismal performance of the newly formed company, stock prices for DaimlerChrysler dropped from about $100 per share in 1999 to less than one-half of its former value in the spring of 2001. The drop in the stock's value added yet another problem to the list: a rebellion by some major shareholders in Europe and in the United States. With projections for further financial losses in 2001, announced job cuts of 26,000 workers (20% of Chrysler's entire workforce) between 2001 and 2003, and strong hints that Chrysler will become just one more division in the larger Daimler corporation, there was little to cheer about in the corporate headquarters in Detroit or Stuttgart.[32]

BENEFITS OF MULTINATIONALS IN THE GLOBAL ECONOMY

Over the past twenty years, the competition among the countries of the world to attract multinationals, and FDI by multinationals, has intensified. The liberalization of cross-border investment policies since the 1980s, including a variety of bilateral and multilateral agreements, is one reason for increased investment. Reductions in burdensome government regulations on FDI have also sparked interest in pursuing M&As and greenfield investments. *UNCTAD's World Investment Report 2000* noted that between 1990 and 1999 countries instituted 1,035 changes in their regulations on FDI, 94% of which were viewed as favorable to foreign investment.[33] Governments have also instituted proinvestment policies such as tax incentives, aggressive privatization, and freer trade between MNCs and their overseas affiliates to attract FDI. The lure of profits, through lower production costs or greater access to foreign markets, is yet another motivation for cross-border investments. Recall from Table 3.2 that total sales, assets, exports, and jobs of MNCs' foreign affiliates rose dramatically during the 1990s. But how does the growth of MNCs translate into benefits for the people of the global economy?

In 2000, the world's most admired companies were:

1. General Electric (U.S.)
2. Cisco Systems (U.S.)
3. Microsoft (U.S.)
4. Intel (U.S.)
5. Wal-Mart Stores (U.S.)
6. Sony (Japan)
7. Dell Computer (U.S.)
8. Nokia (Finland)
9. Home Depot (U.S.)
10. Toyota Motor (Japan)

Source: "Fortune 5 Hundred List of the World's Most Admired Companies," *Fortune* 23 July, 2001, Section F.

One major benefit of MNC investment in the global economy is technology transfer. Technology transfer occurs when an MNC's research and development (R&D), new production techniques, or other innovative products or services are automatically infused into the economy of a host country. In recent years, for example, much of the world's attention has focused on the digital divide between the North and the South. The term "*digital divide*," broadly defined, describes the technology gap that exists between the wealthier industrialized countries (the North) and the poorer developing countries (the South). More specifically, digital divide is used to contrast the North's access to computers, the Internet, and other information and communications technologies that have sped the pace of economic growth, at least among the richer countries that have access to this technology. UNDP's *Human Development Report: 1999* reported: "Globalization's rules have set off a race to lay claim to knowledge. A global map for the new technologies is being drawn up faster than most people are able to understand the implications—let alone respond to them. . . . The global gap between haves and have-nots, between know and know-nots is widening."[34] With the recent expansion of FDI throughout the world, the transfer of technology has accelerated. For example, in Latin America firms such as Delphi, IBM, Hewlett-Packard, and others have opened sophisticated production facilities in Mexico. In eastern Europe, the U.S.–based Flextronics bridged the knowledge gap by modernizing its Hungarian electronics plant to produce quality compact disc players, facsimile machines, and stereos.[35] Clearly, the presence of MNCs in these and other countries makes advanced technology immediately available and, thus, enables firms to compete in global markets.

A second benefit of multinationals in the global economy is the infusion of new real capital into the host nation. *Real capital* refers to the factories, office buildings, farms, machines, and tools that people use to produce goods or services. When MNCs make greenfield investments, they immediately infuse new capital into local economies with the new construction that takes place. In addition, FDI through M&As typically involves plant expansions and the introduction of new management and production techniques. The net effect of foreign investments, which topped $1 trillion in 2000 according to UNCTAD, is an increase in the country's *capital stock*—the total amount of capital goods a country has to produce products. There is a direct relationship between the growth of a country's capital stock on the one hand, and higher worker productivity and economic growth on the other. In the fall of 2000, for example, Exxon Mobil proposed to build a 650-mile-long underground pipeline from landlocked Chad, across neighboring Cameroon, to an offshore terminal—a project estimated to cost about $3.5 billion. That is, Exxon Mobil and its partners—Chevron (U.S.) and Petronas (Malaysia)—planned to make a greenfield investment of about $3.5 billion in the region. Exxon Mobil has also enlisted the support of the World Bank to help maintain a cooperative working relationship with the governments of Chad and Cameroon and to guarantee the investments in the event of war, expropriation, or other disaster. In return, Exxon Mobil and its partners promised to design the pipeline to minimize negative environmental and human impacts. When the pipeline is completed in 2004, it is expected to carry 225,000 barrels of oil per day to the offshore distribution terminal. Over the twenty- to twenty-five-year life of the project, the anticipated economic development value of the pipeline—including tax revenues, royalties, jobs, and business formations—could run as high as $8.5 billion for Chad and nearly $1 billion for neighboring Cameroon.[36]

A third benefit offered by multinationals in the global economy is job creation in the host country. According to UNCTAD's World Investment Report 2000, the number of jobs in MNCs' foreign affiliates jumped from 17.5 million in 1982 to 40.5 million in 1999—an increase of about 23 million jobs (see Table 3.2). To illustrate the employment benefits associated with MNCs, consider the impact of GM's decision to locate an auto manufacturing plant in Gliwice, Poland, in 1998. Gliwice is located in the southern Polish province of Silesia, a region known for its large but inefficient smokestack industries and mines. GM's greenfield investment of about $500 million has built a state-of-the-art plant in Gliwice that employs 2,000 workers. Furthermore, because of the popularity of the Opel Astra Classic model being

Bob Englehart, *The Hartford Courant* (6 July 2000). Reprinted with permission.

manufactured in the Gliwice plant, GM is already contemplating an expansion of the facility, increasing total output from 70,000 to 150,000 automobiles and raising employment by 1,000 workers.[37]

Finally, multinationals benefit the global economy by fostering a more efficient use of scarce resources. Multinationals improve production efficiency by locating affiliates in regions best suited to their manufacture or assembly. In a process called *production sharing*, the successive phases in the production of a good occur at different plants and in different countries by an MNC's affiliates, subcontractors, or other firms. While it may seem time consuming and wasteful to scatter production facilities around the world, consider the efficiency benefits of production sharing. MNCs are free to seek the lowest-cost provider of a necessary resource or intermediate (semifinished) good. MNCs are also able to select the most efficient facility to assemble the finished product and to distribute this product to appropriate markets. In the production sharing process, resources, intermediate goods, and, ultimately, finished products are traded in the global trading system, a system based on countries specializing in the production of those items in which they enjoy a comparative advantage (see chapter 2).

NOTES

1. "Global 5 Hundred: The World's Largest Corporations," *Fortune*, 23 July, 2001, F-1.

2. World Bank, *World Development Report 2000/2001* (New York: Oxford University Press, 2000), 274–275; and "Global 5 Hundred: The World's Largest Corporations (1999)," *Fortune* (*www.fortune.com/ fortune/global500*).

3. "Global 5 Hundred: The World's Largest Corporations," *Fortune*, 23 July 2001, F-1, F-2.

4. "About P&G" (*www.pg.com/about_pg/sectionmain.jhtml*); "Fortune 5 Hundred Largest U.S. Coporations (2000)," *Fortune*, 16 April 2001, F1, F2.

5. United Nations Conference on Trade and Development (UNCTAD), *World Investment Report 2000: Cross-Border Mergers and Acquisitions and Development* (Overview, Table 1) (New York: United Nations Publications, 2000), 2.

6. UNCTAD, *World Investment Report 1999: Foreign Direct Investment and the Challenge of Development* (Table 3.1) (New York: United Nations Publications, 1999).

7. UNCTAD, "FDI–Linked Cross-Border M&As Grew Unabated in 2000" (press release, 27 June 2001) (*www.unctad.org/en/press/ pr0116en.htm*).

8. Alec Klein, "AOL Time Warner Prepare Ad Blitz," *Washington Post,* 31 January 2001 (*www.washingtonpost.com/wp-dyn/articles/A10959–2001 Jan31.html*); "Pfizer and Warner-Lambert Agree to $90 Billion Merger" (*www.pfizer/pfizerinc/investing/announcement.html*); "U.S. approves $82 bn Exxon-Mobil merger," *Company News North America* 5, no 3 (21 February 2000) (*www.gasandoil.com/goc/company/cnn00853.htm*); "Significant Development Report for WorldCom, Inc." (*www.yahoo.marketguide. com/mgi/signdevt.asp?rt=signdevt&rn=50715*).

9. UNCTAD, *World Investment Report 2000,* 2.

10. UNCTAD, "World FDI Flows Exceed US$ 1.1 Trillion in 2000" (press release, 7 December 2000), 2 (*www.unctad.org/en/press/ pr2875en.htm*).

11. UNCTAD, "Bilateral Investment Treaties Quintupled during the 1990s" (press release, 15 December 2000), 1 (*www.unctad.org/en/ press/pr2877en.htm*)

12. Ibid., 1–2.

13. U.S. Department of Commerce, Bureau of Economic Analysis, and Economics and Statistics Administration, *Survey of Current Business* (Washington, DC: U.S. Government Printing Office, September 2000), 40.

14. Ibid., 67.

15. Ibid., 70.

16. Upton Sinclair, *The Jungle* (New York: New American Library, 1906), 136–137.

17. *Legacy of an Oil Spill: 10 Years after* Exxon Valdez (ten-Year Report) (*www.oilspill.state.ak.us/setlment/setlment.htm*) and (*www.oilspill.state. ak.us/history/history.htm*).

18. International Labor Organization (ILO), "Codes of Conduct for Multinationals," 1–11 (*www.itcilo.it/english/actrav/telearn/global/ ilo/guide/main.htm*).

19. ILO Washington Branch Office, "About the ILO: Facts for Americans" (*www.us.ilo.org/aboutilo/facts.html*); ILO, "Codes of Conduct for Multinationals"; and ILO, "Ratifications of the Fundamental Human Rights Conventions by Country," 25 September 2000, 1–6 (*www.ilolex.ilo.ch:1567/ public/english/docs/declworld.htm*).

20. "The 9 Principles" (UN *Global Compact*) (*www. unglobalcompact.org*); and Mark Malloch Brown, "Globalization, Business and Social Responsibility: Partnerships to Reduce Risk and Strengthen Human Development" (United Nations Development Program Address, CARE International UK, London, 6 November 2000), 2 (*www.undp.org/dpa/ statements/administ/2000/november/6nov00.html*).

21. The Reverend Leon H. Sullivan, "Global Sullivan Principles," International Foundation for Education and Self-Help (IFESH) (*www. globalsullivanprinciples.org*).

22. The Reverend Leon H. Sullivan, *The Global Sullivan Principles of Corporate Social Responsibility*, IFESH (*www.globalsullivanprinciples.org*).

23. Paul Raeburn, Sheridan Prasso, Suzanne Timmons, and Michael Shari, "Whose Globe?" *Business Week* (special report), 6 November 2000, 90.

24. Aaron Bernstein, Michael Shari, and Elisabeth Malkin, "A World of Sweatshops," *Business Week*, 6 November 2000, 84–86.

25. United Nations Development Program (UNDP), *Human Development Report: 1999* (New York: Oxford University Press, 1999), 31.

26. Richard McNally, "Pollution for Export?" *UNESCO Courier*, December 1998, 13.

27. Hillary French, *Vanishing Borders: Protecting the Planet in the Age of Globalization* (New York: Norton, 2000), 84–85.

28. "North American Partner Cities," North American Production Sharing, Inc. (*www.napsmexico.com/cities.htm*).

29. McNally, "Pollution for Export?" 1998, 13.

30. Peter Schwartz and Blair Gibb, *When Good Companies Do Bad Things: Responsibility and Risk in an Age of Globalization* (New York: Wiley, 1999), 42 11.

31. "Birth of a Global Company" (Special Reports of DaimlerChrysler), (*www.daimlerchrysler.de/specials/81117birth/sr81117_e.htm*).

32. Keith Naughton and Karen L. Miller, "A Mess of a Merger," *Newsweek*, 11 December 2000, 54–56; Allen Sloan, "A Deal for the History Books," *Newsweek*, 11 December 2000, 57; and "Chrysler Group Announces Next Initiative in Turnaround Plan" (*www.daimlerchrysler. de/news/top/2001/t10129_e.htm*).

33. UNCTAD, *World Investment Report 2000*, 4.

34. UNDP, *Human Development Report: 1999*, 57.

35. Mark L. Clifford et al., "Up the Ladder—Global Trade: Can All Nations Benefit?" *Business Week*, 6 November 2000, 78–84.

36. Paul Raeburn, "A Gusher for Everyone?" *Business Week*, 6 November 2000, 94–95; and "Chad Development Project" (news release) (*www. exxon.mobil.com/em_newsrelease/chad.html*).

37. "New Opel Polksa Plant Inaugurated" (GM news release, 29 October 1998) (*www.generalmotors.org*).

4

Gaps in the Global Web: The "Have" and "Have Not" Countries

UNEVEN ECONOMIC DEVELOPMENT IN THE GLOBAL ECONOMY

The global economy is an international economic web composed of individuals, firms, and governments from over 200 countries and territories, as well as multilateral organizations. Each country and territory within this web has a unique history, culture, institutions, and people. Each also possesses a unique set of social, economic, and political characteristics that have and continue to influence its prospects for sustainable economic development. *Sustainable economic development* refers to the overall advancement of a country's economy, and improvement in the people's quality of life, over time.

The first part of this definition of sustainable economic development—the advancement of the economy—means that the country's economy is growing. Most economists look to the country's real per capita gross national product (GNP) as the best indicator of economic growth. This measure of economic growth calculates the growth of a country's total output of goods and services per person each year. It also calculates any changes in the currency's value over time. Adjusting the per capita GNP for changes in price levels, especially for inflation, makes it a more accurate indicator of the people's well being. Furthermore, advancement of the economy also refers to improvements in all three sectors of the economy—industrial, service, and agricultural—through the use of sophisticated capital goods, skilled workers, innovative management, and so on.

Sustainable economic development also requires improvement in people's quality of life over time. This part of the definition focuses on the overall conditions under which people live, including access to public education, health care, food and water, transportation and communications systems, housing, social programs for the needy, and so on. Furthermore, the economic gains must be maintained over time. The sustainability of a country's economic development hinges on its ability to nurture, rather than exploit, its natural and human resources. It also means that a country is able to infuse appropriate technologies, capital goods, and management techniques into its economy so that the country can fully participate in the fast-paced, dynamic global economy.

Sustainable economic development is a goal for all countries, but in the global economy progress toward this goal has been uneven. Some countries have successfully marshaled their resources to achieve their development goals and have joined the ranks of the more prosperous "have" nations. Most countries in the global economy, however, remain poorer "have not" nations. For convenience, economists have categorized the have and have not countries into three groups: developed, or advanced countries; developing countries; and transition countries. While there is wide variation within these three clusters, countries within each category share some common economic characteristics.

The *developed countries* are the richer, more industrialized countries of the world. They have highly sophisticated economies and are often referred to as the *advanced countries* or *advanced economies*. Nearly all developed countries are *high-income* countries, with a per capita GNP of at least $9,266. The per capita GNPs of most developed countries are significantly higher than this minimum requirement, however, with Luxembourg leading the pack ($44,640). The per capita GNPs of other representative advanced economies include Japan ($32,230), Singapore ($29,610), Sweden ($25,040), Switzerland ($38,350), the United Kingdom ($22,640), and the United States ($30,600).[1] Not all high-income countries are considered advanced economies, however, mainly because they lack the necessary sophistication in one or more of the three economic sectors to qualify. Examples of high-income countries not included in the advanced category are Cyprus, Kuwait, Qatar, Slovenia, the United Arab Emirates, and a number of smaller countries such as Brunei and Liechtenstein. The classifications of countries by per capita GNP is shown in Table 4.1.[2]

Table 4.1
Comparing Countries in the Global Economy by Per Capita GNP,
1999

Classification of Countries	Per Capita GNP (in $US)	Average Per Capita GNP (in $US)	Percentage of the World's Countries	Percentage of the World's People
Low income	$755 or less	$410	30%	40.5%
Lower-middle income	$756–$2,995	$1,200	27%	35.0%
Upper-middle income	$2,966–$9,265	$4,900	18%	9.6%
High income	$9,266 or more	$25,730	24%	14.9%

Note: Includes some territories as separate entities such as Guam (U.S.), and Hong Kong SAR and Macao (China).
Source: World Bank, *World Development Report 2000/2001: Attacking Poverty*.

In the advanced economies, the industrial, service, and agricultural sectors rely on sophisticated capital goods, a highly educated and skilled labor force, and innovative technologies to promote sustainable economic development. In fact, today many of these advanced economies have moved beyond the industrial age where manufacturing dominated the economy into an information age where services dominate. In the United States, for example, nearly 80% of the labor force is employed in service-producing industries, while less than 2% is employed in agriculture, according to the U.S. Commerce Department.[3] There are just twenty-eight advanced economies in the world.[4] The *Group of Seven (G-7) Countries*, which is an organization that comprises the seven major industrialized democracies of the world, has met regularly since the mid-1970s to discuss freer trade, global development, currency stability, and other matters of global concern. The *newly industrialized economies*, sometimes called the Asian tigers, have closed the economic gap between themselves and the more established advanced economies in recent decades. Most of the remaining advanced economies hail from Europe. Because most of developed countries are located in the Northern Hemisphere, they are often called the *North*.

The Advanced Countries

The Group of 7 (G7) Countries

Canada, France, Germany, Italy, Japan, the United Kingdom, and the United States

The Newly Industrialized Countries

Hong Kong SAR*, Singapore, South Korea, and Taiwan

Other Advanced Countries

Australia, Austria, Belgium, Denmark, Finland, Greece, Iceland, Ireland, Israel, Luxembourg, the Netherlands, New Zealand, Norway, Portugal, Spain, Sweden, and Switzerland

*Hong Kong was returned by the United Kingdom to the People's Republic of China (July 1, 1997) and is currently a Special Administrative Region (SAR) of China.

Source: International Monetary Fund (IMF), *World Economic Outlook: 2000.*

The *developing countries*, also called the less developed countries, are the poorer countries of the world. The per capita GNPs of developing countries are significantly lower than the GNPs of the advanced economies. The great majority of developing countries are classified as low-income, lower-middle-income, or upper-middle-income countries. *Low-income countries* have a per capita GNP of $755 or less, and include countries such as Bangladesh, Ethiopia, Haiti, India, Nicaragua, Nigeria, and Vietnam. *Lower-middle-income countries* have a per capita GNP of between $756 to $2,995, and include countries such as China, Colombia, Egypt, Iran, Namibia, the Philippines, and Turkey. *Upper-middle-income countries* have a per capita GNP of between $2,996 and $9,265. Included in this category are countries such as Argentina, Brazil, Gabon, Saudi Arabia, South Africa, and South Korea.[5] The economies of developing countries lack the size and sophistication of the advanced economies. Most developing countries also lack the economic and social infrastructure to speed them toward economic development. As a result, many developing countries tend to concentrate on the production of goods and services that best meet their survival needs—especially food. For example, Haiti, the poorest country in the Western Hemisphere, devotes about two-thirds of its entire labor force to agriculture, while just one-third is employed in services or industry. In the Southeast Asian countries of Lao People's Democratic Republic and Cambodia, about four out of five workers are employed in agriculture.[6] The great majority of the developing countries are located in Africa, Asia, and Latin America, mostly in the Southern Hemisphere. For this reason, economists often refer to the countries of the developing world as the *South*.

The *transition countries* are the countries of Europe and Asia that are in the process of transforming from centrally planned communist economies to market-oriented economies.[7] With the exception of Slovenia (a high-income country), all transition countries are classified as low income, lower-middle income, or upper-middle income.[8] The epic transformation in the twenty-eight European and central Asian transition countries has been in progress since the late 1980s and early 1990s. Adding momentum to the market transition was the collapse of the Union of Soviet Socialist Republics (USSR) in December 1991. With the sudden dissolution of the USSR, the fifteen Soviet Republics became independent countries, twelve of which joined a loose confederation called the Commonwealth of Independent States (CIS). A number of East Asian countries including Cambodia, China, the Lao People's Democratic Republic, and Vietnam are also currently in transition, but because the main challenge for these poorer countries is economic development, rather than converting to capitalism, they are classified as developing countries.[9]

The Transition Countries of Europe and Central Asia

Central and Eastern Europe

Albania, Bosnia and Herzegovina, Bulgaria, Croatia, Czech Republic, former Yugoslav Republic, Macedonia, Hungary, Mongolia, Poland, Romania, Slovak Republic, Slovenia, and Yugoslavia (Serbia/Montenegro)

Baltic States

Estonia, Latvia, and Lithuania

Commonwealth of Independent States (CIS)

Armenia, Azerbaijan, Belarus, Georgia, Kazakhstan, Kyrgyz Republic, Moldova, Russia, Tajikistan, Turkmenistan, Ukraine, and Uzbekistan

Source: IMF, *World Economic Outlook: 2000.*

THE QUALITY OF LIFE: DISPARITIES IN THE GLOBAL ECONOMY

Quality of life refers to the overall conditions under which people live. These conditions include people's access to a variety consumer goods and services, health care, education or other training, clean water, adequate food supplies, sanitation, energy, transportation and communications systems, and other factors that promote economic opportunity and prosperity. Countries that enjoy a relatively high per capita GNP, including the advanced countries and other high-income countries, typically enjoy a higher quality of life because they are better able to provide essential goods and services to their people. The poorer countries, however, are ill prepared to meet society's most basic needs. As a result, they endure economic hardships and a lower quality of life.

The per capita GNP is one of the most widely used indicators to gauge the quality of life for people in the global economy. The average per capita GNP for low-income, lower-middle-income, upper-middle-income, and high-income countries are compared in Table 4.1. Even a quick glance at the data in Table 4.1 reveals several startling economic disparities among the nations of the world. First, while about one-quarter of the countries of the world are classified as high-income countries, just 15% of the world's population resides in these countries. In other words, only about one out of every seven people in the world lives in a high-income country. Second, about 75% of the world's population lives in low-income or lower-middle-income countries. Third, the average per capita GNP for the high-income countries ($25,730) is over sixty times the average per capita GNP of the low-income coun-

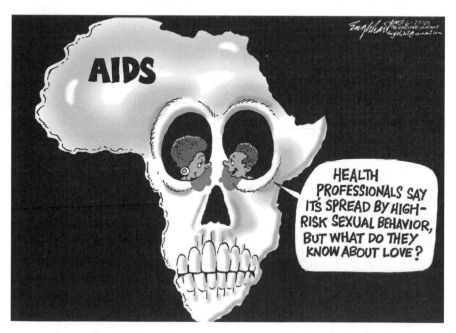

Bob Englehart, *The Hartford Courant* (27 June 2001). Reprinted with permission.

tries ($410), over twenty times the per capita GNP of lower-middle-income countries, and over five times the per capita GNP of the upper-middle-income countries.

The Acquired Immune Deficiency Syndrome (AIDS) epidemic devastates the quality of life for millions of people around the world. By 2000:

- 36 million people had the Human Immunodeficiency Virus (HIV)

- 22 million people had already died of AIDS

- 25 million Africans were living with HIV

- 12 million children had lost one or both parents to AIDS

- 36% of the entire adult population of Botswana was HIV–positive

Source: "An Overview of the AIDS Epidemic: Factsheet," United Nations Special Session on HIV/AIDS, June 2000.

Financial and social statistics can tell us a great deal about the quality of life for people living in the richer and poorer regions of the world. Table 4.2, for example, lists ten key social and economic indicators that are useful in comparing the quality of life for people living in developing countries, transition countries, and high-income countries. For example, people in high-income countries consume far greater amounts of basic goods than do people in the developing world—over four times the number of televisions and ten times the amount of electricity per person. In terms of public health and the health care system, similar disparities exist. For example, the life expectancy for people in the developing countries is thirteen years less than it is for people in high-income countries (64.4 years compared to 77.7 years). The child mortality rate in the developing countries, however, is over fifteen times greater than it is in the high-income countries (93 deaths per 1,000 live births compared to just 6 deaths per 1,000 live births). In the realm of education, adult literacy in the high-income and transition countries far surpasses that of the developing countries, where over one-quarter of the entire adult population can neither read nor write.[10] The contrasts between the richer and the poorer countries become even sharper when quality of life comparisons are made between the high-income countries and the poorest regions of the developing world. In the poorest regions, 1.2 billion people live on less than $1 per day, and an additional 1.6 billion people live on less than $2 per day.[11]

In recent years, governments, international organizations, nongovernmental organizations (NGOs), and others have stressed the

Table 4.2
Disparities in the Quality of Life: Selected Social and Economic
Indicators

Social and Economic Indicators	Developing Countries	Transition Countries	High-Income Countries
Consumption			
Daily calorie intake	2,663	2,907	3,412
TVs (per 1,000 people)	162	379	674
Electricity (kwh per person)	884	4,095	9,531
Health and Health Care			
Life expectancy (years)	64.4	68.7	77.7
Deaths prior to age 40 (%)	14.3%	8.1%	3.0%
Child mortality rate (per 1,000 live births)	93	33	6
Doctors (per 100,000 people)	78	345	252
Education			
Adult literacy (%)	72.3%	98.6%	98.6%
Children in the labor force (ages 10–14 years)	13%	NA	0
Population Growth			
Fertility rate (children per woman)	3.0	1.6	1.6

Sources: United Nations Development Program (UNDP), *Human Development Report, 2000;* and World Bank, *World Development Report 2000/2001: Attacking Poverty.*

importance of quality of life issues in the global economy. In fact, since the early 1990s the United Nations Development Program (UNDP) has developed procedures to measure progress in human development, and to evaluate countries' progress toward sustainable economic development (which includes a higher quality of life). According to the UNDP, *human development* involves the protection of people's human rights, the eradication of poverty, the reduction of gross income inequalities within countries, and the preservation of the natural environment. It also means that countries and people not be marginalized or excluded from the benefits globalization. In its *Human Development Report: 1999*, the UNDP warned:

Stronger policies for human development—more investment to equip people for the globally competitive economy, and to participate in the global network society—are needed to promote human development. But they are also needed to make globalization work. Ultimately, people and nations will reject integration and global interdependence if they do not gain from it and if it increases their vulnerability.[12]

The UNDP's human development index (HDI) ranks countries by level of human development. By 1999, there were forty-eight high, seventy-eight medium, and thirty-six low human development countries.[13]

In 1999, the countries ranking the highest on the HDI were:

- Norway

- Australia

- Canada

- Sweden

- Belgium

In 1999, the countries ranking lowest on the HDI were:

- Ethiopia

- Burkina Faso

- Burundi

- Niger

- Sierra Leone

Source: UNDP, Human Development Report: 2001.

GNP DATA FROM A DIFFERENT PERSPECTIVE: PURCHASING POWER PARITY

There is no foolproof way to measure the quality of life for people in different countries. Historically, economists have used the per capita GNP to provide some general insights about the wealth and well being of people, and have compared GNP data by first converting other currencies into an equivalent number of U.S. dollars. But how do we convert the per capita GNP of Mexico, which is measured in pesos, or Poland, which is measured in zloty, into dollars? Traditionally, to convert foreign currencies into dollars the prevailing foreign exchange rate has been used. For example, in the spring of 2001 the exchange rate of the Polish zloty was about .25. This means that the zloty was worth about 25 cents in U.S. currency or, to put it another way, it would take four zloty to equal one U.S. dollar. Thus, by dividing Poland's per capita GNP (measured in zloty) by 4, it is converted into U.S. dollars. If, for example, the per capita GNP in Poland is 16,000 zloty, its equivalent in U.S. currency is $4,000 (16,000 zloty divided by 4 = $4,000). The process of using prevailing exchange rates to convert GNP data from one country to the next is not without its problems, however. One major problem is that exchange rate calculations cannot account for the actual purchasing power of foreign currencies. That is, it is a poor indicator of how many goods and services a Polish zloty or Mexican peso can buy in its domestic economy.

In recent years, the IMF and other groups have frequently used another measurement technique, purchasing power parity, to calculate nations' per capita GNP. *Purchasing power parity* (PPP) makes adjustments in the exchange rate to account for differences in the cost of living in different countries. In doing so, it more accurately reflects the actual buying power of a currency in a nation. To illustrate the usefulness of measuring GNP data on a PPP basis, consider the following example. In 1999, Switzerland had a per capita GNP of $38,350 (third highest in the world), while the United States' per capita GNP was $30,600 (eighth highest in the world). Based on traditional per capita GDP calculations we would conclude that the Swiss were about $8,000 better off than Americans. Yet, general price levels for goods and services are higher in Switzerland than they are in the United States. Shouldn't this fact be figured into the comparison between the economic well being of Americans and the Swiss? By measuring the per capita GNP on a PPP basis, the difference in price levels is factored into the calculation. On a PPP basis, the 1999 U.S. per capita GNP stood at $30,600 (the U.S. GNP data always remains constant when converting foreign currencies into the U.S. dollar equivalent) while the Swiss per capita GNP dropped to $27,486. Thus, using the PPP method of figuring per capita GNP Americans, on average, were financially better off than the Swiss.

In many developing countries and transition countries, the per capita GNPs, measured on a PPP basis, are considerably higher than the traditional exchange rate calculations would indicate, as shown in Table 4.3.[14] The main reason for the higher per capita GNP numbers in PPP calculations is that the general price level, or cost of living, is lower in

Table 4.3
Comparing Per Capital GNP, 1999: Traditional
Exchange Rate vs. PPP Measurement (in billions of
$US)

Selected Countries	GNP Per Capita, Exchange Rate Measurement	GNP Per Capita, PPP Measurement
Developed		
Japan	$32,230	$24,041
Switzerland	$38,350	$27,486
United States	$30,600	$30,600
Transition		
Czech Rep.	$5,060	$12,289
Hungary	$4,650	$10,479
Poland	$3,960	$7,894
Developing		
Brazil	$743	$6,317
China	$780	$3,291
India	$450	$2,149

Source: World Bank, *World Development Report 2000/2001: Attacking Poverty.*

developing and transition countries. A lower cost of living reflects the reality that these workers typically earn lower wages, and many commonly consumed items are less expensive in developing and transition countries than comparable products are in the United States.

Other GNP data can also be examined through a PPP lens. For instance, if you were asked what the largest economies in the world were, how would you respond? The question seems simple enough. Yet, if we use this same PPP concept to measure the relative size of the world's economies—as measured by their annual GNP—the answer to this simple question may be somewhat surprising, as shown in Table 4.4.[15] The left-hand column ranks the world's largest economies using traditional exchange rate GNP totals for major countries in the global economy. When the GNP data is converted on a PPP basis, however, the list

Table 4.4

Comparing GNP, 1999: Traditional Exchange Rate Measurement vs.
PPP Measurement (in billions of $US)

Rank	Country	GNP, the Exchange Rate Measurement	Rank	Country	GNP, the PPP Measurement
1	U.S	$8,351	1	U.S.	$8,351
2	Japan	$4,079	2	China	$4,112
3	Germany	$2,079	3	Japan	$3,043
4	France	$1,427	4	India	$2,144
5	UK	$1,338	5	Germany	$1,838

Source: World Bank, World Development Report 2000/2001: Attacking Poverty.

changes dramatically, as shown in the right-hand column. Note that China, on a PPP basis, bumped Japan out of the number two position (climbing from number seven on the traditional exchange rate list). Similarly, India's ranking improved from number eleven (on the traditional exchange rate list) to the number four. In doing so, India jumped ahead of Germany, France, the United Kingdom, and all other highly advanced economies of the West except the United States and Japan. The use of two competing methods of comparing GNP data—the exchange rate method and the PPP method—remind us of the limitations inherent in many international comparisons in the global economy.

ECONOMIC DEVELOPMENT: THE ROLE OF GLOBAL INSTITUTIONS

Since the close of World War II, the influence of global institutions on the global economy has grown. Today, there are six main global institutions that guide economic relations among the nations of the world, including: the World Bank Group, IMF, regional development banks, the United Nations (UN) system, the Organization for Economic Cooperation and Development (OECD), and the World Trade Organization (WTO). (See chapter 2 for more on the WTO). Combined, these global institutions promote economic growth and stability in the global economy.

The *World Bank Group* is designed to promote sustainable economic development through five mutually supporting institutions, including:

- International Bank for Reconstruction and Development (IBRD, World Bank). The IBRD makes long-term (fifteen to twenty years) low-interest loans to the more creditworthy governments in developing and transition countries to finance development projects. For instance, the bulk of IBRD loans are designed to strengthen countries' financial institutions, transportation and communication systems, educational systems, agriculture, and social services. IBRD also provides the necessary technical advice and training to ensure that projects are completed and that they are maintained over the long term.

- International Development Association (IDA). The IDA extends even longer-term (thirty-five to forty years) interest-free development loans, called credits, and technical assistance to the poorest and least creditworthy nations. IDA credits are used for infrastructure construction or repair, health services, education, and so on.

- International Finance Corporation (IFC). The IFC, unlike the IBRD and IDA, extends loans to private firms rather than to governments. The IFC actively promotes private domestic investment and foreign direct investment (FDI) to stimulate economic growth. It also assists in the privatization of state-owned businesses.

- Multilateral Investment Guarantee Agency (MIGA). MIGA helps create a more favorable business climate in developing and transition countries. MIGA promotes FDI by insuring foreign investors against non-commercial risks such as civil unrest, war, or expropriation. MIGA also helps poorer countries publicize investment opportunities.

- International Center for Settlement of Investment Disputes (ICSID). The ICSID complements the work of MIGA through its procedures for settling disputes between foreign investors and host governments.

The *International Monetary Fund* (IMF) is a second important international organization designed to promote economic stability within countries and in the global trading system. The work of the IMF is divided into three categories: surveillance, financial assistance, and technical assistance. Surveillance involves active IMF monitoring of developing countries' domestic economies to encourage prudent management of limited financial resources. For instance, countries are expected to maintain sound currencies, avoid excessive budgetary deficits and unsustainable foreign debts, and so on. The IMF's financial assistance involves the granting of loans or credits to help countries in financial distress. Unlike the World Bank's loans, which are used for a variety of development projects, IMF funds are used to help the poorer nations pay for imported goods, service their foreign debts (make payments on debts that are owed to foreign banks , governments, or other investors), and prop up weakening currencies. By the fall of 2000, the IMF had extended credits or loans totaling nearly SDR 46 billion ($60 billion) to ninety countries around the world. (SDR, or Special Drawing Rights, is the IMF's currency. In March 2001, one SDR unit was worth $1.28 in U.S. currency.[16]) The third main role of the IMF is technical assistance, which focuses on institution building, the forming of responsible stabilization policies, and advice on the reform of countries' legal codes. Institution building includes the creation of central banks, national treasuries, and agencies to collect taxes and customs duties. Stabilization policies, including monetary and fiscal policies, address the need for stable prices, a low unemployment rate, and economic growth. Legal reforms stress the creation of policies that promote a dynamic private sector, such as trade liberalization, the privatization of state-owned enterprises, and the rule of law.

In addition to its three primary functions, the IMF also sponsors a number of special programs to combat poverty and promote economic growth. One of these programs is the Poverty Reduction and Growth Facility (PRGF) that, since 1999, has provided low-interest loans to the world's eighty poorest nations. A second special program is the Heavily Indebted Poor Countries (HIPC) Initiative that, since 1996, has committed billions of dollars to debt relief for forty-one low-income countries burdened with *unsustainable debt*—a foreign debt so large that it cannot be repaid without devastating consequences for the country.

The IMF is not without its critics, however, as evidenced by the massive demonstrations at the IMF and World Bank spring meetings (April 2000) in Washington, DC, among numerous other protests. At the center of the storm are the structural adjustment programs (SAPs), or conditions, that developing countries must satisfy before they receive IMF assistance. Critics of the IMF and World Bank contend that SAPs favor the profits of multinational corporations (MNCs) over the well being of people. SAPs have traditionally favored trade liberalization, privatization, reduced regulations or restrictions on foreign investment, and fewer government subsidies and social programs. Combined, critics say that these types of conditions rob local peoples and their governments of the power to deal with multinationals on an equal footing.

Regional development banks, a third type of global institution designed to promote stability and growth in the global economy, are multilateral institutions created to encourage sustainable economic development in a specific region of the world. They generate operating

"NOW, GIVE ME THE BOWL AS COLLATERAL."

Bob Englehart, *The Hartford Courant* (18 April 2000). Reprinted with permission.

capital in three ways: by collecting contributions from member countries, by charging interest on loans to member countries, and by borrowing money from financial institutions in global markets. Combined, regional development banks have made hundreds of billions of dollars in loans to governments and private businesses to stimulate investment in the public and private sectors, encourage entrepreneurship and new business start-ups, and provide short-term financial assistance to distressed economies. The three main regional development banks operating in the world today are the African Development Bank Group (1964), the Asian Development Bank (1966), and the Inter-American Development Bank Group (1959). In 1991, a fourth regional development bank called the European Bank for Reconstruction and Development (EBRD) was founded to assist transition countries in eastern and central Europe and central Asia in their journey from communism toward capitalism and democracy.

The UN is a fourth global institution linked to sustainable economic development in the global economy. Since its founding in 1945, the UN has been universally recognized as the world's leading international peacekeeping organization. Yet, through its specialized agencies and programs, the UN is also heavily involved in creating economic prosperity on a global basis. For example, at the 1992 United Nations Conference on Environment and Development—more commonly called the Rio Earth Summit—the landmark *Agenda 21* was written to set guidelines for sustainable economic development. This 300-page document stressed respect for the natural environment and the need to reduce global poverty and the gross income disparities between the have and have not countries. The specialized agencies and programs within the UN system are responsible for much of the organization's legwork. They are self-governing, have their own staffs, and raise their own money to support economic development. For example, the World Bank Group and the IMF are, technically, specialized agencies within the UN system, although they are rarely associated with the UN because of their autonomy. Other major specialized agencies and programs within the UN system are:

- World Health Organization (WHO): WHO, founded in 1948, today operates in 191 countries. Its mission is to guide and strengthen health and hygiene programs worldwide. Currently, WHO's main challenges are containing the Acquired Immune Deficiency Syndrome (AIDS), the resurgence of tuberculosis (TB), and the perennial problem of malaria. WHO contributes to sustainable economic development by supporting a healthy and productive labor force and by improving the people's overall quality of life.

- United Nations Educational, Scientific, and Cultural Organization (UNESCO): UNESCO was founded in 1945 and formally joined the UN system as a specialized agency a year later. It promotes sustainable economic development through education, the efficient use of local resources, and respect for local peoples and cultures.

- United Nations Development Program (UNDP): The UNDP helps countries plan and implement programs essential to their long-term economic well being. In recent years, much of the UNDP's work has addressed the problems of desertification, gender inequalities in education and the workplace, the technology gap between rich and poor nations, and the inadequate social and economic infrastructure in developing countries.

- United Nations Environmental Program (UNEP): The UNEP is another program in the UN system that stresses the sustainability of economic development. It works with local officials on small-scale projects and on a more global scale to address cross-border environmental challenges, such as global warming, ozone depletion, desertification, deforestation, acid rain, and biodiversity (see chapter 5 for more on global environmental challenges).

- United Nations Conference on Trade and Development (UNCTAD): UNCTAD helps integrate the poorer countries into the global economy, mainly by assisting these countries to benefit from international trade and investment opportunities. For example, UNCTAD's sponsorship of the Generalized System of Preferences (GSP) in 1971 paved the way for preferential treatment of certain exports from developing countries to markets in the developed nations. UNCTAD also sponsored the Agreement on a Global System of Trade Preferences in 1989 to underscore the importance of integrating the developing countries into the global trading system.

The *Organization for Economic Cooperation and Development* (OECD) is a fifth international group concerned with promoting sustainable economic development for member and nonmember nations alike. Since its founding in 1961, the OECD's membership has grown from twenty to thirty nations. The OECD formally discusses and forms policies to address many issues of global concern. For example, in recent years the OECD has focused world attention on the need for freer trade, environmental protection, combating international crime, sharing technology, and promoting economic growth and development. Through its twenty-two-member Development Assistance Committee (DAC), the OECD is also the world's largest provider of *official development assistance* (ODA), which is a type of foreign aid that targets economic development in developing and transition countries. Reflecting its concern for global economic development, DAC countries extended $53 billion in ODA in 2000. Yet, as a percentage of GNP, ODA from the DAC countries has fallen steadily in recent years. On average, DAC countries contributed just 0.22% of their GNPs—less than one-quarter of 1%—to help needy countries by 2000. In fact, only five DAC countries met the ODA target of 0.7% of GNP, including Denmark, Luxembourg, the Netherlands, Norway, and Sweden. The majority of ODA is granted to low-income countries (54%), with lesser amounts allocated to lower-middle income countries (38%), upper middle-income countries (5%), and high-income countries (3%). Close to one-half of this foreign aid was invested in education and health services, other social infrastructure, and the economic infrastructure. In 1999, the top five recipients of DAC assistance were Indonesia, the People's Republic of China, India, Egypt, and Russia.[17]

The Organization for Economic Cooperation and Development (OECD)

Membership in the OECD is based on three criteria: the existence of a market economy, the practice of democratic principles, and the respect for human rights. By 2001, there were thirty member countries in the OECD.

Asia and the Pacific

Australia, Japan, South Korea, and New Zealand

Europe

Austria, Belgium, Denmark, Finland, France, Germany, Greece, Iceland, Ireland, Italy, Luxembourg, the Netherlands, Norway, Portugal, Spain, Sweden, Switzerland, Turkey, and the United Kingdom

North America

Canada, Mexico, and the United States

Transition Countries

Czech Republic, Hungary, Poland, and the Slovak Republic

Source: Organization for Economic Cooperation and Development.

MOBILIZING SOCIETY's RESOURCES: JUMP-STARTING THE VIRTUOUS CYCLE

Countries create different types of economic systems to answer the basic economic questions: What to produce, how to produce, and for whom to produce. As the global economy enters the twenty-first century most countries of the world have jumped onto the capitalist bandwagon and embraced a decentralized decision-making model to give direction to their development efforts. Decentralized decision making relies on the private sector of the economy, mainly households and business firms, to answer the basic economic questions. Under *capitalism*, the private sector owns and controls the vast majority of society's natural, human, and capital resources. Consumers freely determine what should be produced through their demand for certain goods or services. Businesses, in turn, determine how to produce products. An individual's income is the most important factor in answering the for whom to produce question.

In recent years, the collapse of communism and the triumph of capitalism in the global economy have channeled productive resources into more efficient and profitable directions. In some regions of the world, particularly in the advanced countries, the triumph of capitalism has also stimulated the virtuous cycle, which occurs when the development of new technologies and new products spawns an explosion of new business activity. The resulting snowball effect creates new and better jobs, greater demand for society's output, a rising GNP, and an improved quality of life. Let's examine six essential ingredients in promoting the virtuous cycle, including support for technology, human resources, capital deepening, entrepreneurship and innovation, good governance, and democracy.

In today's dynamic global economy, the application of new and better technology is one indispensable stimulant to the virtuous cycle. Consider some of the changes new technologies have already made to the structure and operation of economies worldwide. First, technology has radically altered production methods, including the use of capital within production facilities. For example, computerization and robotics have released some workers from the drudgery of the assembly line and have reduced waste, product defects, and production costs in some assembly plants in the advanced countries. The U.S. pharmaceutical industry has also benefited from technological advances in biomedicine and information technologies, which has enabled these manufacturers to streamline the research, development, and testing of new drugs.[18] Second, the marketing and distribution of products in domestic and global markets have been revolutionized by technology. For example, the Internet and e-commerce (electronic commerce) have helped firms reduce production costs and expand their markets by instantly linking businesses with low-cost suppliers of resources and intermediate goods and with consumers. In fact, the rise of the *virtual firm*—a firm that conducts its business over the Internet—has already removed many traditional costs of production by reducing construction costs and the need to carry large inventories of goods and large numbers of employees. Business-to-business e-commerce accounted for about $43 billion in sales in 1998. By 2003, some experts believe Internet transactions will rise to $1.3 trillion—a thirtyfold increase in just five years.[19] The technology gap between the rich and poor nations is substantial, but the infusion of new technologies into developing countries is essential to the goal of sustainable economic development. The use of advanced technology in the developing world has already resulted in significant changes in traditional agriculture. Since the 1960s, for example, the techniques of the *green revolution* have enabled India to feed its own people and to export food surpluses. The green revolution employs mechanization, hybrid seeds, pesticides and fertilizers, and scientific planting methods to expand crop yields (see chapter 5 for more on the technology gap in the global economy).

A second essential feature to jump-starting the virtuous cycle is the creation of an educated, highly skilled, and motivated labor force. Economists sometimes call labor, *human capital* to highlight the fact that workers' native abilities are enhanced by knowledge and skills they have acquired through formal education or occupational training. It is important to note that education alone is not sufficient to increase worker productivity or economic growth. For instance, the adult literacy rate for the advanced countries and the transition countries is identical (98.6%). Yet, in the ten-year period between 1992 and 2001 the real gross domestic products (GDPs) of the advanced countries increased by a healthy 3.5% per year, on average, while the real GDPs of the transition countries fell by 2.1% per year on average as shown in Table 4.5.[20] For the labor force to become more productive and contribute to sustained economic growth, the proper incentives—such as the right to own private property and the freedom to earn profits—must also be protected. Countries that are unwilling or unable to guarantee equal opportunity and basic economic freedoms in their domestic economies have also suffered from the *brain drain*, a process whereby many of the most skilled workers emigrate from poorer countries to the more advanced countries. The brain drain has plagued the developing countries for decades and, more recently, has undermined the prospects for economic growth in the transition countries. In fact, the World Bank recently reported:

The brain drain has been a ubiquitous feature of the early phases of transition in Central and Eastern Europe and the former Soviet Union. Many of the best and the brightest have left for educational and professional careers in the West. For a long time the hope was that young talent would return once their home countries had turned the corner. Sufficient time has passed to acknowledge that this has not happened. The return flow is, at best, a trickle.[21]

Another major issue in creating a skilled labor force is the continuing population explosion in the developing world. The UN predicts that an additional 3 billion people will inhabit the planet by 2050 and that virtually all of this increase in population will occur in the developing countries. The UN's Population Fund concedes that already "80 countries cannot produce enough food to feed their own populations," and ponders how economic growth can occur when billions of additional mouths demand an even greater share of society's scarce resources.[22] Many experts agree that family planning and greater reproductive rights for women can slow the population explosion (see chapter 5 for more on the population explosion).

A third piece in the creation of the virtuous cycle is *capital deepening*, which occurs when a country is able to increase its *capital stock*—the total amount of productive capital available in an economy. *Capital*, or capital resources, is any item that is designed to produce other goods or services. In the private sector of an economy, airliners, business computers, software, office buildings, manufacturing plants, tractors, supertankers, and delivery trucks are all examples of capital used by businesses. In the public sector of the economy, the government also invests in capital, called *social capital*. Examples of social capital include roads and highways, courts and prisons, airports and seaports, water and sewage systems, dams and bridges, public schools and universities, and other elements of the infrastructure.

The advanced countries have long emphasized the production of private and social capital as a means of improving the overall business climate in their economies and increasing productivity and economic growth. Much of the success of the advanced economies is based on their ability to channel savings into investments in private and social capital. In the United States, for example, gross savings in 2000 topped $1.8 trillion, about $1.3 trillion from private sources (personal savings and business savings) and the remaining $500 billion from government sources. In that same year, $1.4 billion of this money was loaned to individuals and firms for investments in private capital, including nonresidential structures (mines, farms, utilities, and commercial buildings), information processing equipment and software, and other equipment.[23] Social capital is typically financed through tax revenues and other fees collected by governments at the local and national levels.

In 1999, the combined GDPs of countries in the global economy, by income status, were:

- High-Income countries $24.3 trillion

- Upper-middle income countries $2.9 trillion

- Lower-middle income countries $2.6 trillion

- Low-income countries $1.0 trillion

                        Total: $30.8 trillion

Source: World Bank, *World Development Indicators: 2001*, 189.

In the global economy, there is a clear relationship between saving and investment on the one hand, and economic growth and prosperity on the other. Relatively high saving and investment rates by the newly industrialized countries in Asia, such as Singapore and Hong Kong SAR, for example, illustrate the positive impact of capital deepening on economic development.[24] Interestingly, there is a relatively small difference between the savings rates for countries classified as high income (23% of GDP), upper-middle income (23% of GDP), lower-middle income (30% of GDP), and low income (20% of GDP). But, as the World Bank points out, "even high savings rates generate small sums in the poorest countries."[25] Another problem, capital flight, also retards efforts to achieve sustainable economic development. *Capital flight* occurs when savings from one country are invested in safer, more profitable ways abroad. Capital flight, which in Russia has averaged between $10 to $20 billion per year since the early 1990s, remains one of the greatest obstacles to economic growth in this capital-starved country.[26]

A fourth ingredient in promoting the virtuous cycle is entrepreneurship and innovation. *Entrepreneurship* is the risk-taking by innovators, called entrepreneurs, in an economy. Entrepreneurship involves the creation of new products, new ways to produce products, or new businesses. In a recent ground-breaking report, *Global Entrepreneurship Monitor (GEM) 2000*, a direct relationship was drawn between the level of entrepreneurial activity in a country and its level of economic growth. *GEM 2000* also identified characteristics that promote entrepreneurial activity, including the entrepreneur's level of education and motivation; the sophistication of the country's economic infrastructure; the support of political institutions; access to information technologies; the existence of true economic opportunities; and the culture's acceptance of risk-taking, especially for women entrepreneurs, in the creation of new businesses. *GEM 2000* also noted that attitudes about entrepreneurship vary among the countries of the world, even among the advanced economies themselves. Advanced countries that ranked high in entrepreneurial activity included Australia, Canada, Norway, South Korea, and the United States. Advanced economies that ranked low on the scale were France and Japan. *GEM 2000* reported that the lion's share of *venture capital*—money invested in new businesses (but not into mergers and acquisitions [M&As])—was invested in the United States.[27] Another recent study conducted by *Wired* magazine identified forty-six "hubs of innovation" in the global economy. In 2000, the United States had the largest number of hubs (thirteen), and, according to the study, had attracted over $100 billion in venture capital—about thirty-five times the sum that the United Kingdom (ranked second) could muster.[28] Naturally, the inability of the poorer countries to accumulate savings, and the crippling effects of capital flight from some countries, limits innovation and entrepreneurship—and economic growth—in much of the global economy.

A fifth stimulant to the virtuous cycle is *good governance*, which refers to the manner in which a government discharges its responsibilities. Is the government effective and accountable to the people? In today's global economy, good governance is associated closely with the government's ability to stop corruption in the public sector, fight organized crime, end excessive intrusions by government in market activities, and develop procedures that support openness in the political system. Good governance also rests on the *rule of law*, which means that all participants in the economy are subject to a fair and uniform set of laws and regulations. Broadly speaking, the rule of law protects private property rights, enforces contracts, mandates uniform accounting practices, guides bankruptcy proceedings, protects intellectual property, and ensures a fair administration of existing tax codes. In the advanced countries, a tradition of good governance, and the rule of law, have created a stable business climate for investors, entrepreneurs, and existing businesses. In some other regions of the world, significant obstacles to good governance remain. For example, rampant corruption in some developing countries has discouraged FDI by MNCs and has diverted tax revenues and foreign assistance away from productive uses and into the personal bank accounts of corrupt government leaders. Examples include Saddam Hussein in Iraq, Mobutu Sese Seko in Zaire (Democratic Republic of Congo), Ferdinand Marcos in the Philippines, Manuel Antonio Noriega in Panama, and the Somoza family in Nicaragua. In Russia, the largest of the transition countries, the rise of the *gangster economy*—an economy run by organized crime—has discouraged legitimate business investment (including investment by multinationals) and has accelerated capital flight. Recognizing the need for good governance and the rule of law in Russia, the newly elected President Vladimir Putin (2000) pledged to work toward these reforms—reforms that may take years to implement. Sadly, even if Putin's reforms are successful it may take several more years to convince foreign and domestic investors that they are workable and permanent.

A sixth way to support the virtuous cycle is by forming democratic governments. *Democracy* is a type of political system in which the people rule, either directly through the ballot, or indirectly through freely elected representatives. Democracy is important to the advancement of global *capitalism*, a type of economic system based on private ownership and control over most resources, and on people's freedom to answer the basic economic questions of what, how, and for whom to produce. The relationship between democracy and capitalism is a symbiotic one. That is, each system relies on informed, individual decision making and the freedom to pursue one's own political and economic self-interest. While the advanced countries have spearheaded the movement toward democracy and capitalism since World War II, countries throughout the world have come to embrace the movement, especially in recent years. The Freedom House, which has tracked the rise of democracy and freedom in the world since the 1940s, recently reported that the number of democracies in the world has risen from just 22 in 1950 (14% of the 154 countries) to 120 countries by 2000 (62.5% of the 192 countries). Furthermore, in its *Freedom in the World: The Annual Survey of Political Rights and Civil Liberties, 2000–2001*, the Freedom House argued convincingly that there is a direct connection between freedom and economic growth in the advanced countries and the poorer countries alike.[29]

SOME FINAL COMPARISIONS: ADVANCED, TRANSITION, AND DEVELOPING COUNTRIES

As we enter the twenty-first century, it is clear that there are gaps in the economic web that we call the global economy. These gaps are most visible when comparing the have and have not countries of the world. The have countries are mainly the highly advanced nations of the world. They have highly developed industrial, service, and agricultural sectors that help make them the dominant producers of goods and services in the global economy (57.4% of the world's GDP). The advanced economies also dominate the volume of international trade (77.6% of all exports), attract the most FDI (73% of the world's total FDI), and are responsible for the vast majority of all cross-border M&As (94.1% of all purchases of foreign firms). As a consequence, the 1.2 billion people who live in the advanced countries enjoy a high standard of living and quality of life. A summary of key economic data related to countries' participation in the global economy is shown in Table 4.5.[30]

The economic data shown in Table 4.5 show some of the gross disparities between the richer and the poorer countries (developing and transition countries) in the global economy. It should not be surprising, therefore, that many of these poorer nations are currently on the fringes of the global economy, barely touched by the benefits that globalization has offered to their wealthier, more connected neighbors. Is it possible for the poorer countries to compete with the more advanced countries in world markets?

Different groups have analyzed the factors that contribute to a country's competitiveness. One highly recognized competitiveness ranking

Table 4.5
Comparing Economic Data: A Summary

Economic Data*	Advanced Countries	Transition Countries	Developing Countries
Number of countries	28	28	128
World population (%of world total, 1999)	15.5%	6.8%	77.7%
Real GDP (average annual growth, 1992–2001)	3.5%	–2.1%	5.6%
Real GDP (% of world total)	57.4%	5.8%	36.8%
Inflation (average annual growth, 1992–2001)	2.3%	117.9%	21.0%
Exports (% of world total, 1999)	77.6%	4.4%	18.0%
FDI (inflows in billions of $US, 1999)	$636	$23	$208
FDI (inflows as a % of world total, 1999)	73%	3%	24%
Cross-border M&As (purchases in billions of $US, 1999)	$677.3	$1.6	$41.2
Cross-border M&As (purchases as a % of world total, 1999)	94.1%	0.2%	5.7%

*Economic data often vary slightly depending on the source.
Source: IMF, *World Economic Outlook: 2000*, and UNCTAD, *World Investment Report, 2000*.

is designed and published annually by the World Economic Forum (WEF), a nonprofit organization comprising 1,000 of the world's leading corporations and political and cultural leaders from around the world. In its recent study, *The Global Competitiveness Report 2000*, the WEF analyzed factors that contribute to economic growth, productivity, technological advances, and environmental sustainability. Predictably, advanced countries led the pack, with the United States, Singapore, Luxembourg, the Netherlands, and Ireland copping the top five spots in the growth competitiveness ranking.[31] Another annual competitiveness ranking, called the *World Competitiveness Yearbook* (*WCY*), is published by the International Institute for Management Development (IMD). To determine the strength of each country's business environment, the *WCY 2000* examined eight general criteria, including items such as savings and investment, trade, macroeconomic stability, financial institutions, technology, the economic infrastructure, and others. Of the forty-seven countries examined in the report, the advanced economies were again clustered at the top of the ranking while the transition and developing countries lagged behind, as shown in Table 4.6.[32]

There are significant challenges facing the transition and developing countries as they strive to connect themselves with the global economy. Over the past decade, the transition countries have made significant, but uneven, progress. Politically, most have become freer and more democratic. Economically, most have also created the necessary foundation for a successful market transition, including policies that support trade liberalization, privatization, good governance and the rule of law, social programs, and responsible federal budgeting. In fact, the IMF recently reported that the countries of central Europe and the Baltic States "have re-joined the ranks of middle-income countries and can claim to have transition*ed*."[33] But other transition countries, including Russia and most CIS nations, have not kept pace with their neighbors to the West.

The developing countries continue to focus their efforts on sustainable economic development. Here, too, progress toward this elusive goal has been uneven. The success of the newly industrialized countries

Table 4.6
The World Competitiveness Scoreboard, 2000: Selected Countries

Advanced Countries		Transition Countries		Developing Countries	
Rank	Country	Rank	Country	Rank	Country
1	United States	27	Hungary	25	Malaysia
2	Singapore	35	Slovenia	26	Chile
3	Finland	37	Czech Rep.	31	China
4	Netherlands	40	Poland	36	Mexico
5	Switzerland	47	Russia	43	India

Source: International Institute for Management Development, *The World Competitiveness Yearbook 2000*.

of Asia, including Hong Kong SAR, Singapore, South Korea, and Taiwan, provide useful models for others countries to consider—models that are based on market principles and that embrace globalization. In addition, the spectacular economic growth rate of the People's Republic of China in recent decades underscores the importance of market incentives and the need to join the global web of nations. Trade liberalization and openness to FDI by MNCs have added to China's new prosperity. In fact, China's phenomenal rate of economic growth has recently elevated the world's most populated nation from its former low-income status to its present lower-middle-income status. Still, significant regions of the world remain economically depressed and isolated from the global economy, none more so than the nations of sub-Saharan Africa, central Asia, and pockets within Southeast Asia and Central America. As the global economy matures in the twenty-first century, the countries of the world face a dual challenge. For the poorer countries, the challenge is to learn from past mistakes and to initiate reforms to promote sustainable economic development. The challenge for the richer countries is to nurture global development with an eye keenly focused on inclusion and global prosperity.

NOTES

1. International Monetary Fund (IMF), *World Economic Outlook: 2000* (Washington, DC: IMF Publications, 2000), 187; and World Bank, *World Development Report 2000/2001: Attacking Poverty* (New York: Oxford University Press, 2000), 274–75.

2. World Bank, *World Development Report 2000/2001*, 274–275.

3. U.S. Department of Commerce, *Survey of Current Business* 81, no. 2 (February 2001), D34.

4. IMF, *World Economic Outlook: 2000*, 188.

5. World Bank, *World Development Report 2000/2001*, 334–335.

6. *The World Almanac and Book of Facts: 2000* (Mahwah, NJ: World Almanac Books, 1999), 781, 804, 816.

7. IMF, *World Economic Outlook: 2000*, 194.

8. World Bank, *World Development Report 2000/2001*, 334–335.

9. IMF, *World Economic Outlook: 2000*, 194.

10. United Nations Development Program (UNDP), *Human Development Report: 2000* (New York: Oxford University Press, 2000), 160, 171, 189, 193, 201, 203, 226, 240; and World Bank, *World Development Report 2000/2001*, 279.

11. Kofi A. Annan (secretary-general of the United Nations) et al., *A Better World for All: 2000* (*www.paris21.org/betterworld/foreword.htm*).

12. UNDP, *Human Development Report: 1999* (New York: Oxford University Press, 1999), 44.

13. UNDP, *Human Development Report: 2001* (New York: Oxford University Press, 2001), 141–144.

14. World Bank, *World Development Report 2000/2001*, 274–275.

15. Ibid.

16. IMF, "The IMF at a Glance: A Factsheet" (*www.imf.org/external/np/exr/facts/glance.htm*); and IMF, "Special Drawing Rights: A Factsheet," March 2001 (*www.imf.org/external/np/exr/facts/sdr.htm*).

17. Development Assistance Committee (DAC), "Special Factors Explain Lower Official Development Assistance (ODA) Outcome" (press release, 23 April 2001) (*www.oecd.org/media/release/nw01–37a.htm*); DAC, "Frequently Asked Questions about Aid," 24 February 2000 (*www.oecd.org/dac/htm/faq.htm*); and Organization for Economic Cooperation and Development, "Aid at a Glance," 3 January 2001 (*www.oecd.org/dac/htm/agdac.htm*).

18. *Economic Report of the President: 2000* (Washington, DC: U.S. Government Printing Office, 2000), 103–104.

19. Ibid., 116.

20. IMF, *World Economic Outlook: 2000*, 187, 197, 208, 210.

21. Erik Berglof, "Reversing the Brian Drain in Transition Economies," *Transition Newsletter* (*www.worldbank.org/html/prddr/trans/may-aug2000/pg41.htm*).

22. United Nations Population Fund, "Population and Sustainable Development," *Population Issues Briefing Kit*, 3 (www.unfpa.org/modules/briefkit/English/ch03.html).

23. Bureau of Economic Analysis, "Gross Saving and Investment" (*www.bea.doc.gov/bea/dn/nipaweb/TableViewFixed*).

24. UNDP, *Human Development Report: 2000*, 206.

25. World Bank, *World Development Indicators: 2001* (New York: Oxford University Press, 2000), 189.

26. Stanley Fisher (acting managing director of the IMF), "Russian Economic Policy at the Start of the New Administration," 6 April 2000 (*www.imf.org/external/np/speeches/2000/040600.htm*).

27. Babson College, "United States Dominates Venture Capital Investments" (press release, 13 November 2000) (*www.babson.edu/press/gem/vc2000.html*).

28. UNDP, *Human Development Report: 2001*, 38.

29. Freedom House, "Global Democracy Continues Forward March" (press release, 20 December 2000) (*www.freedomhouse.org/media/pressrel/121900.htm*); Freedom House, "Freedom and Economic Growth" (*www.freedomhouse.org/research/freeworld/2001/essay1g.htm*); and Freedom House, "Freedom in the World: Table of Countries" (*www.freedomhouse.org/rresearch/freeworld/2001/tracking.htm*).

30. IMF, *World Economic Outlook: 2000*, 187, 197, 208, 210; and United Nations Conference on Trade and Development, *World Investment Report 2000: Cross-Border Mergers and Acquisitions and Development* (New York: United Nations Publications, 2000), 7–8, 15.

31. World Economic Forum, *The Global Competitiveness Report 2000* (New York: Oxford University Press, 2000), 11 (*www.weforum.org/pressre . . . ? theglobalcompetitivenessreport2000introducesanewfocus*).

32. International Institute for Management Development (IMD), "Executive Summary" (*www.imd.ch/wcy/pressrelease/pressrelease.cfm*); IMD, "The World Competitiveness Scoreboard," May 2000 (*www.imd.ch/wcy/ranking/ranking.cfm*); and IMD, "Input Factors Scores and Contents" (*www.imd.ch/wcy/factors/factors.cfm*).

33. IMF, "Transition Economies: An IMF Perspective on Progress and Prospects," 3 November 2000, 8 (*www.imf.org/external/np/exr/ib/2000/110300.htm*).

5

A Planet at Risk: Global Challenges for the Twenty-First Century

The globalization process has radically altered the economic, political, and cultural landscape of the planet, especially since World War II. Often, when people speak of globalization they automatically attach an economic lens. In this economic context, globalization refers to the complex economic web that constitutes the global economy. This economic web has been strengthened in recent years by the exuberant growth in international trade, foreign direct investment (FDI), and other economic linkages. In a broader context, however, globalization also embraces the integration of local peoples, their cultures and institutions, and even their ways of thinking within the larger global community. Globalization's powerful allies, including multinational corporations (MNCs), multilateral organizations, and most national governments, have smoothed the path for the globalization juggernaut. Modern technology, particularly in the fields of computerization and information technologies (IT), has quickened globalization's pace and strengthened its roots.

What impact will globalization have on the planet and its peoples as we wade into the uncertain waters of the twenty-first century? Will we stroll through a wading pool that is clear, calm, and predictable? Or will we be tossed and battered by a global rip tide? Clearly, how we choose to confront today's global challenges—including the inevitable stresses on the planet and its peoples—will affect the human condition in the future. This chapter will explore seven formidable challenges for humankind in the third millennium. Included in this list are issues and problems related to the environment, energy production and consumption, overpopulation and the cycle of poverty, the global financial architecture, the North-South digital divide, cultural homogenization, and global terrorism. Many of these complex challenges are interconnected. For example, in the World Resource Institute's *World Resources 2000–2001, People and Ecosystems: The Fraying Web of Life*, it is argued that "[b]ehind all the pressures impinging on ecosystems are two basic drivers: human population growth and increasing consumption."[1] Understanding these overlapping challenges is an important foundation on which to build an effective global response.

ENVIRONMENTAL STRESSES

Stresses on the natural environment stem from abrupt disruptions in ecosystems. The landmark *World Resources 2000–2001* defines *ecosystems* as "systems combined of organic and inorganic matter and natural forces that interact and change," and identifies five categories of ecosystems: grasslands, forests, agrosystems (areas used for agriculture), freshwater systems, and coastal systems.[2] Many natural factors affect ecosystems, including climate and the amount of sunlight and water in a region. These factors, in turn, determine what types of life the ecosystem can sustain, whether human, plant, animal, or insect. While ecosystems are dynamic and have evolved over time, the disruptions caused by humans have tested the limits of ecosystems to adapt and survive. Factors such as overpopulation, industrialization and urbanization, pollution, agriculture and animal domestication, aquaculture and overfishing, and global consumption of resources and products have resulted in a general degradation of the environment.[3] The following are several of the specific environmental stresses confronting the peoples of the world on the land, in the atmosphere, and in the seas.

Desertification is the transformation of fertile land to desert. In part, it is caused by natural forces such as drought, wind erosion, and proximity to existing deserts. But it is the actions of humans including intensive farming, herding (overgrazing), timbering, and stripping natural land covers (vegetation) that have accelerated the pace of desertification in recent years. Desertification has swallowed hundreds of thousands of square miles of land in the Sahel region of Africa—on the southern fringe of the world's largest desert, the Sahara. Desertification is also evident in the countries of southern Africa, which border the Namib and Kalahari Deserts, and in northern China and Mongolia, which border the Gobi Desert. Desertification threatens the survival of

Bob Englehart, *The Hartford Courant* (18 April 1999). Reprinted with permission.

millions of people that rely on the land for their livelihoods, especially subsistence farmers and small-scale herders in the developing world.

Deforestation is the clearing of timber and brush from a region. There are many reasons why people harvest trees and brush. In Haiti, hillsides have been cleared of timber to make way for small-scale agriculture. In Brazil, forests have been leveled to make way for ranches, mines, and plantations. In India, the United States, and Canada, extensive logging has taken place for commercial purposes. In many African countries, timber and brush are collected for fuel. The destructive consequences of deforestation are readily observable and include soil erosion, desertification, and the destruction of vulnerable ecosystems—each of which has a negative impact on local economies. On a more global level, the systematic destruction of tropical rain forests in Brazil and in central Africa also has implications for the planet's supply of oxygen and for the rich variety of tropical plants that, in the past, have proven valuable in the creation of new medicines.

Ozone depletion is the weakening or destruction of the protective ozone layer in the earth's atmosphere. The ozone layer, which is positioned ten to twenty-five miles above the planet's surface, protects all life from the sun's dangerous ultraviolet (UV) radiation. The main cause of ozone depletion is the release of certain chemicals into the atmosphere. The most destructive of these chemicals are chlorofluorocarbons (CFCs), which are made up of chlorine, fluorine, and carbon atoms. CFCs have been used in aerosol spray cans, air conditioners, styrofoam packaging, and other commonly consumed items for much of the twentieth century. By 1985, scientists had discovered a hole in the ozone layer over Antarctica—a hole that had grown to a record 10.5 million square miles by 1998 according to the National Aeronautics and Space Administration (NASA). This hole shifted northward, exposing people in Australia to UV rays. More recently, a second hole in the ozone was discovered over the North Pole, exposing some people in Canada, Russia, and the northernmost reaches of the United States to UV radiation. Exposure to UV rays can cause skin cancer and damage immune systems in humans and is harmful to animal and plant life depending on the intensity of UV exposure. In 2000, NASA researchers reported a modest decline in the size of the hole over Antarctica, reflecting some progress in controlling CFC emissions.[4]

Global warming refers to a gradual warming of global surface temperatures over time. Evidence suggests that global warming started at the dawn of the Industrial Revolution a couple centuries ago when early industrialists began using fossil fuels such as oil and coal to power the emerging factory system. Emissions of gases from these factories, especially carbon dioxide, methane, and nitrous oxide, soon collected in the atmosphere. Heavy concentrations of these gases trapped some of the earth's heat, much like a greenhouse, preventing it from radiating back into space—a process many scientists today refer to as the *greenhouse effect*. As the use of fossil fuels expanded during the twentieth century to power motor vehicles and to heat homes and businesses, even higher concentrations of the greenhouse gases resulted. Not surprisingly, the relatively small number of industrialized countries produced about one-half of all carbon emissions by the late 1990s. The United States alone produced 25% of all greenhouse gases in 1997. The possible impacts of the greenhouse effect are troubling. A partial meltdown of the polar ice caps, for example, has already resulted in rising sea levels—a matter of grave concern for low-lying countries such as Bangladesh. In fact, the Environmental Protection Agency (EPA) recently reported that sea levels increased by four to ten inches globally during the twentieth century. The EPA also projected a rise in global temperatures of between 1.6 and 6.3 degrees Fahrenheit by 2100, which could result in sea-level rises of two feet by the close of the twenty-first century.[5]

The ecological stability of the oceans is another major environmental concern. Oceans cover about 70% of the earth's surface. For most of recorded history, the oceans were viewed as almost limitless in their potential to supply humans with food. Yet today, even the oceans are succumbing to human-induced stresses. For instance, the oceans have long been viewed as a convenient dumping ground for wastes such as industrial effluent, sewage, and the toxic fallout from acid rain. Oceans have also been overharvested by highly mechanized fishing fleets in the oceans and by intensive small-scale coastal fishing. As a result, the stock of fish in the Mediterranean Sea, North Atlantic, North Pacific, and other regions of the world has been reduced or depleted. In fact, the United Nations's (UN) Food and Agriculture Organization (FAO) recently reported that "more than a quarter of all fish stocks are already depleted as a result of past overfishing or are in imminent danger of depletion from current overharvesting. Almost half of all fish stocks are being fished at their biological limit and are therefore vulnerable to depletion if fishing intensity increased."[6] Another disruption in the ecosystems of the oceans is rising sea levels caused by global warming. While all coastal regions would be affected by rising sea levels, the most significant impacts would likely be felt in low-lying regions and island countries.

Resource degradation has occurred at an alarming rate. Today:

- 40% of the world's population experiences serious water shortages

- 65% of all land used for crops has experienced some soil degradation (40% is strongly or very strongly degraded)

- 50% of the world's wetlands have been lost during the twentieth century

- 50% of the world's forests have been lost to agriculture, logging, or other uses

Source: World Resources Institute, World Resources: 2000–2001, 54, 88, 104, 110.

What is being done to combat environmental degradation in the global economy? How successful have past efforts been in addressing global environmental concerns? Who is spearheading these global environmental efforts? The answers to these questions are elusive and the results to date have been mixed. There have been a number of major *multilateral environmental agreements* (MEAs) negotiated in recent years. MEAs have dealt with global environmental issues such as global warming, biodiversity, and ozone depletion, as shown in Table 5.1. The most recognized international authority in combating environmental degradation is the United Nations Environmental Program (UNEP), which was founded in 1972. In 1997, the Nairobi Declaration further solidified the UNEP's central role by labeling it "the principal United

Table 5.1
Major Multilateral Environmental Agreements (MEAs)

MEA	Date	Goals of the Agreement	Status of Compliance
Montreal Protocol	1987	to halt ozone depletion by regulating and eventually eliminating the production of CFCs and other ozone-depleting substances	the production of most ozone-depleting substances was banned in the industrialized countries by 1996, and will be phased out in developing countries by 2010; the ozone will likely recover by 2050
Agenda 21	1992	to promote sustainable economic development; to support freer trade; to reduce poverty, illiteracy, and disease; to promote responsible uses of resources, including energy resources; and to promote respect for workers, indigenous peoples, and local cultures	created the Commission on Sustainable Development (CSD) to monitor the Agenda 21 agreements (which were approved at the Rio Earth Summit in 1992); the Earth Summit +5 in 1997 adopted a comprehensive plan of action for the CSD to strengthen implementation of Agenda 21; disagreements over implementation remain, particularly between nations of the North and South
Framework Convention on Climate Change	1992	to stabilize emissions of greenhouse gases such as carbon dioxide, methane, and nitrous oxide; and to slow global warming that results from greenhouse emissions	compliance was generally lax; the goal of reducing carbon dioxide emissions to 1990 levels by 2000 was noble, but unrealistic; disagreements about the severity of global warming hurt compliance
Kyoto Protocol	1997	to control global warming by limiting the emissions of greenhouse gases; specific targets were set for emissions reductions for 38 industrialized countries and some countries in transition, ranging from 6–8% by 2008 to 2012; developing countries were exempted from meeting specific emissions reduction targets	Kyoto Protocol support was strongest among the EU countries; in 2001 President George W. Bush pledged to remove the United States from the treaty (which had never been ratified by the Senate); at best the treaty was designed to slow the emissions of greenhouse gases in the coming years; without U.S. support the success of this protocol (which was intended to strengthen the 1992 UN Convention on Climate Change) remains doubtful

Nations body in the field of the environment" and "an authoritative advocate for the global economy."[7] Among the UNEP's primary functions are to coordinate global environmental programs, monitor compliance with existing MEAs, and create and implement sound environmental policies that represent the views of other UN agencies (United Nations Development Program [UNDP], World Health Organization [WHO], FAO, and so on), nongovernmental organizations (NGOs), national governments, multilateral organizations (World Bank, International Monetary Fund [IMF], and so on), and others. Still, the UNEP lacks the size, resources, and stature of some of the larger and better-financed international agencies. For instance, inadequate funding deprives the UNEP of the financial clout held by its larger cousins in the UN system such as the World Bank or IMF. Nor does the UNEP have the authority to rule on international environmental disputes, depriving it of the legal clout held by organizations such as the World Trade Organization (WTO).

FUELING THE GLOBAL ECONOMY: ENERGY PRODUCTION AND CONSUMPTION

It is a truism that energy fuels the global economy, and without reliable sources of energy the global economy would grind to a halt. There are numerous issues related to the production and consumption of energy in the world today. One production issue is the use of nonrenewable fossil fuels such as oil, coal, and natural gas. Fossil fuels are not only are finite in supply, but also have negative impacts on the environment when they are burned. A second issue questions the power of the Organization of Petroleum Exporting Countries (OPEC), a producer cartel. How much control should OPEC have on the world's most important energy resource? A third production issue focuses on nuclear energy. Here, controversies tend to concentrate on the proper disposal of nuclear wastes and on the inherent dangers in producing nuclear energy. The ghosts of Three-Mile Island and Chernobyl are inescapable. A fourth production issue centers to the desirability, and the limitations, of incorporating renewable energy sources into the mix of energy alternatives on the local, national, and global levels.

Energy production continues to be dominated by the big three—petroleum (40% of the total energy supply), coal (23%), and natural gas (22%). During the 1990s, the production of petroleum and natural gas climbed steadily, while coal production dropped slightly. It is interesting to note that about 63% of the world's supply of petroleum, coal, and natural gas was produced by non-Organization for Economic Cooperation and Development (OECD) countries. The OECD is composed mainly of the wealthy, industrialized countries of the North. The non–OECD countries are mainly the developing and transition countries. Other forms of energy including hydroelectric power, nuclear electric power, and other renewable sources (biomass, geothermal, solar, and wind) comprised the remaining 15% of the world's energy supplies.[8]

Energy consumption in the global economy also creates some high-profile issues and controversies. The central consumption issue revolves around the gross disparity between energy consumption in the North and the South. That is, the industrialized countries of the North consume the lion's share of the energy that is produced—and enjoy a high standard of living that plentiful energy can help provide. The United States, for example, consumes close to one-quarter of all energy used for commercial purposes in the world.[9] The countries of the South resent the skewed distribution of scarce energy resources that tend to favor the industrialized countries. Global energy consumption has grown steadily over time to meet the needs of a growing global economy and a growing world population. Measured in British thermal units (Btu), the world's consumption of energy will nearly triple during a fifty-year span of time, from 207 quadrillion Btu in 1970 to 608 quadrillion Btu by 2020.[10]

Experts predict some major shifts in global energy consumption over the next twenty years. One shift involves the dramatic growth of energy consumption by developing countries in the early twenty-first century. In 1990, for example, the developing countries of Africa, Asia, the Middle East, and Central and South America consumed just 25% of the world's supply of energy. The highly industrialized countries of the West consumed 53%, and the Soviet Union and East European countries consumed 22%. According to the U.S. Department of Energy (DOE), by 2020 energy consumption by the developing world (45%) will overtake that of the industrialized countries (43%), and will far outdistance energy consumption by the transition countries of the former Soviet Union and eastern and central Europe (12%). On a related note, as energy consumption rises in the developing world carbon emissions from these regions will also rise. In fact, the DOE predicted that in the absence of an enforceable international carbon emissions treaty, carbon emissions by developing countries will surpass those of the industrialized countries by 2010. In 2020, 10 billion metric tons of carbon emissions will be spewed into the atmosphere, 49% of which will come from developing countries (compared to just 28% in 1990), and the remainder from the industrialized (39%) and transition (12%) countries.[11]

A second shift in global energy consumption involves the types of energy sources people will rely on in the future. The following are some of the highlights of energy use during the early twenty-first century, as reported by DOE's *International Energy Outlook 2000*.[12]

- Oil: Crude oil is currently the dominant energy source in the global economy and will hold this dominant position in the early twenty-first century. DOE predicts that the consumption of crude oil will satisfy about 38% of the world's energy needs through 2020. World consumption will jump from 73 million barrels per day (1997) to about 113 million barrels per day in 2020. Furthermore, consumption of oil will rise in virtually all parts of the world for use in business, transportation, and other needs.

- Coal: Coal, which currently supplies 24% of the world's energy needs, will decline slightly as a percentage of global energy consumption by 2020. The consumption of coal declined in some parts of the world as early as the 1980s and 1990s. For instance, the drop in coal consumption in some west European countries resulted from the switch to other energy sources, including nuclear energy. The decline in coal consumption in the transition countries of eastern and central Europe since the early 1990s, stemmed from sluggish business activity. Over the next twenty years, coal consumption is expected to remain strong throughout Asia, and will rise dramatically in the world's two most populous countries—China and India. These two countries alone will account for almost all of the world's total increase in coal use by 2020.

- Natural gas: Of the three dominant energy sources, the consumption of natural gas will show the steepest climb, increasing by more than 100% between 1997 and 2020. Hence, natural gas will account for a larger share of the world's total energy consumption, jumping from 22% in 1997 to 29% in 2020. The rise in natural gas use will be especially strong in the industrialized countries, mainly because it is a relatively efficient and clean energy source. The industrialized countries will also increase their consumption of natural gas as their aged nuclear power facilities are retired.

- Nuclear power: The global nuclear capacity, which stood at 349 gigawatts in 1998, is expected to peak at 368 gigawatts in 2010, and then decline steadily after that. Most of the increased output of nuclear generated electricity over the next decade will come from East Asia. Many industrialized countries, however, will continue to retire aged nuclear plants, hence accounting for the global decline in nuclear power after 2010.

- Renewable energy sources: The major renewable energy sources will increase by 54% between 1997 and 2020, and will hold steady at 8% of global energy consumption during this period of time. Included in renewable energy sources are hydroelectric, biomass, geothermal, solar, and wind power. Regional trends offer the most insights into the use of renewable energy sources. For example, over the next twenty years the greatest expansion in hydroelectric power will be in East Asia, where massive hydroelectric plants are under construction or in the planning stages. China's controversial Three Gorges Dam, which should be completed by 2009, is the most spectacular example of the region's commitment to hydropower. Wind power is making the greatest headway in the industrialized countries such as Germany, the United States, Spain, and Denmark. It is also important to note that while renewable energy sources comprise just 8% of the global consumption, these sources have a major impact on the lives of billions of people. For instance, biomass, which includes woodfuels, agricultural byproducts, and animal wastes, "are an important source of energy, particularly in the developing world," according to the *International Energy Outlook 2000*.

OVERPOPULATION AND THE CYCLE OF POVERTY

The growth of human population is at the heart of many problems currently facing the global economy, including the cycle of poverty that plagues billions of people. For instance, rising populations, especially in lower-income countries, place stresses on fragile ecosystems as large numbers of people compete for dwindling supplies of fresh water, arable land, and energy sources. In addition, money spent to provide for people's rudimentary survival needs such as food, clothing, and shelter diverts financial resources away from savings and productive investments in new capital and technology. Prospects for breaking the cycle of poverty are further dimmed by an underdeveloped and overburdened social infrastructure, which is unable to adequately meet people's needs for a quality education, adequate health care, or social services.

As we enter the twenty-first century, a number of population trends are readily observable. The first is that the world's population, which is currently increasing by 83 million people each year, will continue to rise into the foreseeable future. Historically, it wasn't until 1850 that the world's population hit 1 billion people. By 2000, 6 billion people inhabited the planet. By 2050, the world's population is estimated to jump to 9 billion. What factors contributed to this remarkable growth—what some demographers have called the population explosion? Certainly, access to modern medical care and medicines, improved nutrition, knowledge about hygiene and sanitation, and a better communications and transportation network contributed to a lower mortality rate and a longer life expectancy. In addition, fertility rates among women remained relatively high in many parts of the world, mainly the developing world. Combined, these factors have paved the way for the growth of human populations, as shown in Figure 5.1.[13]

Over the next fifty years, virtually all of the world's population growth will occur in the developing world, as shown in Figure 5.1. The most rapid population growth will occur in the forty-eight countries classified as least developed, where population is expected to triple from 2000 to 2050, rising from 658 million to 1.8 billion people. By 2050, India will overtake China as the world's most populous country, showing an increase of over 600 million people from 2000 to 2050. The populations of many developed countries, however, will decline by the middle of the twenty-first century. Included in this list of thirty-nine countries expected to see a drop in population are Japan, Germany, Italy, Russia, and the Ukraine.[14] The population of the United States will continue to climb, however, topping 400 million by 2050. Accounting for this rise in the U.S. population are a relatively high fertility rate (2.1

Figure 5.1
World Population Growth, 1950–2050 (in billions)

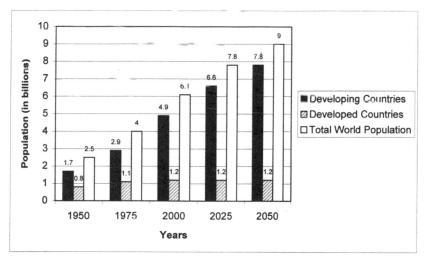

Sources: Population Reference Bureau, *2000 World Population Data Sheet* and United Nations Development Program (UNDP), *Human Development Report 2001.*

births per woman) and high numbers of immigrants (over 26 million foreign-born residents lived in the United States in 1999). A comparison of the world's largest countries in 2000 and 2050, as projected by the Population Reference Bureau, is shown in Table 5.2.[15]

As the world's population climbs by 83 million annually, additional pressures will be placed on the environment, on the process of sustainable economic development, and on the efficient functioning of the global economy. Furthermore, these stresses will be felt mainly in the developing world, which will absorb a disproportionate share of this population growth. Already about 1.3 billion people live in absolute poverty in the developing countries, subsisting on less than $1 per day, according to the United Nations Population Fund (UNFPA). An additional 1.6 billion people subsist on less than $2 per day. UNFPA also noted that the 20% of the world's population living in the high-income countries consumes about 86% of all private goods, compared with the poorest 20% of the world's population that consumes just 1.3% of all private goods. Is there anything that can be done to slow population growth in the developing world and, in doing so, help these countries break the cycle of poverty?

Table 5.2
The World's Largest Countries, 2000 and 2050 (in millions of people)

	Ranking in 2000			Ranking in 2050	
Rank	Country	Population	Rank	Country	Population
1	China	1,265	1	India	1,628
2	India	1,002	2	China	1,369
3	United States	276	3	United States	404
4	Indonesia	212	4	Indonesia	312
5	Brazil	170	5	Nigeria	304
6	Pakistan	151	6	Pakistan	285
7	Russia	145	7	Brazil	244
8	Bangladesh	128	8	Bangladesh	211
9	Japan	127	9	Ethiopia	188
10	Nigeria	123	10	Congo, DR	182

Source: Population Reference Bureau, "2000 World Population Data Sheet."

In 1999, the quality of life for people in the least developed countries lagged far behind that of other nations.

- 164 out of every 1,000 children will die before their fifth birthday

- life expectancy is just fifty-one years

- 47% of the total adult population is illiterate

- 57% of all people have inadequate sanitation facilities

- the 4.9% fertility rate is the highest of any classification of countries (the fertility rate is 1.6% in the industrialized countries)

Source: United Nations Children's Fund (UNICEF), *The State of the World's Children: 2001*, 81, 89, 97.

The conclusions reached at the International Conference on Population and Development (ICPD), which took place in Cairo in 1994, recognized the link between population growth and its role in perpetuating poverty in the developing world. In its Program of Action, which was strengthened by the UN General Assembly in 1999 (ICPD + 5), a number of specific recommendations were adopted to slow population growth rates. These interrelated recommendations focused on the need for education, gender equity, family planning, and respect for reproductive rights.[16]

- Education: This goal focuses on the need to equalize educational opportunities between males and females and to expand basic educational services for all people. Better education for females is viewed as essential to empowering women within the family, in the workplace, and in society.

- Gender equity through legislation: This goal stresses the need to empower women through government legislation. Included in this legislation should be specific guarantees in the areas of property rights, inheritance, employment, and protections against gender-based violence. In short, this goal seeks to elevate the status of women in society.

- Family planning: This goal centers on the need to increase family planning services as a means of preventing unwanted or mistimed pregnancies. The UNFPA estimates that up to 80 million pregnancies per year are unwanted or mistimed. Good family planning programs require strong government support, well-trained medical and support personnel, and access to a variety of contraceptive methods. They must also be respectful of clients' needs and cultural conditions. At the heart of effective planning is free choice, not coercion or control.

- Respect for reproductive rights: This goal stresses the right of women to choose how many children they will have and how they will manage their own lives. Women's freedom of choice will reduce unwanted pregnancies and the number of abortions. It should also expand educational and career possibilities.

REFORMING THE GLOBAL FINANCIAL ARCHITECTURE: A WORK "IN PROGRESS"

The *global financial architecture* refers to the institutions and to the practices of governments, businesses, and individuals when they engage in financial activities in global markets. For instance, international trade, FDI, and financial investments by people in foreign stock or bond markets are all examples of financial activities in global markets. The institutions that oversee the operation of the global economy are also key components of the global financial architecture. For example, overseeing the economic relations among countries are the Big Three: the WTO, which promotes freer trade; the IMF, which supports currency stability; and the World Bank, which promotes sustainable economic development.

In recent years, the operation of the global financial architecture has been scrutinized and, in some cases, criticized for its inability to avert financial crises or remedy economic problems such as poverty. The intensity of people's outcry for reform of the global financial architecture stems from the rapid changes that are occurring in the global economy, what economists have called economic globalization. Globalization, which is built on the liberalization of international trade and investment, and on advanced information technologies and transportation systems, has altered the pace and conduct of business on the international scene. The wave of financial crises since the mid-1990s, starting in Mexico (1994–1995) and reappearing in East Asia (1997–1998), Brazil (1998–1999), and Russia and eastern Europe (1998–1999), underscored the need to reexamine and reform certain domestic policy failures as well as the global financial architecture. The overriding goals of these reforms are "to strengthen the international financial system and to better manage the risks associated with globalization."[17]

The debate about "how to" reform the global financial architecture has been joined by national governments, NGOs, international financial institutions (IFIs) such as the IMF and regional development banks, regional trade organizations such as the European Union (EU), the UN and its specialized agencies, and others. To date, no blueprint for the reform of the global financial architecture has emerged. The following is a summary of some proposals and directions—a list that should be considered a work in progress.[18]

- Establish international standards and codes of good practice: In 1999, the IMF created codes governing the collection and sharing of financial data and transparency in countries' monetary and fiscal policies. The IMF has also piloted reports on the observance of standards and codes (ROSCs) to assess compliance with these codes. In conjunction with the World Bank, the IMF established financial sector assessment programs (FSAPs) in 1999 to identify weaknesses in countries' financial systems. The UN, historically, has also set certain standards in the areas of international statistics, trade laws, aviation, shipping, and telecommunications. The challenges for the future include setting uniform standards in the areas of accounting and auditing, bankruptcy procedures, corporate governance, and the regulation of securities markets. Some experts have even supported the creation of a global financial authority to set, implement, and enforce regulations related to the flow of money and capital across national borders.

- Improve transparency: Transparency refers to the openness of financial transactions to public examination and scrutiny. Countries must be more transparent in terms of sharing accurate and timely financial data with IFIs, potential investors, and others. International organizations such as the IMF, World Bank, and WTO must likewise become more open and inclusive in their decision-making processes. MNCs, local and international financial institutions, and other business concerns must become more transparent in their business operations, including loaning practices that in the past were often influenced by cronyism, favoritism, and corruption. Greater transparency on the part of offshore financial centers (OFCs), which have been used as tax havens and as conduits for untold billions of dollars, is essential.

- Strengthen international financial institutions (IFIs): Stronger financial institutions, with the authority to supervise and regulate the conduct of countries and businesses, are necessary to enforce the still-evolving rules of the game in the global economy. Broadly speaking, this proposal includes expanding the authority and the resources of the IMF and World Bank and the strengthening of the WTO's voice in settling trade disputes. It also includes enlarging the regional development banks (Inter-American Development Bank [IDB], African Development Bank, Asian Development Bank), and increasing their role in solving regional financial crises or problems. Cooperation and the coordination of IFIs' policies with those of other international organizations such as the UN (and its specialized agencies and programs such as the WHO, the FAO, and so on) and the OECD and Group of Eight (G-8) countries, is necessary.

- Strengthen the financial sector in countries: The financial sector in an economy is composed mainly of its banks and other depository institutions and its securities markets. Stronger surveillance and regulatory powers by the Basle Committee on Banking Supervision and by IFIs, especially the IMF and the regional development banks, would enhance equity and efficiency in loaning practices by banks. It would also reduce international financial crimes such as money laundering, drug trafficking, tax evasion, bribery, and other corrupt practices. Special protections for developing countries and transition countries to regulate or control inflows and outflows of money, including foreign investments in securities markets such as bond or stock markets, would help prevent herd behaviors by investors, financial crises within countries, and financial contagion in the global economy.

- Avoid moral hazard: In the world of finance, moral hazard occurs when a country, business, bank, or investor takes above-normal risks because there is a rescue mechanism in place should the business activity sour. The financial crises of the 1990s were, in part, a result of people's recognition that the IMF, regional development banks, and wealthy countries would intervene if certain economies were in danger of collapse. Many experts believe that private firms, individual investors, banks, and national governments should more carefully consider the risks inherent in their decisions and must accept the financial consequences of their actions. In short, they should look before they leap.

- Promote the inclusion of marginalized people: While globalization has raced into the twenty-first century, large segments of the world's population remain on the sidelines as spectators. The financial architecture of the twenty-first century must include the marginalized people of the world. One positive step toward inclusion was the creation of the Group of Twenty (G-20) in 1999, which brought major developing and transition countries under the same roof as the G-8 countries to discuss and debate global issues. The need for inclusion also applies to the globalization process itself. That is, billions of spectators are entitled to take part in the bounty that the global economy can offer. The inclusion of the poorer regions of the world into the global trading system is essential in this regard. Njoki Njoroge Njehu, the director of the 50 Years Is Enough Network—an international NGO—summarized the sentiment of marginalized peoples when she explained:

  > The WTO is supposed to create a "level playing field" in trade. But let me use an analogy that Americans will understand: A basketball court may be level. The basket is at a certain height. But if you put me against Michael Jordan, it isn't an equal contest. This is what happens at the WTO. Even if Haiti or Kenya won a case against the United States, neither has the power to hurt the American economy.
  >
  > In Africa, we have a saying: "When the elephants are fighting, the grass gets hurt." In global trade, the United States and Europe are like the elephants, and we—too often—are like the grass.[19]

Programs such as the General System of Preferences (United States) and the EU's recent pledge to open its markets (except military equipment) to the world's forty-eight poorest countries by 2009 are concrete steps toward inclusion. Another important step is to create a framework to channel responsible FDI by multinationals into the developing world. This framework would involve local people in corporate decision making. Steps toward this goal have been taken by the United Nations Conference on Trade and Development (UNCTAD), which is currently preparing business investment guides to attract FDI to the forty-eight least developed countries (LDCs).

- Encourage grassroots initiatives: Related to the goal of inclusion are financial reforms geared toward elevating people's standard of living, particularly in the developing world. For example, many experts favor the expansion of microloans (loans sometimes less than $100) to entrepreneurs in developing countries. The MicroStart Program, which is sponsored by the UNDP and supported by a number of international banks, is one step in the right direction. The IDB has been active in extending microloans in Latin America. The G-8 countries have also voiced their support for microenterprises in the developing world and for the construction of the necessary infrastructure—especially transportation systems—to help integrate these microenterprises into the national and global economies.

- Increase foreign aid: Foreign aid involves a cross-border transfer of money, capital equipment, goods or services, information, technology, or advisors to help the recipient country. For some of the LDCs, foreign aid is the largest infusion of outside money into the country—greater than the value of the country's exports and greater than the FDI the country can attract. In recent years, official development assistance (ODA), which supports development projects in developing countries, has fallen as a percentage of the richer countries' gross national products (GNP). The goal of contributing ODA of 0.7% of the GNP (less than 1% of GNP) has been met by only a handful of countries. Reforms in the global financial architecture must consider the responsibilities of the wealthier countries to expand ODA. Mechanisms must be installed to ensure that foreign aid is used to benefit the people, rather than to enrich corrupt government officials or their private-sector henchmen.

CONNECTIVITY: CLOSING THE DIGITAL DIVIDE

Another major challenge confronting the global economy in the twenty-first century is the growing digital divide between the countries of the industrialized North and the developing South. *Digital divide* refers to the widening technological gap, particularly the gap in information and communications technologies (ICTs), that have been the wellspring for economic growth and productivity in the North. The digital divide is apparent in virtually all aspects of life: how we learn, how we work and conduct business, how we receive and disseminate information, how we travel around town or around the world, and so on. In short, the North has embraced connectivity, while the South remains in relative isolation.

The technological gulf between the North and the South is staggering. For instance, the World Bank's *World Development Report 2000/2001: Attacking Poverty* noted that in 2000 there was fewer than one Internet host for every 10,000 people in low-income developing countries, 10 Internet hosts per 10,000 people in middle-income developing countries, and 777 Internet hosts per 10,000 people in high-income countries. In the most highly developed economies the gap was even larger. Internet hosts in the United States, for example, numbered 1,940 per 10,000 people—about 1 Internet host for every 5 people in the country. Similar disparities existed in access to personal computers, telephone service, and other forms of information and communication.[20]

Why is the digital divide a problem? At the heart of the problem is that connectivity is vital to economic growth and development. For example, a country's technological infrastructure is a major criterion that MNCs consider before they invest in a country. FDI provides instant access to skilled managers and new technologies, capital, and jobs. Likewise, technological connectivity is essential to creating and maintaining profitable trade relationships with foreign businesses. This is because businesses are increasingly linked to suppliers of resources and intermediate goods, and to consumers, through the Internet and e-commerce. The economic successes of the newly industrialized Pacific Rim—Singapore, Taiwan, and South Korea—illustrate how connectivity with the global economy has promoted economic development and improved people's living standards.

Can the poorer regions of the world get connected and join the global economy? A recent forum sponsored by the UN Economic and Social Council (ECOSOC) grappled with this question and concluded "that wealthy nations face huge obstacles in spreading technology in a world where half the population does not have a telephone and four out of ten adults cannot read."[21] But it would be a mistake to conclude that infusing new ICTs into developing economies is a hopeless task. For example, in recent years the Peace Corps has adapted to twenty-first-century needs by launching its own "e-initiative." Commenting on the necessity of bringing information technologies to the developing world, Peace Corps director Mark L. Schneider remarked:

In the twenty-first century, I am convinced that Peace Corps is even better prepared and better positioned than virtually any other agency or institution to bring information technology to the task of poverty reduction. To be sure, technology is no panacea—it will not solve all of the problems that confront people in the developing world. Yet if the poor are unable to participate in the information technology revolution that we now take for granted, the equity gap will widen even further.[22]

While the Peace Corps' e-initiative is a promising start, the organization's 7,000 volunteers who operate in 77 countries is just the first drop in the bucket. Massive assistance from IFIs, multilateral organizations such as the UN, and multilateral and bilateral financial and technical assistance is also required. Developing economies' use of domestic and international resources must also be transparent and wise, laying the foundation for an information society. According to the Information Society Index, there are four critical components for this foundation: wide access to information (telephone, television, radio, and fax), computers, the Internet, and certain social conditions (universal education, freedom of the press, and civil liberty).[23]

It is clear that globalization, and the technology that supports it, has increased productivity and economic growth for the countries that have been able to plug into the system. It is equally clear, as the UNDP notes, that "[t]he voices and concerns of people already living in human poverty—lacking incomes, education and access to public institutions—are being increasingly marginalized."[24] What remains is uncertain. What sacrifices are people willing to make to ensure that countries, regardless of geographic location or income level, are connected to the global economy?

CULTURAL HOMOGENIZATION: IS IT AN INEVITABLE BY-PRODUCT OF GLOBALIZATION?

Cultural homogenization is the process by which local cultures are transformed or absorbed by a dominant outside culture. Of course, recorded history has documented many examples of dominant civilizations spreading their culture traits to others through trade, exploration, migrations, missionary activity, and empire building. For example, 2,000 years ago the ancient Romans shared their language, legal system, values and beliefs, and other culture traits with peoples throughout their vast empire. Today, cultural homogenization has been nurtured by the globalization juggernaut—by the unprecedented movement or people, goods and services, money and capital, and ideas across national borders. Technology is the lubricant that facilitates these cross-border movements. Communications satellites, computers and the Internet, mobile and cell phones, television and radio, high-speed rail transport and supersonic airplanes, and other technological marvels of the twentieth century connect people with greater ease and at a lower cost than at any other time in human history. What has yet to be determined is how globalization will affect the cultures it touches. Will it destroy the rich cultural diversity that has defined the different peoples of the world? Or will it create a more prosperous planet, enabling people to experience and appreciate other cultures? Let's explore some of the main issues related to globalization and its impact on cultures.

What does the emerging global culture look like? At its core is a Western orientation. That is, the emerging global culture has its roots firmly planted in the United States and, to a lesser degree, in western Europe. Some experts have even described the rapid infusion of Western culture traits into other countries as the *Americanization* of the global culture. The main components of this global culture fall into three categories: values and beliefs, lifestyles, and the consumer culture.

- Values and beliefs: Ingrained in the Western tradition are the importance of the individual, civil, and human rights for all people—including gender equity—and the freedom of choice. Institutions have been created to support these values and beliefs, including democratic governments and the free market mechanisms associated with capitalism.

- Lifestyles: The Western lifestyle is not uniform for all people, but some general tendencies about life in a highly industrialized society are observable. For instance, the Western lifestyle tends to be fast-paced, forward-looking, and urban. Its language is English. Above all, people are technologically aware and connected in their personal and business lives.

- Consumer culture: The wellspring of the consumer culture is the mass production and mass consumption of goods and services. Driven by the lure of profits, businesses cater to the fast-changing wants and needs of consumers. Consumers, in turn, cast their dollar votes for or against products—with currency, plastic (credit or charge cards), or e-commerce transactions. The media fuels the buying frenzy through mass advertising and, in the process, reinforces brand loyalties to the icons of capitalism—McDonald's, IBM, Disney, Nike, Levis, Coca-Cola, and many others.

There is a mountain of evidence that cultural homogenization is influencing the way people around the globe see themselves and their world. The impact of globalization can be seen in peoples' preferences in clothing styles, entertainment (including the dominance of Hollywood movies and American television shows), foods, and the stores where they shop. Did you know that there are about 28,000 McDonald's restaurants located in 119 countries? But the degree of cultural homogeneity varies greatly in the global economy. For instance, Western cultural influences tend to be felt most by the urban youth throughout the world, who are more technologically connected and less tied to traditional values and lifestyles. Western culture has had a far smaller impact on people living in more remote regions, such as rural areas in the LDCs where modern communications and transportation networks are less accessible. Western culture has also been limited in countries where religious fundamentalism is powerful, such as Afghanistan and Iran, and in countries that have been isolated for political reasons, such as Cuba and North Korea. Can cultural diversity coexist with a fast-spreading global culture? Perhaps, as a recent article from *National Geographic* suggests, "[in] the end the cultures that survive will be those that are willing and able to embrace the new on their own terms, while rejecting anything that implies the total violation of their way of life."[25]

Already, there is a grassroots movement to slow the globalization juggernaut. The movement comprises some NGOs, labor and human rights activists, environmentalists, and others who believe that the economic, social, and cultural costs of globalization far outweigh the benefits. The massive antiglobalization protests that occurred at the WTO ministerial conference in Seattle (1999), at the World Bank and IMF's annual meeting in Washington, DC (2000), and at the World Economic Forum's annual meeting in Davos, Switzerland (2001) illustrate the growing discontent with policies that value economic integration and corporate profits above the interests of local communities and peoples. In fact, in recent years efforts to relocalize economic activity have sprung up around the world. *Relocalization* favors smaller-scale community-based production, which is adaptable to local needs, including environmental and employment needs. Supporters of relocalization believe that the actions of governments (freer trade policies), MNCs (cross-border investments), and multilateral organizations (structural adjustment programs), have been irresponsible and destructive to the nations of the South. That is, their actions extend the promise of global prosperity but create conditions that crush local businesses and make poorer countries dependent on the countries of the North. Relocalization is also sensitive to local cultures, respecting the customs and institutions that have evolved over the centuries. Thus, it opposes the emergence of a global culture. What remains is a challenge—the challenge of creating an integrated global economy with realistic opportunities for all countries of the world to participate, on their own terms, within this global web.

TERRORISM AND THE GLOBAL ECONOMY: THE ECONOMIC IMPACT OF THE SEPTEMBER 11 ATTACKS

Terrorism is any act of terror, or threat used to gain a political advantage. Terrorists have operated in virtually all regions of the world over the centuries. On September 11, 2001 the largest terrorist attack in the history of the United States occurred. Airliners, hijacked by terrorists, were deliberately crashed into the World Trade Center complex in New York City, and the Pentagon in Washington, DC. Another airliner crashed in Pennsylvania when passengers attempted to retake control of the craft from the terrorists. Blame for these horrific attacks fell on Osama bin Laden, head of the al-Qaeda terrorist organization—a group with its roots in Afghanistan and terrorist cells operating throughout the world. The unparalleled destruction in New York City and Washington, DC caused many to wonder how these tragedies would affect the global economy. Shortly after the events of September 11 Alan Greenspan, Chairman of the Federal Reserve System in the United States, conceded that "[t]errorism poses a challenge to the remarkable record of globalization."[26] Some of the immediate and long-term effects included:

- *Sluggish economic growth.* The World Bank predicted that the events of September 11 would slow economic growth in high-income and developing countries alike, as shown in Table 5.3.[27] Terrorism can cause economic downturns by reducing consumer and investor confidence, thereby stunting international trade and foreign direct investment. A further drag on economic growth is the adverse effects of terrorism on key services such as tourism, transportation, and insurance.
- *Higher poverty rate.* The World Bank estimated that an additional 10 million people would fall into desperate poverty in 2002 as a result of the September 11 terrorist attacks on the United States, and that an additional 20,000 to 40,000 children could die in 2002 as people sunk deeper into poverty. These anticipated consequences were linked to slower growth rates in the richer countries.

Table 5.3
GDP Growth Forecasts, 2001–2002 (annual percentage change)

	Actual	Before Sept. 11		After Sept. 11	
	2000	2001	2002	2001	2002
High-income countries	3.4	1.1	2.2	0.9	1–1.5
Developing countries	5.5	2.9	4.3	2.8	3.5–3.8

Source: The World Bank.

- *Reduced international trade.* Almost immediately after September 11 signs of a slowdown in global trade were apparent. This slowdown in trade was due mainly to lower demand for exported products by the industrialized nations as consumer confidence declined. Trade also slowed due to increased costs of trade, including higher insurance and security costs, longer delays at customs, and the revival of protectionist trade policies in some countries. In addition, reduced trade was expected to weaken the demand for many commodities, such as cotton, causing commodity prices to plummet—an economic hardship that would be most keenly felt by the poorer regions of the world.

- *Reduced foreign direct investment (FDI).* The events of September 11 were expected to further reduce FDI in the developing world. This would occur if cautious investors sought safer havens in the advanced countries for their investments. The World Bank predicted that FDI in developing countries would fall from about $240 billion in 2000 to just $160 billion in 2001.

- *Unstable capital markets.* The September 11 attacks unnerved many investors in global financial markets. The New York Stock Exchange, which suspended stock trading from September 11 to September 14, 2001, was socked with a 684-point drop in the Dow Jones Industrial Average when trading resumed on September 17. Before the selling spree ended, the Dow had fallen by 1,369 points. It took nearly two months before jittery investors brought the Dow back to its pre–September 11 level.

- *Contraction of sensitive industries.* Certain industries in the global economy were hurt more severely than others, including tourism, travel and transportation, petroleum, and insurance. For instance, shortly after the tragedies of September 11 lower demand for airline tickets caused many major airlines to lay off tens of thousands of workers. Tourism-dependent states such as Hawaii and Florida, along with traditional resort locations in the Caribbean and elsewhere, were hardest hit.

At the dawn of the twenty-first century the menace of global terrorism forced the countries of the world to join together in opposition to terrorists and the nations that harbored them. Steps in that direction took concrete form in the fall of 2001. A global coalition headed by the United States and the United Kingdom conducted a military, diplomatic, and financial assault on the terrorist al Qaeda organization in Afghanistan—and on the ruling Taliban government that had protected al Qaeda and its leader Osama bin Laden. Reflecting the economic significance of confronting terrorism, Fed Chairman Alan Greenspan said, "[i]f we allow terrorism to undermine our freedom of action, we could reverse at least part of the palpable gains achieved by postwar globalization. It is incumbent upon us not to allow that to happen."[28]

NOTES

1. World Resources Institute, *World Resources 2000–2001, People and Ecosystems: The Fraying Web of Life* (Washington, DC: World Resources Institute, United Nations Development Program, United Nations Environment Program, and the World Bank, 2000), 18.

2. Ibid., 10–11.

3. Ibid.

4. National Aeronautics and Space Administration, "The Ups and Downs of Ozone" (*www.spacescience.com/headlines/y2000/ast26jun_1m.htm*).

5. Environmental Protection Agency, "Global Warming: Climate" (*www.epa.gov/globalwarming/climate/index.html*).

6. World Resources Institute, *World Resources 2000–2001*, 78.

7. United Nations Environment Program (UNEP), "Nairobi Declaration" (*www.unep.org/documents/default.asp?documentid-111&articleid-1728*).

8. The Energy Information Administration (EIA) and the U.S. Department of Energy (DOE), "Table 2.9: World Production of Primary Energy by Selected Country Groups (Btu), 1989–1998," *International Energy Outlook 2000* (Report #: DOE/EIA-0484 [2000]), (*www.eia.doe.gov/emeu/iea/table29.html*).

9. World Bank, *World Development Report 2000/2001: Attacking Poverty* (New York: The Oxford University Press, 2000), 292–293.

10. EIA/DOE, "Figure 2: World Energy Consumption, 1970–2020," *International Energy Outlook 2000* (Report #: DOE/EIA-0484 [2000]) (*www.eia.doe.gov/oiaf/ieo/images/figure_2.jpg*).

11. EIA/DOE, "Table 1: Energy Consumption and Carbon Emissions by Region, 1990–2020," *International Energy Outlook 2000* (Report #: DOE/EIA-0484 [2000]) (*www.eia.doe.gov/oiaf/ieo/tbl_1.html*).

12. EIA/DOE, "World Oil Markets," *International Energy Outlook 2000* (Report #: DOE/EIA-0484 [2000]) (*www.eia.eia.doe.gov/oiaf/ieo/oil.html*); "Coal" (*www.eia.doe.gov/oiaf/ieo/coal.html*); "Natural Gas" (*www.eia.doe.gov/oiaf/ieo/nat_gas.html*); "Nuclear Power" (*www.eia.doe.gov/oiaf/ieo/nuclear.html*); and "Hydroelectricity and Other Renewable Sources" (*www.eia.doe.gov/oiaf/ieo/hydro.html*).

13. Population Reference Bureau, "2000 World Population Data Sheet" (poster) (Washington, DC: Population Reference Bureau, 2000); Lori Ashford, "Is the 'Population Explosion' Over?" *Population Bulletin* 56, no. 1 (March 2001) (*www.prb.org/pubs/population_bulletin/bu56-1/56_1_popexplosion.html*); and United Nations Development Program (UNDP), *Human Development Report: 2001* (New York: United Nations Publications, 2001), 154–157.

14. United Nations Population Fund (UNFPA), "World Population Prospects: The 2000 Revision," 27 February 2001 (*www.un.org/news/press/docs/2001/dev2292.doc.htm*); and UNFPA, "Population of Poorest Countries Will Triple by 2050: United Nations," 28 February 2001 (*www.unfpa.org/news/pressroom/2001/2000revision.htm*).

15. Population Reference Bureau, "2000 World Population Data Sheet."

16. UNFPA, *The State of World Population 2000* (*www.unfpa.org/swp/2000/english/ch01.html*); and UNFPA, "Reproductive Health and Rights," and "Challenges for the 21st Century," *Population Issues Briefing Kit* (*www.unfpa.org/modules/briefkit/English.html*).

17. International Monetary Fund (IMF), *Report of the Managing Director of the International Monetary and Financial Committee on Progress in Strengthening the Architecture of the International Financial System and Reform of the IMF*, 2 (*www.imf.org/extrenal/np/omd/2000/02/report.htm*).

18. Group of Eight, *Global Poverty Report* (Executive Summary, July 2000), 1–15 (*www.g8kyushu-okinawa.go.jp/e/theme/gpoverty.html*); *Economic Report of the President: 2000* (Washington, DC: U.S. Government Printing Office, 2000), 225–231; IMF, "Progress in Strengthening the Architecture of the International Financial System," 31 July 2000 (*www.imf.org/external/np/exr/facts/arcguide.htm*); "A New International Financial Architecture?" *UN Chronicle* no. 2 (1999), 45; and Organization for Economic Cooperation and Development, "Aid at a Glance," 3 January 2001 (*www.oecd.org/dac/htm/agdac/htm*).

19. Njoki Njorge Njehu, "The Elephants and the Grass," *The National Voter* (League of Women Voters) (December 2000/January 2001), 28.

20. World Bank, *World Development Report 2000/2001*, 310–311.

21. Nii Armah Addy, "Globalization—Focus on Developing Countries" (Africa News Service, 23 September 2000), 2 (*library.northernlight.com/FB20000923410000053.html?cb=0&dx=1006&sc=0*).

22. Mark L. Schneider, "Globalization, Information Technology, and the Peace Corps in the 21st Century" (Washington, DC: Woodrow Wilson International Center for Scholars, 7 June 2000), 4.

23. Cited in UNDP, *Human Development Report: 1999* (New York: Oxford University Press, 1999), 66.

24. Ibid., 63.

25. Wade Davis, "Vanishing Cultures," *National Geographic* (August 1999), 89.

26. Alan Greenspan, "Remarks by Chairman Alan Greenspan on Globalization," Washington, DC, Institute for International Economics' Inauguration of the Peter G. Peterson Building, 24 October, 2001, in *International Information Programs,* U.S. Department of State, 7.

27. World Bank, "Poverty to Rise in Wake of Terrorist Attacks in U.S.," *International Information Programs, U.S. Department of State,* 1–2.

28. Alan Greenspan, "Remarks by Chairman Alan Greenspan on Globalization," 7.

Primary Documents on the Global Economy

Document 1

THE ECONOMIST PROPOSES "THE CASE FOR GLOBALISATION" (SEPTEMBER 23, 2000)

The Economist is among the most respected economic publications in the world. In a recent article, "The Case for Globalisation," *The Economist* highlights two critical features propelling globalization as we enter the twenty-first century—technology and economic freedom.

Globalization, in its broadest sense, is the process by which people's economic, political, and cultural identities are integrated with those of the larger global community. In recent years the economic component of globalization has drawn the most attention. Issues related to international trade, foreign direct investment, and investments in global capital markets have a direct and immediate impact on the lives of billions of people. In the following article, *The Economist* supports the world's movement toward freer and more integrated markets as a moral imperative. It also warns that the globalization juggernaut could be derailed by protectionism or other government actions designed to restrict the free flow of goods, people, or capital across national borders.

The anti-capitalist protesters who wrecked the Seattle trade talks last year, and who hope to make a great nuisance of themselves in Prague next week when the city hosts this year's annual meeting of the World Bank and the International Monetary Fund, are wrong about most things. However, they are right on two matters, and the importance of these points would be difficult to exaggerate. The protesters are right that the most pressing moral, political, and economic issue of our time is third-world poverty. And they are right that the tide of "globalisation," powerful as the engines driving it may be, can be turned back. The fact that both these things are true is what makes the protesters—and, crucially, the strand of popular opinion that sympathizes with them—so terribly dangerous.

International economic integration is not an ineluctable process, as many of its most enthusiastic advocates appear to believe. It is only one, the best, of many possible futures for the world economy; others may be chosen, and are even coming to seem more likely. Governments, and through them their electorates, will have a far bigger say in deciding this future than most people appear to think. The protesters are right that governments and companies—if only they can be moved by force of argument, or just by force—have it within their power to slow and even reverse the economic trends of the past 20 years.

Now this would not be, as the protesters and their tacit supporters must reckon, a victory for the poor or for the human spirit. It would be just the opposite: an unparalleled catastrophe for the planet's most desperate people, and something that could be achieved, by the way, only by trampling down individual liberty on a daunting scale. Yet none of this means it could never happen. The danger that it will come to pass deserves to be taken much more seriously than it has been so far.

PANDERING AS THEY GO

The mighty forces driving globalisation are surely, you might think, impervious to the petty aggravation of street protesters wearing silly costumes. Certainly, one would have hoped so, but it is proving otherwise. Street protests did in fact succeed in shutting down the Seattle trade talks last year. More generally, governments and their international agencies—which means the IMF and the World Bank, among others—are these days mindful that public opinion is anything but squarely behind them. They are not merely listening to the activists but increasingly are pandering to them, adjusting both their policies and the way these policies are presented to the public at large. Companies too are bending to the pressure, modest as it might seem, and are conceding to the anti-capitalists not just specific changes in corporate policy but also large parts of the dissenters' specious argument.

These outbreaks of anti-capitalist sentiment are meeting next to no intellectual resistance from official quarters. Governments are apologizing for globalisation and promising to civilize it. Instead, if they had any regard for the plight of the poor, they would be accelerating it, celebrating it, exulting in it—and if all that were too much for the public they would at least be trying to explain it.

Lately, technology has been the main driver of globalisation. The advances achieved in computing and telecommunications in the West offer enormous, indeed unprecedented, scope for raising living standards in the third world. New technologies promise not just big improvements in local efficiency, but also the further and potentially bigger gains that flow from an infinitely denser network of connections, electronic and otherwise, with the developed world.

The "gains" just referred to are not, or not only, the profits of western and third-world corporations but productive employment and higher incomes for the world's poor. That is what growth-through-integration has meant for all the developing countries that have achieved it so far. In terms of relieving want, "globalisation" is the difference between South Korea and North Korea, between Malaysia and Myanmar, even (switching timespan) between Europe and Africa. It is in fact the difference between North and South. Globalisation is a moral issue, all right.

If technological progress were the only driver of global integration, the anti-capitalist threat would be less worrying. Technological progress, and (it should follow) increasing global integration, are in some ways natural and self-fuelling processes, depending chiefly on human ingenuity and ambition: it would be hard (though, as history shows, not impossible) to call a halt to innovation. But it is easier to block the effects of technological progress on economic integration, because integration also requires economic freedom.

The state of the developing countries is itself proof enough of this. The world is still very far from being a single country. Even the rich industrialized economies, taken as a group, by no means function as an integrated whole. And this is chiefly because governments have arranged things that way. Economic opportunities in the third world would be far greater, and poverty therefore vastly reduced, right now except for barriers to trade—that is, restrictions on economic freedom—erected by rich- and poor-country governments alike. Again, the protesters are absolutely right: the governments are not powerless. Raising new barriers is as easy as lowering existing ones. Trade ministers threaten to do so on an almost daily basis.

The likelihood of further restrictions has increased markedly of late. Rich-country governments have all but decided that rules ostensibly to protect labour and the environment will be added to the international trading regime. If this comes about, it will be over the objections of developing country governments—because most such governments have come round to the idea that trade (read globalisation) is good. Europe and the United States are saying, in effect, that now that the poor countries have decided they would like to reduce poverty as quickly as possible, they can't be allowed to, because this will inconvenience the West.

If that reason were true, it would be a crime to act on it. But it isn't true, or even all that plausible. Rich-country governments know very well that the supposed "adjustment problems" of expanded trade are greatly exaggerated: how convincing is it to blame accelerating globalization for the migration of jobs from North to South, when America has an unemployment rate of less than 4% and real wages are growing right across the spectrum? Yet even under these wonderful circumstances, politicians in Europe and America (leftists, conservatives, Democrats and Republicans alike) are wringing their hands about the perils of globalisation, abdicating their duty to explain the facts to voters, and equipping the anti-capitalists with weapons to use in the next fight.

It would be naïve to think that governments could let integration proceed mainly under its own steam, trusting in technological progress and economic freedom, desirable as that would be. Politics could never be like that. But is defending globalisation boldly on its own merits as a truly moral cause—against a mere rabble of exuberant irrationalists on the streets, and in the face of mild public skepticism that is open to persuasion—entirely out of the question? If it is, as it seems to be, that is dismal news for the world's poor.

Source: "The Case for Globalisation," *The Economist*, 23 September 2000, 19–20.

Document 2

THE *ECONOMIC REPORT OF THE PRESIDENT*, "OPPORTUNITY AND CHALLENGE IN THE GLOBAL ECONOMY" (2000)

The *Economic Report of the President* is an annual U.S. government publication that represents the viewpoint of the current administration on economic issues. The *Economic Report of the President: 2000,* which reflects the views of the Clinton administration, comments on the global economy and on the benefits of highly integrated global markets.

But is economic integration inevitable? Will the globalization juggernaut continue to weave its web of interdependence? These are difficult questions to answer. Recall, however, that the three pillars of globalization—international trade, foreign direct investment, and capital market flows—are the result of intentional government policies, not of irreversible natural laws. This document focuses on the globalization process as a means to an end—a path toward prosperity. But, like the first great age of globalization during the pre-World War I era, the choices people make today could steer the world onto a different path for tomorrow.

What an extraordinary episode in the economic progress of man that age was which came to an end in August, 1914! . . . life offered, at a low cost and with the least trouble, conveniences, comforts, and amenities beyond the compass of the richest and most powerful monarchs of other ages. The inhabitants of London could order by telephone, sipping his morning tea in bed, the various products of the whole earth . . . he could at the same moment and by the same means adventure his wealth in the natural resources and new enterprises of any quarter of the world . . . But, most important of all, he regarded this state of affairs as normal, certain, and permanent, except as the direction of further improvement, and any deviation from it as aberrant, scandalous, and avoidable.
    —John Maynard Keynes, *The Economic Consequence of the Peace* (1919), writing about the pre–World War I economy

For centuries, rising prosperity and rising integration of the global economy have gone hand in hand. The United States and much of the rest of the world have never before been as affluent as today. Nor has economic globalization—the worldwide integration of national economies through trade, capital flows, and operational linkages among firms—ever before been as broad or as deep. Keynes's words in the epigraph describe London at the beginning of the 20th century, yet they ring truer for the United States and many other countries as we look to the 21st century. This conjuncture of rising wealth and expanding international ties is no coincidence. The United States has gained enormously from these linkages, which have helped drive the unprecedented prosperity of the economy. Indeed, future improvements in Americans' living standards depend in part on our continued willingness to embrace international economic integration. . . .

One reason why prosperity and economic globalization have risen together is that dramatic improvements in technology have contributed to both. . . . [T]echnological advances have raised living standards, enabling each worker to produce more and better goods and services. Meanwhile innovations in transportation, communications, and information technology have made international economic integration ever easier.

Quite apart from the impact of technology, openness to the world itself makes us more prosperous. The freedom of firms to choose from a wider range of inputs, and of consumers to choose from a wider range of products, improves efficiency, promotes innovation in technology and management, encourages the transfer of technology, and otherwise enhances productivity growth. All these benefits, in turn, lead to higher real incomes and wages. Through trade, countries can shift resources into those sectors [in which they are] best able to compete in international markets, and so reap the benefits of specialization and scale economies. Opening domestic markets to global capital can improve efficiency of investment, which can promote economic growth. Through firms' direct investment in foreign affiliates, countries can adopt international best practices in production, including managerial, technical, and marketing know-how.

Given the momentum of the economic and technological forces behind globalization, its rise many seem inevitable. But policy can play a critical role in either helping or hindering its advance. The experience of the 20th century reinforces this lesson. International linkages in the United States and elsewhere were fairly developed at the beginning of the century: as Keynes observed, raising prosperity and increasing economic integration had come to seem the natural state of affairs. Yet from 1914 until mid-century, war as well as mistakes of economic policy thwarted this normalcy. In the trade arena, governments actively promoted protectionism through high tariffs and non-tariff barriers, and so inadvertently contributed to the slowed pace of world growth and development.

For the past half century, in contrast, policy has worked actively to remove barriers and distortions that impede the market forces underpinning trade and investment. For example, the General Agreement on Tariffs and Trade (GATT) and, more recently, the World Trade Organization (WTO) have championed trade liberalization. Since the 1970s, most industrialized countries have removed most of their controls on international capital movements, and many developing countries have greatly relaxed theirs as well. Given the very real benefits of open markets in both trade and finance, we should continue to embrace and encourage this trend toward liberalization.

Of course, economic globalization is not an end in itself, but rather a means to raise living standards. Like other sources of economic growth, including technological progress, economic integration involves natural tradeoffs. It provides real benefits by increasing the choices available to people and firms, but it also raises legitimate concerns. Increased trade re-sorts each country's resources, directing them toward their most productive uses, but some industries and their workers may find themselves facing sharp competition from other countries. Broader global capital flows can increase efficiency and speed development, but when these flows reverse course, they can temporarily upset whole economies.

Sound policy plays an important role in ensuring that the benefits of international economic integration are shared as widely as possible, raising living standards within and across all countries that take part. Even in an increasingly global economy, each nation controls its own destiny. In large measure, active participation in international markets for goods, services, and capital strengthens the case for policies that make sense even without integration. Among these are policies that encourage a flexible and skilled work force, provide an adequate social safety net, reward innovation, and ensure that the financial system is sound and that financial markets are deep.

Source: *Economic Report of the President: 2000* (Washington, DC: U.S. Government Printing Office, 2000), 199–202.

Document 3

CANDIDO GRZYBOWSKI, "NGOs: SEARCHING FOR SOLID GROUND" (SEPTEMBER 2000)

Candido Grzybowski, a sociologist and director of the Institute of Social and Economic Analysis (IBASE) in Rio de Janeiro, examines the role of nongovernmental organizations (NGOs) in the emerging global economy in this reading. Grzybowski argues that NGOs have created a grassroots power base that is difficult for multinational corporations, international organizations, and governments to ignore.

In recent years, NGOs have become an important new voice—or, more accurately, a chorus of new voices—in discussions dealing with global economic issues. NGOs played a major role at the Rio Earth Summit in Rio de Janeiro in 1992. In the late 1990s, Secretary-General Kofi A. Annan of the United Nations referred to NGOs as "indispensable partners" in global decision making. By the late 1990s and early 2000s, NGOs had also taken to the streets of Seattle, Washington, DC, Prague, Czech Republic, and Davos, Switzerland, to name a few locations, to voice their many concerns about the fate of the planet. The NGO chorus, however, is unique in that its participants aren't obliged to sing the same tune. Rather, it expresses a multitude of viewpoints and values the right to be heard. Can the tens of thousands of NGOs in operation truly democratize global decision making? Can they compete with the economic and political muscle of multibillion dollar multinationals and the other major players in the global economy? The following reading provides some insights on these and other questions as NGOs search for solid ground.

NGOs were not born yesterday, but the rising number of conflicts that have reverberated in recent decades around the world globalized in the neo-liberal mold has led them to multiply and diversify into highly visible bodies.

Who are the main players in this process of globalization? Governments (politics) and the market (the economy) are the twin pillars supporting the productive systems and structures of modern societies. So who has the legitimate right to change them? The societies themselves, for they alone are made up of citizens grouped together as a people, a nation or a country. The right does not belong to governments, state structures, corporate executives or markets. This is why, as NGOs, our attention is directed at civil society itself.

At the global level, our basic task is to foster the emergence of a worldwide civil society as a precondition to calling for a new style of globalization: "world governance." Our mission is to encourage the re-founding of globalization along more democratic lines by taking part in public debate and promulgating the concept of world citizenship. The political stances we take and our lobbying activities, therefore, do not come out of the blue, but are efforts to transmit the main currents and aspirations of public opinion and make this opinion stronger and clearer.

THE TRIPARTITE MIRAGE

All NGO actions are based on an obvious priority, namely that of supporting social protests and public pressure during major negotiations taking place within the main circles of power. That is why the agreements we conclude and the alliances we forge are above all else aimed at organizations and movements arising from civil society.

That is also why we build forums, coalitions and networks that straddle national borders. On the basis of our approach, we can think globally, set up links between the particular and the universal, swap experiences and keep ourselves regularly informed.

Today, global power is monopolized by major multilateral organizations, and is fundamentally anti-democratic in its structure and workings. In their current form, these organizations' claims to embody democracy and universal citizenship ring hollow. In fact, their only possible claim to legitimacy is through the vote. But not all the national governments represented in international organizations have been elected by popular suffrage, and very few of them represent all the different social forces that go into making up their nations.

Does this mean that NGOs, which are supposed to embody civil society, should claim to represent these peoples? Does it mean that our goal should be to win a place at the heart of a future new world democratic order? Does it mean that we are fully entitled to a seat in some new tripartite structure—made up of government, companies and civil society—that some people are campaigning for? In my opinion, all of that is just a mirage; even worse, we risk losing sight of our most useful and most legitimate purpose if we embrace that vision.

SMALL PLAYERS, BIG ISSUES

NGOs are not out to conquer power or win elections, be they world, national or local bodies. We are not set up like political parties, even though our actions are public and seem highly politicized. We cannot even present ourselves as representatives of civil society because civil society has not yet entrusted us with any such mandate.

So what do we want? To reach out, mobilize, educate, get across messages, suggest, innovate, persuade and politically strengthen various groups in civil society and, more specifically, those excluded from the decision-making process. We want to give a voice to ideas, values, questions and proposals that involve social justice, a more equitable distribution of wealth, respect for the environment, the struggle against poverty and social exclusion.

Who are we? Small players, compared to the other pillars of civil society, such as trade unions and professional organizations, or bodies in the state or the market. But we are also—and this is something new—"big" players, because our mission and our field of action are not limited to a given society, national economy or single government. Our task is to form a bridge between the local and the global: in other words, to deal with what is universal, with what is common to all humanity. Human rights, social crises and environmental protection are global issues. We deal with them in specific situations, but our perspective is always planetary.

So where does our legitimacy lie? In the quality of the values, principles and ideals we defend. In the relevance and the importance of the issues we raise. In the inventiveness of the proposals we put forward. Our only source of legitimacy is our ability to develop ideas aimed at action—ideas that are up to the standards of public duty to which we aspire.

Source: Candido Grzybowski, "NGOs: Searching for Solid Ground," *UNESCO Courier*, September 2000, 35–36.

Document 4

THE WORLD BANK REPORTS ON "LESSONS FROM EAST ASIA AND EASTERN EUROPE" [CREATING A DEVELOPMENT AGENDA] (2000)

The World Bank has assisted economic development, mainly in the developing world, since the mid-1940s. Over the past half-century, the original World Bank (called the International Bank for Reconstruction and Development (IBRD) has expanded into the World Bank Group. This group comprises the IBRD, the International Development Association, the International Finance Corporation, the Multilateral Investment Guarantee Agency, and the International Center for Settlement of Investment Disputes.

The World Bank's stated mission is to help create "a world free of poverty." To this end, the World Bank has loaned nearly $400 billion to countries over the past fifty years. In recent years, the World Bank has also sought ways to become more transparent and inclusive in its dealings with recipient countries. For instance, it is more receptive to local participation in decision making and solicits input from nongovernmental organizations. In the following selection from *Entering the 21st Century: World Development Report: 1999/2000*, the World Bank highlights a number of lessons it has learned from successful and unsuccessful development strategies, and considers how these lessons could be important in creating development strategies to meet the unique needs of developing countries.

The success of East Asia provides some notable lessons on successful development strategies.

- Savings. All the East Asian countries had much higher savings rates than other developing countries. From 1990 to 1997, for example, gross domestic savings in the countries of East Asia and Pacific were 36 percent of GDP, compared with 20 percent in Latin America and the Caribbean and 17 percent in Sub-Saharan Africa.

- Investment. The East Asian countries managed to invest these savings productively, so that the return on capital investment remained higher than in most other developing countries (at least until the mid-1990s).

- Education. These economies invested heavily in education—including female education. The investments paid off in contributions to growth.

- Knowledge. The East Asian countries managed to narrow the knowledge gap with high-income countries by investing heavily in science and engineering education and by encouraging foreign direct investment.

- Global integration. The experience of East Asia's economies shows that developing countries have a greater ability to enter global markets for manufactured goods than many believed possible several decades ago.

- Macroeconomic policy. The East Asian countries implemented sound macroeconomic policies that helped contain inflation and avoid recessions. Indonesia and Thailand had positive real growth from 1970 to 1996. Over that same period Malaysia and the Republic of Korea each had only one year of negative real GDP growth.

Each of these points opens up a number of new issues. For instance, the high savings rate might have been generated by personal preferences, government policies, or a combination of the two. And while these countries invested their savings well, many others do not. Nonetheless these elements of overtly successful policies point the way toward a partial development agenda.

Failures as well as successes can provide positive lessons for development. Among the most recent (and sometimes spectacular) examples of such failures are Russia, some of the economies in transition in Central and Eastern Europe, and several East Asian countries affected by the economic and financial crisis of the mid-1990s. Their experiences point to other factors that can influence economic growth, including corporate and public governance and competition.

- Legal frameworks. A sound legal framework helps ensure that managers and majority shareholders in the corporate realm focus on building firms rather than on looting them.

- Corruption. Reducing corruption in the public sphere makes a country more attractive to investors. Many privatization efforts have been racked by corruption, undermining confidence in both the government and the market economy. The loans-for-shares scheme in Russia was so widely perceived as raising corruption to new heights that much of the resulting wealth is considered illegitimate.

- Competition. Competition is essential. It encourages efficiency and provides incentives for innovation, but monopolies may try to suppress it unless the government steps in.

Source: World Bank, "Lessons from East Asia and Eastern Europe" (Box 1), *Entering the 21st Century: World Development Report: 1999/2000* (New York: Oxford University Press, 2000), 17.

Document 5

THE FREEDOM HOUSE, "FREEDOM AND ECONOMIC GROWTH" (2000)

The Freedom House is a nonprofit, nonpartisan organization dedicated to promoting democracy and freedom around the world. It was founded in 1941 by prominent Democrats such as Eleanor Roosevelt, leading Republicans such as Wendel Wilkie, and other Americans who were alarmed by the rising tide of aggressive dictatorships and antidemocratic forces in the world. Freedom House has championed numerous struggles for freedom including support for the American civil rights movement, the Vietnamese boat people, the anti-apartheid movement in South Africa, and Poland's Solidarity movement.

Since 1972, Freedom House has surveyed the state of people's political and civil rights in the world and has published its findings in annual editions of *Freedom in the World*. Over the past three decades, Freedom House has noted significant progress. For example, the number of democracies in the world has more than doubled. In addition, by 2000 about three-quarters of all countries were classified as either "free" or "partly free." What does this mean for the global economy? Freedom House has analyzed the connections between political freedoms and liberties on the one hand, and economic prosperity on the other—and has shown a correlation between the two. The following reading presents the results of the survey and, in doing so, makes a compelling case for expanding freedom in the world.

While the Survey findings already suggest that high levels of respect for political rights and civil liberties are attainable by poorer countries, it is nevertheless important to examine whether the large number of prosperous countries in the Free category suggest that freedom is [a] consequence of prosperity and development or whether prosperity is a consequence of basic political and civic freedoms.

To attempt to answer this question, we looked at all countries with a population of one million or more and examined their records of average annual growth over a ten year period. The data found that among all such Free countries the average annual GDP growth rate was 2.56 percent, compared to 1.7 percent for Partly Free countries, and 1.46 percent for Not Free countries. But such data might reflect the dynamism of the advanced industrial countries, which are almost universally free and democratic.

The differences in the growth indicators of poorer countries were even more dramatic. Our survey found that for all Free countries with a per capita GDP of under $5,000, the average ten-year annual growth rate was 3.23 percent. This was more than double the 1.39 average ten-year annual growth rates of the Partly Free poorer countries (with a per capita GDP of under $5,000). Finally, among the less developed Not Free countries, average per capita GDP growth over a ten year period stood at 1.52 percent, again less than half that of the Free poorer countries. Less developed Free countries that achieved average annual growth rates above four percent over a ten year period included Benin, Bolivia, the Dominican Republic, El Salvador, India, and Papua New Guinea.

From this data, it appears that repressive countries with high sustained economic growth rates, such as China, are the exception rather than the rule. Indeed, it is possible to conclude that as a general principle, economic growth is accelerated in an environment of political freedom. Thus, the Survey findings support the position of such economists as Nobel laureate Amartya Sen who view "development as freedom."

From these findings it is possible to consider some of the reasons why economic development is promoted by greater levels of political freedom. A primary factor is the evidence that political freedom tends to reinforce economic freedom and a vibrant private sector based on property rights. Indeed, there is a high and statistically significant correlation between the level of political freedom as measured by Freedom House and economic freedom as measured by the Wall Street Journal/Heritage Foundation survey.

A second important reason is that open and free societies benefit from an active and engaged citizenry and lively investigative news media to expose and help combat corruption. Moreover, the natural rotation of alternative political elites reduces the opportunities for cronyism and for patrimonial relations between politicians and the business community. Additionally, free societies are characterized by a neutral and independent judiciary, which is essential in the enforcement of contracts and the honest adjudication of differences among parties. It can be argued—as the Harvard scholar Dani Rodrik has shown—that free societies that protect the right to association and collective action create an environment conducive to a more balanced distribution of wealth and income. This, in turn, improves social stability and serves as an internal economic engine for prosperity by creating a vibrant working middle class.

Source: Freedom House, *Freedom in the World: The Annual Survey of Political Rights and Civil Liberties, 2000–2001* (New York: Freedom House, 2000).

Document 6

MIKE MOORE SPEAKS ON "TRADE, POVERTY, AND THE HUMAN FACE OF GLOBALIZATION" (JUNE 16, 2000)

Mike Moore, the current director-general of the World Trade Organization, is a proponent of international trade and other economic linkages between the countries of the world. Moore, like many leaders in the global community, recognizes the value of trade to expanded global output and consumption in the global economy.

In Moore's view, international trade and the larger globalization process have remained abstract concepts to many people. That is, many people perceive the forces that integrate the global economy as having little to do with their own lives. In a speech delivered at the London School of Economics, he challenges this perception and offers examples of how international trade and globalization have dramatically improved the standard of living and quality of life for billions of people around the world. The following passage summarizes the global impact of global integration—the "human face of globalization."

Few topics are as controversial as globalization. That is hardly surprising. It is the defining feature of our time. Bringing distant markets and people across the world closer together is a huge change that affects everyone, whether they are peasants in India, students in London, or bankers in New York. Such an enormous upheaval is unsettling, especially when it seems unpredictable and uncontrollable. People tend to assume the worst: that what they value most will be lost, and that what replaces it can only be bad.

We need to reassure people that globalization is generally a force for good. The last 20 years have seen a dramatic rise in living standards for many countries across the world. But those gains can be lost. Of course, the Internet cannot be uninvented. But governments can, and do, intervene to prevent products, money, people and ideas from flowing freely across national borders. They can slow or block progress. In the first half of the 20th century, the globalization of the 19th century was rolled back. We cannot rely on people's grudging acceptance of the perceived inevitability of globalization. We must not shrink from making our case.

Some people say that the problem with globalization is that it lacks a "human face."

Perhaps they are trying to say that the benefits of globalization mean little to ordinary people. After all, no-one has ever manned a barricade demanding that efficiency be maximized. But although the terminology may not have a human face, the reality does. Inefficiency is never a good thing: it means people are wasting their talents and countries are squandering their scarce resources. Maximizing efficiency means getting the most out of what you've got. It means enabling people to fulfill their potential and helping countries make the most of their resources and conserve the environment. Those are truly noble aims.

The evidence of people doing better for themselves is captured in economic statistics. There is overwhelming evidence that trade boosts economic growth. Just compare the protectionist nightmare of the 1930s with the long boom in America and Europe as trade barriers fell in the 1950s and 1960s. Or read the famous study by Jeffrey Sachs and Andrew Warner of Harvard University which finds that developing countries with open economies grew by 4.5% a year in the 1970s and 1980s, while those with closed economies grew by 0.7% a year. At that rate, open economies double in size every 16 years, while closed ones must wait a hundred. Or cast an eye on the countless country studies that support their results. When people say globalization lacks a human face, they may also mean that it doesn't benefit ordinary people. But that is simply not true.

It is not just Wall Street traders, management gurus and international civil servants like myself who gain from globalization.

It is also everyone with a pension who enjoys a more comfortable retirement because their savings are more fruitfully invested abroad, as well as everyone abroad who benefits from that foreign investment.

It is people in Britain who can talk on Finnish mobile phones, use Japanese cameras, drive American cars, drink Colombian coffee and wear clothes made in Asia.

It is poor people everywhere who can buy cheaper food and clothes produced abroad.

It is Indian computer programmers who can sell their services to American companies, and earn enough to give their children a good education and decent healthcare.

And it is poor people in poor countries who are grasping the opportunities provided by trade and technology to try to better their lives.

Mexican farm hands who pick fruit in California, Bangladeshi seam-stresses who make clothes for Europeans, and South African phone-shop owners who hawk time on mobile phones to their fellow township dwellers. They and countless other real people everywhere are the human face of globalization.

It is true that in general living standards in poor countries are not catching up with rich ones. It is a tragedy that 1.2 billion people—a quarter of the world's population—survive on less than a dollar a day and that a further 1.6 billion—another third of the world's popula-tion—make do with between one and two dollars a day.

Reducing such extreme poverty must be a priority. Of course, it is easier said than done. But we can learn from the example of those devel-oping countries that are catching up with rich ones. Take South Korea. Thirty years ago, it was as poor as Ghana; now, it is as rich as Portugal. Or consider China, where 100 million people have escaped from ex-treme poverty over the past decade.

What do these fortunate countries have in common? Openness to trade. That is the main finding of a new World Trade Organization study on trade and poverty by Dan Ben-David of Tel Aviv University and Alan Winters of Sussex University which will be launched on Mon-day.

The bottom line is this: the developing countries that are catching up with rich ones are those that are open to trade; and the more open they are, the faster they are converging. That is particularly good news for China. The liberalization that joining the WTO requires will give an-other big boost to Chinese living standards.

Trade alone is not enough to eradicate poverty. For instance, abol-ishing trade barriers will not help much if countries are at war and farm-ers cannot get their crops to market. But freer trade is essential if poor people are to have any hope of a brighter future.

Even so, critics of free trade argue that poor people within a country lose out when it liberalizes. Not so. The new WTO study finds that the poor tend to benefit from the faster economic growth that trade liberal-ization brings. It concludes that "trade liberalization is generally a strongly positive contributor to poverty alleviation—it allows people to exploit their productive potential, assists economic growth, curtails ar-bitrary policy interventions and helps to insulate against shocks." This concurs with the finding of a new study by David Dollar and Aart Kray of the World Bank which, using data from 80 countries over four de-cades, confirms that openness boosts economic growth and that the in-comes of the poor rise one-for-one with overall growth.

Of course, in the short term some people do lose from globalization. As trade barriers fall, foreign competition forces domestic firms to specialize in what they do best, rather than making goods which are more efficiently produced elsewhere. Those who are no longer gainfully employed have to find new jobs. Some are fat cats grown rich from cozy deals with governments. But others are poor farmers who lose their subsidies or unskilled workers who lose their jobs and take time to find another one.

Their plight must not be forgotten. But their hardship, like that of anyone who loses their job, should be eased with welfare benefits and job retraining, not by putting a halt to liberalization. The temporary losses of a few should not prevent a country from reaping the much bigger—and permanent—gains from free trade. After all, the interests of candle makers were not allowed to stop the introduction of electricity. Freeing trade, like new technology, causes change. That is how it boosts economic growth. Some of us lose at first, but eventually we all gain.

Although the WTO is not a development organization, it does a lot to alleviate poverty. After all, free trade is not an end in itself. It helps to raise living standards, which lifts people out of poverty.

Even so, the WTO could do more to help the poor. Poor countries do not always make the most of the world trading system, and sometimes their interests are overlooked. That is why in my first speech as director-general last September I called on WTO members to do more to help the world's poorest countries reap greater benefits from the world trading system. I am glad to report that we have made progress on that front, with a package that includes better access to rich-country markets, increased technical assistance, and closer co-operation between the WTO and other global institutions that promote development, notably the World Bank.

These are important steps. But the surest way to do more to help the poor is to continue to open markets. A new round of multilateral trade negotiations would bring huge benefits. As Kofi Annan, the Secretary General of the United Nations, has said: "Whatever cause you champion, the cure does not lie in protesting against globalization itself. I believe the poor are poor not because of too much globalization, but because of too little." He is right. The poor as well as the rich need globalization.

Source: Mike Moore, "Trade, Poverty and the Human Face of Globalization," Speech delivered at the London School of Economics, 16 June 2000.

Document 7

THE INTERNATIONAL LABOUR ORGANIZATION DECLARES "TERMS AND CONDITIONS OF WORK" (1998)

The International Labour Organization (ILO) was founded in 1919 as a part of the Versailles Treaty—the treaty that officially ended World War I. In 1946, the ILO became a specialized, independent agency of the newly formed United Nations. Today, the ILO headquarters is located in Geneva, Switzerland, and comprises representatives from 175 countries, who represent the interests of workers, employers, governments, and a number of nongovernmental organizations.

The overriding goal of the International Labour Organization is to promote justice for workers in the global economy. This broad goal involves identifying the basic rights of workers, encouraging equal opportunities for men and women in the workplace, strengthening social safety nets, and promoting constructive dialogue among workers, businesses, and governments. Since 1919, the ILO has been the world's leading voice for workers. The following excerpt summarizes the ILO's position on the "terms and conditions of work" for employers—particularly multinational enterprises—in the fast changing global economy. This excerpt is part of a larger document that also identifies other fundamental principles such as workers' right to form unions and bargain collectively, and the right to transparency in the company's financial matters.

TERMS AND CONDITIONS OF WORK

- Promote equality of opportunity and treatment in employment, with a view to eliminating any discrimination based on race, colour, sex, religion, political opinion, national extraction or social origin;

- Make qualifications, skill and experience the basis for the recruitment, placement, training and advancement of their staff at all levels;

- Endeavor stable employment for their employees and should observe freely negotiated obligations concerning employment stability and security. In view of the flexibility which multinational enterprises may have, they should strive to assume a leading role in promoting security of employment, particularly in countries where the discontinuation of operations is likely to accentuate long-term unemployment;

- Avoid arbitrary dismissal procedures;

- Provide some form of income protection for workers whose employment has been terminated;

- Develop national policies for vocational training and guidance, closely linked with employment;

- Ensure that relevant training is provided for all levels of their employees in the host country, as appropriate, to meet the needs of the enterprise as well as the development policies of the country. Such training should, to the extent possible, develop generally useful skills and promote career opportunities. This responsibility should be carried out, where appropriate, in cooperation with the authorities of the country, employers' and workers' organizations and the competent local, national or international institutions;

- Participate, along with national enterprises, in programmes, including special funds, encouraged by host governments and supported by employers' and workers' organizations. Wherever practicable, multinational enterprises should make the services of skilled resource personnel available to help in training programmes organized by governments as part of a contribution to national development;

- Offer wages, benefits and conditions of work not less favourable to the workers than those offered by comparable employers in the country concerned;

- When multinational enterprises operate in developing countries, where comparable employers may not exist, they should provide the best possible wages, benefits and conditions of work, within the framework of government policies. These should be related to the economic position of the enterprise, but should be at least adequate to satisfy basic needs of the workers and their families. Where they provide workers with basic amenities such as housing, medical care or food, these amenities should be of good standard;

- Provide adequate safety and health standards for their employees;

- Cooperate in the work of international organizations concerned with the preparation and adoption of international safety and health standards;

- Cooperate fully with the competent safety and health authorities, the representatives of the workers and their organizations, and established safety and health organizations.

Source: International Labour Organization (ILO), "Terms and Conditions of Work," *Summary of ILO Tripartite Declaration of Principles Concerning Multinational Enterprises*, Copyright International Labour Organization, Geneva, Switerland, 1998.

Document 8

UNITED NATIONS SECRETARY-GENERAL KOFI A. ANNAN OF THE UNITED NATIONS PROPOSES *THE GLOBAL COMPACT: THE 9 PRINCIPLES* (JANUARY 31, 1999)

> Secretary-General Kofi A. Annan of the United Nations (UN) proposed *The Global Compact* in a speech at the World Economic Forum in Davos, Switzerland, on January 31, 1999. The *Compact* challenges business leaders to abide by nine principles, which lay a sound foundation for the new global economy.
>
> The nine principles outlined in *The Global Compact* ask businesses around the world to practice good corporate citizenship. That is, the *Compact* appeals to corporations to practice social responsibility by protecting human rights, labor rights, and the natural environment on a global level. The nine principles were drawn from existing documents including "The Universal Declaration of Human Rights" (UN), "The Fundamental Principles on Rights at Work" (International Labor Organization), and the "Rio Principles on Environment and Development" (UN). The goal is to enlist 100 major multinationals and 1,000 other firms from around the world to integrate the nine principles into their business practices by 2002. Excerpts from *The Global Compact*'s nine principles are provided here.

"THE 9 PRINCIPLES"

1 The Secretary-General asked world business to support and respect the protection of internationally proclaimed human rights within their sphere of influence.

Corporate leadership in human rights is good for the community and for business. The benefits of responsible engagement merit being spelled out.

For business they include: being more in touch with markets, customers and consumers by better understanding the opportunities and problems of the social context; the advantages of a good social reputation; a greater chance of a stable and harmonious atmosphere in which to do business; a reduction of damaging criticism, which, in the extreme, can lead to lost investment, contracts or customers. And there is the long-term benefit of a more stable and peaceful society in which investments can prosper.

For society, the benefits of corporate social responsibility include: less adverse impacts from ill-thought-through business initiatives; a gearing-up of social partnerships; capacity and innovation brought to bear on problems; and the full contribution of influential citizens to the general well-being.

*2 The Secretary-General asked world business to make sure they
are not complicit in human rights abuses.*

An effective human rights policy will help companies avoid being im-
plicated in human rights violations.

*3 The Secretary-General asked world business to uphold
freedom of association and effective recognition of the right to
collective bargaining.*

Businesses face many uncertainties in a rapidly changing global market. Establishing genuine dialogue with freely chosen workers' representatives enables both workers and employees to understand each
other's problems better and find ways to resolve them. Security of rep-
resentation is a foundation for building trust on both sides.

*4 The Secretary-General asked world business to promote the
elimination of all forms of forced and compulsory labour.*

Forced labour robs societies of the opportunities to apply and develop human resources for the labour market of today, and develop the
skills in education for the labour markets of tomorrow. . . . Forced labour retards the proper development of human resources, reduces lifetime earnings of whole families, lowers the level of productivity and
economic growth for society generally, and produces social unrest.

*5 The Secretary-General asked world business to promote the
effective abolition of child labour.*

Child labour involves depriving children of their childhood and their
dignity. Of particular concern are children who work long hours for low
or no wages, often under conditions harmful to their health, physical
and mental development, who are deprived of an education and who
may be separated from their families. . . . Protecting a child from economic exploitation involves protecting him or her from performing any
work that is likely to interfere with education, or is harmful to a child's
health or well-being.

*6 The Secretary-General asked world business to uphold the
elimination of discrimination in respect to employment and
occupation.*

Discrimination in employment and occupation restricts the available
pool of workers and skills, and isolates an employer from the wider
community. Non-discriminatory practices help ensure the best quali-
fied person fills the job. Discriminatory practices can damage a com-

pany's reputation, potentially affecting profits and stock value. Discrimination in the world of work slows economic growth as a whole. The lack of a climate of tolerance results in missed opportunities for development of skills and infrastructure to strengthen competitiveness in the global economy.

7 The Secretary-General asked world business to support a precautionary approach to environmental challenges.

Prevention rather than cure—it is more cost-effective to take early actions to ensure that the irreversible environmental damage does not occur. This requires developing a life-cycle approach to business activities to:

Manage the uncertainty

Ensure transparency

8 The Secretary-General asked world business to undertake initiatives to promote greater environmental responsibility.

As outlined in *Agenda 21*, environmental responsibility is " . . . [the] responsible and ethical management of products and processes from the point of view of health, safety and environmental aspects. Towards this end, business and industry should increase self-regulation, guided by appropriate codes, charters and initiatives integrated into all elements of business planning and decision-making, and fostering openness and dialogue with employees and the public." Given the increasingly central role of the private sector in global governance issues, the public is demanding that business manage its operations in a manner which will enhance economic prosperity, ensure environmental protection and promote social justice.

9 The Secretary-General asked world business to encourage the development and diffusion of environmentally friendly technologies.

Environmentally sound technologies (ESTs), as defined by *Agenda 21* " . . . protect the environment, as less polluting, use all resources in a more sustainable manner, recycle more of their wastes and products, and handle residual wastes in a more acceptable manner than the technologies for which they were substitutes. [ESTs] are not just individual technologies, but also systems which include know-how, procedures, goods and services, and equipment as well as organizational and managerial procedures."

Source: The Global Compact: The 9 Principles, Announced by Secretary-
General Kofi A. Annan of the United Nations, 31 January 1999
(www.unglobalcompact.org/gc/unweb.nsf/content/prin12.htm).

Document 9

50 YEARS IS ENOUGH CALLS FOR GLOBAL ECONOMIC JUSTICE (1994)

50 Years Is Enough is an international nongovernmental organization (NGO) dedicated to reforming the global financial architecture and thereby promoting economic justice in the global economy. This NGO was founded in 1994—the fiftieth anniversary of the founding of the World Bank and the International Monetary Fund (IMF) at the Bretton Woods Conference. Since the mid-1990s, 50 Years Is Enough has challenged many of the policies and practices of the World Bank, the IMF, and other international organizations.

50 Years Is Enough, like many other NGOs, has formed alliances with numerous partner organizations in dozens of countries around the world. As an advocate for global justice, 50 Years is Enough has actively promoted and participated in protests against the World Bank, IMF, and other organizations. It has also proposed alternative strategies to deal with global economic problems—particularly those of the global South. NGOs have become a major force in shaping policies and in influencing the decision making of multinational corporations, international organizations, and governments. A summary of 50 Years Is Enough's vision for the future is described in the following reading.

PLATFORM SUMMARY

1) Institutional reform to make openness, full public accountability and the participation of affected populations in decision making standard procedure at the World Bank and the IMF.

- Full openness and systematic consultation by the World Bank and IMF with local populations potentially affected by the policy reforms, programs and projects they support.

- Full disclosure of information at the World Bank and IMF.

- Legal and structural changes at the IMF to permit an increase in its openness and accountability.

2) A shift in the nature of economic-policy reform programs and policies to support equitable, sustainable and participatory development.

- A halt to World Bank and IMF structural adjustment programs as currently constituted so as to limit further damage to poor and working people and the environment.

- The reorientation of World Bank and IMF lending for economic-policy reform to support development that is equitable and sustainable and that addresses the root causes of poverty.

3) An end to all environmentally destructive lending and support for more self-reliant, resource-conserving development that preserves biodiversity.

- The reorientation of all World Bank and IMF lending to ensure consistency with the agreements reached at the 1992 United Nations "Earth Summit."

- An immediate moratorium on the preparation of any World Bank–supported project involving forced resettlement in countries that do not have in place policies and legal frameworks that will lead to income restoration for those who will be resettled.

- A moratorium on World Bank funding for the construction of large dams.

- Substantial shifts in World Bank lending towards alternative, cost-effective, resource-conserving energy, water-supply, transportation and sanitation projects.

- A shift in World Bank lending away from agricultural export production and operations which directly or indirectly accelerate forest destruction.

4) The scaling back of the financing, operations, role and, hence, power of the World Bank and the IMF and the rechanneling of financial resources thereby made available into a variety of development assistance alternatives.

- The denial of future capital requests for the IBRD and the IMF's Enhanced Structural Adjustment Facility (ESAF).

- A narrowing of the policy-making roles of the IMF and the World Bank.

- The establishment of an independent IDA [International Development Association], operationally and financially independent of the World Bank.

- The establishment of a fully independent Global Environmental Facility, legally, operationally and financially split off from the World Bank.

5) A reduction in multilateral debt to free up additional capital for sustainable development.

- The immediate cancellation of 100 percent of the outstanding debt owed the IBRD and IMF by the Severely Indebted Low-Income Countries and 50 percent of that owed by Severely Indebted Lower-Middle Income Countries.

- The write-off of World Bank loans made for projects and programs that have failed in economic terms, particularly those which have had severe adverse impact on local populations and the environment.

- An international agreement to ensure that future borrowing by governments from the IMF and the World Bank is based on the informed consent of its citizens to accept and repay the debt.

Source: "Platform Summary," 50 Years Is Enough: US Network for Global Economic Justice (*www.50years.org/platformsummary.html*).

Document 10

RUTH KAGIA PROPOSES "PROJECTS FOR ACCELERATING HUMAN DEVELOPMENT IN THE 21st CENTURY" (2000–2001)

Ruth Kagia is the director of Human Development at the World Bank. In her article Ms. Kagia comments on the fragile nature of human development in the global economy. Yet, despite many obstacles and some recent disappointments, she maintains that human development goals are worthwhile and achievable.

Human development includes the protection of human rights, poverty reduction, a more equitable distribution of wealth within and between countries, and the preservation of the natural environment. Thus, human development is closely linked with improving the quality of life for people and promoting sustainable economic development. By the late 1990s, just 46 countries (mostly the wealthier industrialized nations) out of 174 surveyed were classified as high human development countries by the United Nations Development Program. What are the main obstacles to reaching human development goals? What can be done to advance human development in the global economy, especially in the poorer regions of the world? Why is human development important to global prosperity? Ms. Kagia shares insights on these and other questions in this reading.

On the threshold of the new millennium, human development is at a major crossroad. The twenty-first century will be shaped by the development choices we make today. Those choices will either lead to the eradication of poverty or will deepen it. They will determine whether all economies become truly integrated or whether some of them become increasingly marginalized. At this juncture, the development path that countries will take is not predestined.

Progress in human development is fragile and can be reversed. As we start the twenty-first century, all regions have lost the momentum for achieving poverty reduction goals and the number of poor people in most developing nations is rising. This reflects faltering growth in East Asia and Latin America, continuing slow growth in sub-Saharan Africa and a sharp decline in living standards in Eastern Europe and the former Soviet Union during the difficult transition to modern market economies. Human development is being further halted by the emergence of new health problems, in particular HIV/AIDS, which now is the number one overall cause of death in Africa and has moved up to fourth place among all causes of death worldwide. While the epicenter of the disease is in Southern Africa, it is spreading fast to other regions.

Ten years ago, the private sector invested $35 billion in developing countries, while official development assistance (ODA) was $65 billion. Today, private sector investment in developing countries has grown to $300 billion, while ODA has dwindled to $45 billion. But 70 per cent of those private capital flows went to 12 out of 108 developing countries. Sub-Saharan Africa received less than 5 per cent of that share. More than 80 countries in sub-Saharan Africa and Eastern Europe have lower per capita incomes than a decade ago.

In an increasingly interdependent world, the manifestation of extreme poverty and the growing gap between the rich and the poor decrease the prospects for global integration and peace and security. The challenges of development can only be met through coordinated and adequately funded international efforts. The international community, led by the United Nations family, should spearhead these efforts to assist countries unleash the positive forces of the global market, attract private capital, accelerate the momentum for poverty reduction and reduce the risk of increased marginalization and inequality.

The next century could be shaped into one of unprecedented improvement in the quality of life for people everywhere. Success is within reach of national Governments and their internal and external partners if they take effective public actions to develop policies and institutions that promote inclusive growth. Such actions include: creating enabling conditions for all economies to compete fairly in the global economy; establishing strategic partnerships with all stakeholders; and supporting national Governments to design and implement human-centred, equitable and participatory programmes.

Globalization can unleash the positive forces of the global market if effective public action is taken at the national and international levels to develop institutions and policies that would bring about inclusive growth. In addition, globalization can also facilitate the unleashing of our combined efforts and expertise to reach global solutions. This would reduce the disparities across and within countries, bring more and more people into the economic mainstream and promote equitable access to the benefits of development.

Human development and economic growth are mutually reinforcing; for development to be sustainable, both should be accelerated in tandem. Markets must, therefore, be supplemented with investments in human capital at four levels. Firstly, in order to build secure foundations for growth and development, countries need to complete the unfinished agenda of the twentieth century by accelerating expansion of equitable, broad-based and quality basic services: education, especially of girls; primary health care; adequate food; clean water; and sanitation. Secondly, countries will need to simultaneously address the agenda of the twenty-first century in order to become competitive participants in a global economy and bridge the digital divide. They will need to develop policies and institutions that promote science, technology and enterprise, actions which encourage high levels of private and public investment as a means of creating jobs and stimulating economic growth. Thirdly, the poor need to be active participants in the design and implementation of development programmes. This is not just good for building social capital, but it also ensures that resources benefit the most needy. And, finally, these actions must be rooted in processes that are socially inclusive and responsive to changing circumstances and which work in the interests of the poor, for example, by providing adequate basic services.

Several global initiatives demonstrate the importance of developing strategic alliances. UNAIDS—the joint United Nations Programme on HIV/AIDS—has rapidly become a powerful global force in the fight against the disease. The Onchocerciasis Control Programme, established to eliminate river blindness, and the international programme to eliminate polio are outstanding examples of successful and value-enhancing partnerships. The "Education for All" initiative, launched 10 years ago, has proved to be an effective mechanism for galvanizing international and national actions towards the attainment of education for all.

Some new players have altered the dynamics of the development agenda. The current debt relief programme was reshaped and strengthened, in part because of sustained pressure from several non-governmental organizations. Oxfam has proposed a Global Action Plan for Basic Education that would mobilize resources, push harder for debt relief, and engender national commitment and reform in education, with emphasis on sub-Saharan Africa. The private sector is becoming an increasingly important player in the social sectors, especially in health. For example, the Bill and Melinda Gates Foundation supports vaccine research, while the SmithKline Beecham company offers a free drug supply for the treatment of filiaris. All these relationships need to be effectively managed and leveraged.

Countries need integrated policy packages and institutional environments that foster transparency and accountability, reward hard work and creativity, and facilitate participation. The World Bank has scaled up its efforts to strengthen the interdependence of policies through the Comprehensive Development Framework, which is being piloted in 13 countries. It aims to sharpen the focus on the major goals of development, highlight the integrated nature of policy-making, emphasize institutional processes to sustain development and coordinate development efforts. The framework underscores the growing realization that the many elements that make up the development process must be planned together and coordinated in order to obtain the best results. It seeks a better balance in development efforts by emphasizing the interdependence of all elements of development—economic, financial, social and structural—governance and the environment. It is anchored in the principles of ownership of the policy agenda and on a long-term holistic vision.

International development goals have been agreed upon as global milestones against which progress towards the goal of poverty elimination can be measured.

Progress on attaining these goals, however, has been disappointing, and most of them will not be met by the target date. Current forecasts indicate that only South Asia and China will be able to grow at such a rate as to achieve the international goal of a 50 per cent reduction in poverty by 2015. Such progress can be accelerated through renewed emphasis on quality social service delivery, with increased focus on the poorest countries in Africa and South Asia, which are also most vulnerable to the forces of globalization. Developing countries also need financial and technical assistance to support economic reform efforts, invest in growth and expand access and quality. At a time when many countries have been undertaking fundamental reforms, the level of ODA has been steadily declining: between 1992 and 1997, it fell 20 per cent in real terms and declined by 7 billion in 1997. Appropriate and effective aid levels need to be established to give Governments the space they need to put economic reforms on a self-sustaining path. In addition, development assistance needs to be restructured to focus on people-centred, inclusive development.

The Heavily Indebted Poor Countries (HIPC) initiative arose out of a recognition that high levels of debt act as a serious break to sustainable development. It was launched in 1996 by the World Bank, with support from other partners and endorsed by 180 governments worldwide. Following the Cologne Summit in June 1999, HIPC was expanded to provide more debt relief to more countries and redesigned to link debt relief to poverty reduction. The World Bank and the International Monetary Fund are collaborating closely to integrate poverty reduction into the debt programme.

When all is said and done, responsibility and accountability for poverty reduction and human development rest with the countries. Strong political and intellectual leadership is a necessary condition for effectively utilizing international support. There must be a vision and the political will to design and implement the policies needed to establish the foundations for economic growth and reduce poverty, promote good governance and the rule of law. The international community, however, should remain an effective catalyst for change, sharing international experiences on what works and what does not work, and supporting countries to customize global standards into local situations.

Source: Ruth Kagia, "On the Threshold: Projects for Accelerating Human Development in the 21st Century," *UN Chronicle* no. 4, (2000–2001), 21–22.

Document 11

UNICEF REPORTS ON THE STATE OF THE WORLD'S CHILDREN: MAKING "A NECESSARY CHOICE" (2001)

The United Nations Children's Fund (UNICEF) is a specialized agency within the United Nations System dedicated to the welfare of the world's children. In 1946, UNICEF—then called the United Nations International Children's Emergency Fund—focused on relieving suffering in the aftermath of World War II. Since the 1950s, UNICEF's attention has shifted to improving the quality of life for children mainly in the developing world. Programs have dealt with a wide range of issues related to health, nutrition, education, emergency relief, and even land-mine awareness (in Kosovo).

In recent years, there has been a growing consensus in the international community that the mutually supporting goals of poverty reduction and sustainable economic development are pivotal to the success of a truly global economy. It is also widely acknowledged that the vicious cycle of poverty limits opportunities for poorer countries and poorer people to reap the benefits of globalization. The following reading tells the story of one typical family from Tanzania, and its struggle for survival. It also introduces the Early Childhood Care and Development (ECD) program—a comprehensive program to guarantee children proper health care, nutrition, education, and access to clean water, sanitation, and a safe environment—and why the cycle of poverty remains a fixture in today's global economy.

"A NECESSARY CHOICE"

In Tanzania, Febronia, a 35-year-old woman, has given birth to seven children. Four have survived: Martha 10, Angela, 8, Colman, 6, and Grace, 9 months. Two sons died at age 7, one from yellow fever and the other from an unknown cause. Another child, born prematurely, died shortly after birth. Her husband, Damas, 42, sporadically works at a coffee plantation and the family survives on a cash income of about 80,000 shillings a year ($125).

Febronia and her family live in a shanty made of wood, mud and tin. The area around the house is thick with red mud that crusts on the shoeless feet of the mother, father and their four children. Spending an hour each day fetching water from a stream about 3 kilometers away from her home, Febronia worries about leaving her young children alone at home. But what worries her most is being away from her baby for stretches of three hours or longer. While Febronia collects grass for the family's small herd of cows, Grace is left with Febronia's eight-year-old daughter after she returns from her half-day of school.

Like many mothers in many countries, Febronia spends each day from dawn to dusk struggling to feed and protect her children, with few resources and little support. She begins her day at 6 A.M. preparing porridge for her family. Besides collecting grass for the cows and water and food for the family, Febronia searches for firewood for cooking. Each day, she takes her small children to bathe in the stream. During the rainy season she tries in vain to keep them clean. Like many in the community, the family does not have a permanent latrine, so the muddy water that swirls past their hut is mixed with feces.

From morning to night, Febronia's every waking moment is spent in the service of others. Her tasks are endless. Hours on end, Febronia, a sturdy woman with close-cropped hair, can be seen walking, posture-perfect, carrying heavy loads on her head. Once back home, she cooks, cleans and cares for her family. She works in their small vegetable garden. In between chores, she breastfeeds her baby. After the day's work is done and the last child is bedded down for the night, she says her prayers and goes to sleep.

Like millions of women worldwide, Febronia is unsafe in her home. She is afraid of her husband, who she says drinks too much alcohol. Sometimes he punches and kicks her.

The seeds of male privilege and female servitude have already been planted in Febronia's family. While her mother works in the fields, Angela, the shy eight-year-old who still sucks her thumb, takes care of the baby. When 10-year-old Martha with the furrowed brow and pensive eyes returns from school, she washes the dishes, helps cut grass for the cows and works in the garden. And what does Febronia's son do while the girls are working? Colman, a boy with a cherubic face and an impish smile, plays in the mud and climbs trees.

Like 1.1 billion people worldwide, Febronia lacks access to clean water. After her daily trek for water, she must boil it to protect her children from cholera and other water-borne diseases. The family, like 2.3 billion adults worldwide, does not have access to a decent latrine. Without clean water and a permanent latrine, maintaining good hygiene is yet another hardship for Febronia and her family. They risk diarrhoeal and other diseases, including trachoma, an eye infection that is easily spread among children and their mothers and which, with repeated occurrences, eventually leads to blindness.

Although the family has a small vegetable garden and a couple of cows, poverty robs the family of adequate nutrition. The three oldest children show signs of being malnourished, with patches of bald spots on their heads. The oldest child, Martha, has sunken eyes with deep dark, puffy circles underneath.

The children are not the only ones: in this village of 2,448 people there are 10 licensed bars but no child-feeding centers since 1995. Here, children without day care are often without food for stretches, in some cases for as long as eight hours.

While all but the infant have completed their immunizations against the six major childhood killer diseases, Febronia and Damas have watched three of their children die. A health worker visits their home each week, and there is a missionary hospital less than a kilometer from the village. But Damas bemoans, "The hospital is there, but without money, you will die on its doorstep."

Ten-year-old Martha is in the second grade of primary school, and the eight-year-old and six-year-old are involved in pre-school for two hours each morning. The parents recognize the benefits of pre-school, boasting that the children can count, sing and tell stories. But Damas, a gaunt man in oversized clothes, fears that he will not be able to afford to keep his children in school. When he was a child, education in Tanzania was free, he says, and it provided him with lunch. Today, there are fees for books and uniforms, and lunch must be brought from home. Damas believes that education will provide a better future for his children, but without money their chances are lost.

CHALLENGES OF ECD

Why has the decision to invest in ECD, so seemingly the best public policy for responsible leaders, not been made in every community in every country?

Because poverty is a merciless foe. In a time of unprecedented global prosperity, the World Bank estimates that in 1998, 1.2 billion people, including more than half a billion children, lived in poverty on less than $1 a day. In the poorest nations, money that could go to education, health care and infrastructure improvement is spent on debt repayment. Developing nations owe more than $2 trillion to the World Bank, the International Monetary Fund (IMF), other lenders and industrialized countries. Loans that were meant to lift countries out of poverty—that could lift them in a generation if their monies were invested in ECD today—are instead dragging them further into debt.

Because of the ever-present threat or reality of violence. The rights to survival, growth and development of millions of children throughout the world are at risk along a continuum of violence that stretches from households, where children are often exposed to or are victims of violence and abuse on a routine basis, to international policies where infants and children die as a result of economic sanctions, to the horrors of modern warfare, where millions are killed and millions more survive only to be haunted by their memories.

And because by killing more than 2 million adults each year, HIV/AIDS strips a front line of protection from the thousands of children who are orphaned each day. HIV/AIDS is a global emergency of devastating impact, taking the lives of adults and children in every region of the world and leaving child survivors to cope without parents and grandparents, aunts and uncles and siblings, teachers and health care workers.

The disease spares no continent. In 1998 alone, 2.2 million Africans died from HIV/AIDS. In 1999, nearly a quarter of a million people in Ukraine had the virus. In Latin America and the Caribbean, 1.7 million people are HIV infected, 37,600 of them children. And in Asia, 6.1 million people, including 205,200 children, were living with HIV at the end of 1999.

THE EFFECTS OF POVERTY ON EARLY CHILDHOOD

When poverty engulfs a family, the youngest are the most affected and most vulnerable—their rights to survival, growth and development at risk. A child born in the developing world has a 4 out of 10 chance of living in extreme poverty. This poverty defines every aspect of the child's existence, from malnutrition, lack of clean water, inadequate sanitation, to life expectancy. It is the main underlying cause of millions of preventable deaths and the reason why children are malnourished, miss out on school or are abused and exploited. And it is at the core of a pervasive violation of children's rights. . . .

Poverty's cycle does not stop in one lifetime. A girl born to poverty is more likely to marry early and have a child while still an adolescent. A malnourished girl becomes a malnourished mother, who will give birth to an underweight baby. And, like their parents, poor children are likely to transmit their poverty to the next generation. . . .

Source: United Nations Children's Fund, "A Necessary Choice," in *The State of the World's Children: 2001* (New York: United Nations Children's Fund, 2001), 30–33.

Document 12

THE UNITED NATIONS ISSUES THE "RIO DECLARATION ON ENVIRONMENT AND DEVELOPMENT" (JUNE 3–14, 1992)

In 1992, the United Nations Conference on Environment and Development—more commonly called the Rio Earth Summit—brought leaders from more than 100 nations to Rio de Janeiro, Brazil, to work toward the goal of sustainable economic development. A central piece in the deliberations was the Earth Summit's commitment to environmental protection.

The Rio Earth Summit of 1992 was groundbreaking in a number of ways. First, it gained wide consensus among the leaders of the world that "capacity building"—the creation of institutions capable of spearheading countries' development process—could be achieved while respecting the environment, workers' rights, and human rights. Many of the principles designed to guide the process of sustainable development are recorded in *Agenda 21*, which was adopted by the conference. Second, the summit encouraged participation not only by official representatives of governments, but also by hundreds of nongovernmental organizations that had assembled in Rio for the conference. Hence, the Rio Earth Summit is viewed as a model for more inclusive, democratic forums for public debate on global issues. Finally, the

Commission on Sustainable Development was created to monitor and report on the implementation of Earth Summit agreements. The following reading summarizes the main environmental principles agreed to at the Rio Earth Summit.

The United Nations Conference on Environment and Development,
   Having met at Rio de Janeiro from 3 to 14 June 1992,
   Reaffirming the Declaration of the United Nations Conference on the Human Environment, adopted at Stockholm on 16 June 1972, and seeking to build upon it,
   With the goal of establishing a new and equitable global partnership through the creation of new levels of cooperation among States, key sectors of societies and people,
   Working towards international agreements which respect the interests of all and protect the integrity of the global environment and developmental system,
   Recognizing the integral and interdependent nature of Earth, our home,
   Proclaims that:

Principle 1 Human beings are at the center of concerns for sustainable development. They are entitled to a healthy and productive life in harmony with nature.

Principle 2 States have, in accordance with the Charter of the United Nations and the principles of international law, the sovereign right to exploit their own resources pursuant to their own environmental and developmental policies, and the responsibility to ensure that activities within their jurisdiction or control do not cause damage to the environment or other States or of areas beyond the limits of national jurisdiction.

Principle 3 The right to development must be fulfilled so as to equitably meet developmental and environmental needs of present and future generations.

Principle 4 In order to achieve sustainable development, environmental protection shall constitute an integral part of the development process and cannot be considered in isolation from it.

Principle 5 All States and all people shall cooperate in the essential work of eradicating poverty as an indispensable requirement for sustainable development, in order to decrease the disparities in standards of living and better meet the needs of the majority of the people in the world.

Principle 6 The special situation and needs of developing countries, particularly the least developed and those most environmentally vulnerable, shall be given special priority. International actions in the field of environment and development should also address the interests and needs of all countries.

Principle 7 States shall cooperate in a spirit of global partnership to conserve, protect and restore the health and integrity of the Earth's ecosystem. In view of the different contributions to global environmental degradation, States have common but differentiated responsibilities. The developed countries acknowledge the responsibility that they bear in the international pursuit of sustainable development in view of the pressure their societies place on the global environment and of the technologies and financial resources they command.

Principle 8 To achieve sustainable development and a higher quality of life for all people, States should reduce and eliminate unsustainable patterns of production and consumption and promote appropriate demographic policies.

Principle 9 States should cooperate to strengthen endogenous capacity-building for sustainable development by improving scientific understanding through exchanges of scientific and technological knowledge, and by enhancing the development, adaptation, diffusion and transfer of technologies, including new and innovative technologies.

Principle 10 Environmental issues are best handled with the participation of all concerned citizens, at the relevant level. At the national level, each individual shall have appropriate access to information concerning the environment that is held by public authorities, including information on hazardous materials and activities in their communities, and the opportunity to participate in decision-making processes. States shall facilitate and encourage public awareness and participation by making information widely available. Effective access to judicial and administrative proceedings, including redress and remedy, shall be provided.

Principle 11 States shall enact effective environmental legislation. Environmental standards, management objectives and priorities should reflect the environmental and developmental context to which they apply. Standards applied by some countries may be inappropriate and of unwarranted economic and social cost to other countries, in particular developing countries.

Principle 12 States should cooperate to promote a supportive and open international economic system that would lead to economic growth and sustainable development in all countries, to better address the problems of environmental degradation. Trade policy measures for environmental purposes should not constitute a means of arbitrary or unjustifiable discrimination or a disguised restriction on international trade. Unilateral actions to deal with environmental challenges outside the jurisdiction of the importing country should be avoided. Environmental measures addressing transboundary or global environmental problems should, as far as possible, be based on an international consensus.

Principle 13 States shall develop national law regarding liability and compensation for the victims of pollution and other environmental damage. States shall also cooperate in an expeditious and more determined manner to develop further international law regarding liability and compensation for adverse effects of environmental damage caused by activities within their jurisdiction or control to areas beyond their jurisdiction.

Principle 14 States should effectively cooperate to discourage or prevent the relocation and transfer to other States of any activities or substances that cause severe environmental degradation or are found to be harmful to human health.

Principle 15 In order to protect the environment, the precautionary approach shall be widely applied by States according to their capabilities. Where there are threats of serious or irreversible damage, lack of scientific certainty shall not be used as a reason for postponing cost-effective measures to prevent environmental degradation.

Principle 16 National authorities should endeavor to promote internationalization of environmental costs and the use of economic instruments, taking into account the approach that the polluter should, in principle, bear the cost of pollution, with due regard to the public interest and without distorting international trade and investment.

Principle 17 Environmental impact assessment, as a national instrument, shall be undertaken for proposed activities that are likely to have a significant adverse impact on the environment and are subject to a decision of a competent national authority.

Principle 18 States shall immediately notify other States of any natural disasters or other emergencies that are likely to produce sudden harmful effects on the environment of those States. Every effort shall be made by the international community to help States so afflicted.

Principle 19 States shall provide prior and timely notification and relevant information to potentially affected States on activities that may have a significant adverse transboundary environmental effect and shall consult with those States at an early stage and in good faith.

Principle 20 Women have a vital role in environmental management and development. Their full participation is therefore essential to achieve sustainable development.

Principle 21 The creativity, ideals and courage of the youth of the world should be mobilized to forge a global partnership in order to achieve sustainable development and ensure a better future for all.

Principle 22 Indigenous people and their communities and other local communities have a vital role in environmental management and development because of their knowledge and traditional practices. States should recognize and duly support their identity, culture and interests and enable their effective participation in the achievement of sustainable development.

Principle 23 The environment and national resources of people under oppression, domination and occupation shall be protected.

Principle 24 Warfare is inherently destructive of sustainable development. States shall therefore respect international law providing protection for the environment in times of armed conflict and cooperate in its further development, as necessary.

Principle 25 Peace, development and environmental protection are interdependent and indivisible.

Principle 26 States shall resolve all their environmental disputes peacefully and by appropriate means in accordance with the Charter of the United Nations.

Principle 27 States and people shall cooperate in good faith and in a spirit of partnership in the fulfillment of the principles embodied in this

Declaration and in the further development of international law in the field of sustainable development.

Source: "Rio Declaration on Environment and Development," *Report of the United Nations Conference on Environment and Development* (United Nations Department of Economic and Social Affairs, 1999).

Document 13

THE WORLD RESOURCES INSTITUTE ADOPTS AN ECOSYSTEM APPROACH TO MANAGING THE WORLD'S RESOURCES (SEPTEMBER 15, 2000)

The World Resources Institute, the United Nations Development Program, the United Nations Environment Program, and the World Bank recently joined ranks to publish *World Resources 2000–2001, People and Ecosystems: The Fraying Web of Life*. This landmark report was initially presented to the world's environmental ministers in Bergen, Norway, on September 15, 2000. In the report, the sponsoring institutions not only chronicled the current state of the planet, but also introduced the ecosystem approach to managing the world's limited resources.

The ecosystem approach represents a comprehensive plan of action for responsible, sustainable development. It recognizes that past human interactions with the environment have altered and degraded many critical ecosystems. We continue to rely on ecosystems, however, to provide humanity with the essentials of life—the clean water that we drink, the food that we eat, the air that we breathe, and so on. The following excerpt from *World Resources 2000–2001* comments on the importance of protecting our ever-fraying web of life and proposes concrete steps to guide us toward this goal.

ADOPTING A HUMAN PERSPECTIVE

All organisms have intrinsic value; grasslands, forests, rivers, and other ecosystems do not exist to serve humans alone. Nonetheless, *World Resources 2000–2001* deliberately examines ecosystems, and their management, from a human perspective because human use is the primary source of pressure on ecosystems today, far outstripping the natural processes of ecosystem change. In the modern world, virtually every human use of the products and services of ecosystems translates into an impact on those ecosystems. Thus, every use becomes either an opportunity for enlightened management or an occasion for degradation.

Responsible use of ecosystems faces fundamental obstacles, however. Typically, we don't even recognize ecosystems as cohesive units because they often extend across political and management borders. We look at them in pieces or concentrate on the specific products they yield. We miss their complexity, the interdependence of the organisms—the very qualities that make them productive and stable.

The challenge for the 21st century, then, is to understand the vulnerabilities and resilience of ecosystems, so that we can find ways to reconcile the demands of human development with the tolerances of nature. That requires learning to look at our activities through the living lens of ecosystems. In the end, it means adopting an ecosystem-oriented approach to managing the environment—an approach that respects the natural boundaries of ecosystems and takes into account their interconnections and feedbacks.

• • •

WHAT IS AN ECOSYSTEM APPROACH?

An ecosystem approach broadly evaluates how people's use of an ecosystem affects its functioning and productivity.

- *An ecosystem approach is an integrated approach.* Currently, we tend to manage ecosystems for one dominant good or service such as fish, timber, or hydropower without fully realizing the tradeoffs we are making. In doing so, we may be sacrificing goods and services more valuable than those we receive—often those goods and services that are not yet valued in the marketplace such as biodiversity and flood control. An ecosystem approach considers the entire range of possible goods and services and attempts to optimize the mix of benefits for a given ecosystem. Its purpose is to make tradeoffs efficient, transparent, and sustainable.

- *An ecosystem approach reorients the boundaries that traditionally have defined our management of ecosystems.* It emphasizes a systemic approach, recognizing that ecosystems function as whole entities and need to be managed as such, not in pieces. Thus it looks beyond traditional jurisdictional boundaries, since ecosystems often cross state and national lines.

- *An ecosystem approach takes the long view.* It respects ecosystem processes at the micro level, but sees them in the larger frame of landscapes and decades, working across a variety of scales and time dimensions.

- *An ecosystem approach includes people.* It integrates social and economic information with environmental information about the ecosystem. It thus explicitly links human needs to the biological capacity of ecosystems to fulfill those needs. Although it is attentive to ecosystem processes and biological thresholds, it acknowledges an appropriate place for human modification of ecosystems

- *An ecosystem approach maintains the productive potential of ecosystems.* An ecosystem approach is not focused on production alone. It views production of goods and services as the natural product of a healthy ecosystem, not as an end in itself. Within this approach, management is not successful unless it preserves or increases the capacity of an ecosystem to produce the desired benefits in the future.

Source: World Resources Institute, *World Resources 2000–2001, People and Ecosystems: The Fraying Web of Life* (Washington, DC: World Resources Institute, the United Nations Development Program, the United Nations Environment Program, and the World Bank, 2000), 10–11, 226.

Document 14

THE POPULATION REFERENCE BUREAU ASKS, "IS THE 'POPULATION EXPLOSTION' OVER?" (MARCH 2001)

The Population Reference Bureau (PRB) is a widely recognized authority in identifying population trends in the United States and in the world. By 2000, the PRB reported that world population was growing by 83 million people per year and that the total world population would grow by an additional 3 billion people over the next half century.

The growth of human population is one of the most important challenges of today's global economy. Statistically, virtually all population growth during the coming century will occur in the developing world—regions where sustainable economic development is already threatened by population pressures on scarce resources, fragile ecosystems, and inadequate social services. "Overpopulation" describes an imbalance between the number of people in a region and the region's ability to supply these people with the essentials of life in the long term. What is the state of the world's population? Is the so-called population explosion over, or will its momentum carry it into the twenty-first century? The following PRB document by Lori Ashford, a senior policy analyst at the PRB, deals with these and other questions.

Recent international debates about population policy have downplayed the significance of world population growth, even though the population is still growing rapidly in many parts of the world. The earliest population policies were propelled primarily by fears that rapid population growth would hinder socioeconomic progress. These concerns surfaced during a period of unprecedented population growth that began in the 1950s in less developed countries—setting off what was often referred to as the "population explosion." In these countries, the availability of modern health care, improved nutrition, and expanded transportation networks, among other factors, contributed to the rapid declines in mortality. Fertility remained relatively high. As births outnumbered deaths by even larger margins, the population of less developed countries shot up from 1.7 billion in 1950 to 4.9 billion in 2000. The population in more developed countries rose from 0.8 billion to 1.2 billion over the same period. While the total for more developed countries is expected to fall slightly by 2050, the number is still rising for less developed countries and is projected to exceed 8 billion by 2050. World population will rise from 6 billion in 2000 to 9 billion by 2050.

The world population growth rate peaked in the 1960s, then began a slow descent as fertility levels declined in many world regions. Between the 1960s and 1990s, social and economic advances reinforced the idea that couples could control their family size, and that smaller families were preferable. Expanded education and job opportunities for women encouraged later marriage and delayed childbearing—which also slowed the pace of population growth.

Population policies and family planning programs were important contributors to the widespread fertility declines. These programs fostered greater access to modern contraceptives and enabled couples to control the timing of their childbearing more effectively than ever before.

Some countries in East and Southeast Asia and in Latin America experienced robust economic development during this period. Governments in some of the largest countries—including China, Indonesia, Thailand, and Mexico—also had explicit policies to lower population growth by promoting smaller families. Fertility dropped rapidly in many of these countries.

The marked declines in fertility in some countries in Asia and Latin America, as well as in more developed countries, have led some observers to declare that "the population explosion is over."[1] But there are two parallel worlds: one world in which fertility is low and declining as economic development advances, and another world where fertility remains high and where much of the population is mired in poverty.

U.S. couples average about two children each—the number required to just replace each couple in the population and avoid long-term population growth. Most industrialized societies now have an average of less than two children per couple and some countries are headed for population decline. Some of the larger less developed countries—China, South Korea, Thailand, and Brazil, for example—also have fertility rates close to or below the two-child average. In the 1990s, the UN twice revised population growth projections downward to take into account unexpected rapid declines in fertility in several regions. This slowing of growth has contributed to commentary that "too few babies is emerging as a bigger worry in many countries—not all of them rich ones—than too many."[2]

This perspective ignores the "second world" of population made up of countries in sub-Saharan Africa, South Asia, and elsewhere, where fertility (and mortality) are still relatively high. It also overlooks the effect of population momentum. Decades of rapid growth mean that there are now more young men and women of childbearing age than ever before; just behind them is another large generation of children who will enter childbearing age in the next decade. This huge generation of young people provides the momentum for continued population growth well into the 21st century, even though couples are likely to have fewer children than in earlier generations. The world's population reached 6 billion in 1999 and could exceed 9 billion by 2050, assuming that the average family size falls from 2.8 children per woman today to 2.1 by 2050.

The population will eventually stop growing if fertility falls to a two-child average worldwide ("replacement-level fertility"). Births would balance out deaths, yielding a stable population size. But reaching replacement-level fertility will require widespread access to family planning and major social tranformations in some countries. In the poorest regions, women have five to six children on average. In India—the world's second-largest country—fertility fell substantially over the past few decades, but remains well above replacement at 3.2 children per couple. Even after countries reach replacement level, population momentum ensures future growth. China, for example, has had a two-child average or less for about a decade, yet the momentum provided by the age structure means that 11 million more people were born than died each year in the 1990s. At current fertility levels, China's population will continue to grow until about 2030, according to UN projections.

When media stories alternate between "the population explosion" and "birth dearth," the public is likely to be confused and policymakers may question the need for population policies and programs. Recent UN conferences have sidestepped the issue of rapid population growth (and population momentum), framing the issue instead as that of enhancing individual health and well-being. A lingering question is whether policymakers will invest the sums required to improve individual health and well-being whether or not they perceive a population crisis.

REFERENCES

1. Ben Wattenberg, "The Population Explosion Is Over," *The New York Times Magazine*, Nov. 25, 1997.

2. "The Empty Nursery," *The Economist*, Dec. 23, 2000. Accessed online at: *www.economist.com*, on Jan. 26, 2001.

Source: Lori Ashford, "Is the 'Population Explosion' Over?" *Population Bulletin* 56, no. 1 (March 2001).

Document 15

ERLA ZWINGLE AND *NATIONAL GEOGRAPHIC*, "A WORLD TOGETHER" (AUGUST 1999)

Erla Zwingle, a former *National Geographic* editor, comments on globalization's recent impact on global cultures in "A World Together." In Zwingle's words: "Goods move. People move. Ideas move. And cultures change." Is the world heading for a global culture? Is cultural homogenization already a reality?

Globalization is not a new phenomenon. Economic, political, and cultural integration has occurred, in fits and starts, for thousands of years. At the heart of globalization are the linkages between the global and the local. Yet it is the speed with which we are making these linkages, and the strength of the resulting bonds, that distinguish today's globalization from that of the past. With lightning speed, most economies have turned toward capitalism, and political systems toward democracy. And cultural changes—with a distinctly Western orientation—are reflected not only in the items we buy, but also in our lifestyles and ways of thinking. In the following reading, Zwingle discusses this "cultural assault" and questions whether cultural identities are being erased or adapted to meet the new challenges of the twenty-first century.

Once I started looking for them, these moments were everywhere: That I should be sitting in a coffee shop in London drinking Italian espresso served by an Algerian waiter to the strains of the Beach Boys singing "I wish they all could be California girls. . . ." Or hanging around a pub in New Delhi that serves Lebanese cuisine to the music of a Filipino band in rooms decorated with barrels of Irish stout, a stuffed hippo head, and a vintage poster announcing the Grand Ole Opry concert to be given at the high school in Douglas, Georgia. Some Japanese are fanatics for flamenco. Denmark imports five times as much Italian pasta as it did ten years ago. The classic American blond Barbie doll now comes in some 30 national varieties—and this year emerged as Austrian and Moroccan.

Today we are in the throes of a worldwide reformation of cultures, a tectonic shift of habits and dreams called, in the curious argot of social scientists, "globalization." It's an inexact term for a wild assortment of changes in politics, business, health, entertainment. "Modern industry has established the world market. . . . All old-established national industries . . . are dislodged by new industries whose . . . products are consumed, not only at home, but in every quarter of the globe. In place of the old wants . . . we find new wants, requiring for their satisfaction the products of distant lands and climes." Karl Marx and Friedrich Engels wrote this 150 years ago in *The Communist Manifesto.* Their statement now describes an ordinary fact of life.

How people feel about this depends a great deal on where they live and how much money they have. Yet globalization, as one report stated, "is a reality, not a choice." Humans have been weaving commercial and cultural connections since the first caravan ventured afield. In the 19th century the postal service, newspapers, transcontinental railroads, and great steam-powered ships wrought fundamental changes. Telegraph, telephone, radio, and television tied tighter and more intricate knots between individuals and the wider world. Now computers, the Internet, cellular phones, cable TV, and cheaper jet transportation have accelerated and complicated these connections.

Still, the basic dynamic remains the same: Goods move. People move. Ideas move. And cultures change. The difference now is the speed and scope of these changes. It took television 13 years to acquire 50 million users; the Internet took only five.

Not everyone is happy about this. Some Western social scientists and anthropologists, and not a few foreign politicians, believe that a sort of cultural cloning will result from what they regard as the "cultural assault" of McDonald's, Coca-Cola, Disney, Nike, MTV, and the English language itself—more than a fifth of all people in the world now speak English to some degree. Whatever their backgrounds or agendas, these critics are convinced that Western—often equated with American—influences will flatten every cultural crease, producing, as one observer terms it, one big "McWorld."

Popular factions sprout to exploit nationalists anxieties. In China, where xenophobia and economic ambition have often struggled for the upper hand, a recent book called *China Can Say No* became a best-seller by attacking what it considers the Chinese willingness to believe blindly in foreign things, advising Chinese travelers not to fly on a Boeing 777 and suggesting that Hollywood be burned.

There are many Westerners among the denouncers of Western cultural influences, but James Watson, a Harvard anthropologist, isn't one of them. "The lives of Chinese villagers I know are infinitely better now than they were 30 years ago," he says. "China has become more open partly because of the demands of ordinary people. They *want* to become part of the world—I would say globalism is the major force for democracy in China. People want refrigerators, stereos, CD players. I feel it's a moral obligation not to say: 'Those people out there should continue to live in a museum while we will have showers that work.'"

Westernization, I discovered over months of study and travel, is a phenomenon shot through with inconsistencies and populated by very strange bedfellows. Critics of Western culture blast Coke and Hollywood but not organ transplants and computers. Boosters of Western culture can point to increased efforts to preserve and protect the environment. Yet they make no mention of some less salubrious aspects of Western culture, such as cigarettes and automobiles, which, even as they are being eagerly adopted in the developing world, are having disastrous effects. Apparently westernization is not a straight road to hell, or to paradise either.

But I also discovered that cultures are as resourceful, resilient, and unpredictable as the people who compose them. In Los Angeles, the ostensible fountainhead of world cultural degradation, I saw more diversity than I could ever have supposed—at Hollywood High School the student body represents 32 different languages. In Shanghai I found that the television show *Sesame Street* has been redesigned by Chinese educators to teach Chinese values and traditions. "We borrowed an American box," one told me, "and put Chinese content into it." In India, where there are more than 400 languages and several very strict religions, McDonald's serves mutton instead of beef and offers a vegetarian menu acceptable to even the most orthodox Hindu.

"I used to say that Peoria will look like Paris, and Beijing will look like Boston," said Marshall W. Fishwick, professor of American Studies at Virginia Tech, "but now I'm not so sure. . . ."

Change: It's a reality, not a choice. But what will be its true driving force? Cultures don't become more uniform; instead, both old and new tend to transform each other. The late philosopher Isaiah Berlin believed that, rather than aspire to some utopian ideal, a society should strive for something else: "not that we agree with each other," his biographer explained, "but that we can understand each other."

In Shanghai one October evening I joined a group gathered in a small, sterile hotel meeting room. It was the eve of Yom Kippur, the

Jewish Day of Atonement, and there were diplomats, teachers, and businessmen from many Western countries. Elegant women with lively children, single men, young fathers. Shalom Greenberg, a young Jew from Israel married to an American, was presiding over his first High Day as rabbi of the infant congregation.

"It's part of the Jewish history that Jews went all over the world," Rabbi Greenberg reflected. "They received a lot from local cultures, but they also kept their own identity."

The solemn liturgy proceeded, unchanged over thousands of years and hundreds of alien cultures: "Create in me a clean heart, O God, and renew a right spirit within me," he intoned. I'm neither Jewish nor Chinese, but sitting there I didn't feel foreign—I felt at home. The penitence may have been Jewish, but the aspiration was universal.

Global culture doesn't mean just more TV sets and Nike shoes. Linking is humanity's natural impulse, its common destiny. But the ties that bind people around the world are not merely technological or commercial. They are the powerful cords of the heart.

Source: Erla Zwingle, "A World Together," *National Geographic* 196, no. 2 (August 1999), 12–13, 16, 33.

Glossary of Selected Terms

Absolute advantage   occurs when one region or nation can produce a good more efficiently than a second region or nation.

Advanced countries   the richer, more industrialized countries of the world. The advanced countries are often referred to as the developed countries or advanced economies.

Affiliate   a company that has been purchased by another company, often by a multinational corporation. The purchasing company determines how much autonomy the affiliate will retain.

Agenda 21   a landmark document adopted at the Rio Earth Summit (1992), which established guidelines for sustainable economic development in the world.

Americanization   the infusion of American culture traits into other countries. Americanization often refers to the movement toward cultural homogenization.

Association of Southeast Asian Nations (ASEAN)   a regional trade organization that comprises ten countries: Brunei, Cambodia, Indonesia, Laos, Malaysia, Myanmar, Philippines, Singapore, Thailand, and Vietnam.

Basic economic questions   the fundamental questions that all economies must answer, including what to produce, how to produce, and for whom to produce.

Big Three   the three dominant multilateral organizations that oversee the economic relations among countries, including the World Trade Organization, World Bank, and International Monetary Fund.

Bilateral investment treaties (BITs)   formal agreements between two nations designed to protect and promote foreign investments.

Brain drain   a process whereby many of the most educated and skilled workers from one country (usually the poorer countries) emigrate to more advanced countries.

Bretton Woods Conference (of 1944)   the meeting of forty-four countries that laid the foundation of a more stable post–World War II international monetary system. Both the International Monetary Fund and the World Bank were created at the conference.

Business climate   refers to factors that might encourage or discourage business activity in a region or nation. Such factors include a stable government, a fair tax system, a sound infrastructure, the rule of law, adequate private-sector incentives, and so on.

Capital   any item that is designed to produce other goods or services. Capital is also called capital resources or capital goods.

Capital deepening   occurs when a country is able to expand its capital stock.

Capital flight   occurs when savings from one country are invested in safer, more profitable ways in another country.

Capitalism   a type of economic system in which individuals and firms own and control the great majority of the nation's resources and are free to answer the basic economic questions of what, how, and for whom to produce.

Capital stock   the total amount of real capital a country has to produce goods and services.

Cartel a formal agreement or organization among firms or nations that produce an identical product. The main goal of a cartel is to influence the price of the product by limiting its supply. The world's leading cartel is the Organization of Petroleum Exporting Countries.

Code of conduct for multinationals   a set of rules established by an individual or group outside of a corporation to guide the business behaviors of multinational corporations. The most widely recognized code of conduct for multinationals was authored by the International Labor Organization.

Cold War   the post–World War II tensions and hostilities between the West (the United States and other advanced democracies) and the East (Soviet Union and the communist satellite nations of central and Eastern Europe). The collapse of the Soviet Union in 1991 typically marks the end of the Cold War.

Commonwealth of Independent States (CIS)   a loose confederation of twelve former Soviet republics.

Communism a type of economic system in which the government owns and controls the great majority of the means of production—the factories, farms, and other businesses—and dictates the answers to the basic economic questions of what, how, and for whom to produce.

Comparative advantage occurs in the production of a product in which a region or nation has its greatest advantage, or at least a lesser disadvantage. Resources are used most efficiently when regions or nations specialize in the production of products in which they have a comparative advantage.

Conglomerate a highly diversified corporation.

Corporate code of conduct a set of rules established by a corporation to guide its business behaviors.

Cultural homogenization the process by which local cultures are transformed or absorbed by a dominant outside culture.

Customs union a type of regional trade bloc that not only reduces trade barriers among member nations, but also creates a uniform set of customs duties or other trade restrictions on imports from nonmembers. An example is the European Union.

Deforestation the clearing of timber and brush from a region.

Democracy a type of political system in which the people rule either by a direct vote on issues or through freely elected representatives.

Depression a prolonged economic downturn in an economy, characterized by a drop in the country's gross domestic product, a low level of investment, a high unemployment rate, many business failures, and a mood of pessimism.

Desertification the transformation of fertile land into desert, typically caused by a combination of human actions and natural forces.

Developed countries the richer, more industrialized countries of the world. The developed countries are often referred to as the advanced countries or advanced economies.

Developing countries the poorer countries of the world. The developing countries are often referred to as the less developed countries.

Development Assistance Committee (DAC) a twenty-two-member subgroup within the Organization for Economic Cooperation and Development that extends official development assistance to poorer countries.

Digital divide the technology gap that exists between the wealthier advanced countries and the poorer nations of the world, especially the gap in the use of computers, the Internet, and other information technologies.

East Asian crisis (of 1997–1998) a financial contagion that began in Thailand and spread quickly to other East Asian countries including Malaysia, South Korea, and Indonesia.

Economic Community of West African States (ECOWAS)   a regional trade organization comprised of sixteen countries of West Africa.

Economic globalization   the deliberate movement by individuals, multinational corporations, transnational organizations, and governments to increase the flow of goods, services, people, real capital, and money across national borders in order to create a more integrated and interdependent world economy.

Economic sanctions   any restrictions on trade, investments, or foreign aid that are designed to pressure a country to change a policy or an action.

Ecosystems   systems combined of organic and inorganic matter and natural forces that interact and change. Types include grassland, forest, agriculture, freshwater, and coastal systems.

Efficiency   the effective use of scarce factors of production by businesses so that resources aren't wasted, and the production of goods and services that people want to buy. Sometimes called allocative efficiency.

Embargo   a type of trade barrier that cuts off some or all trade with another nation.

Entrepreneurship   refers to the risk-taking by innovators, called entrepreneurs, in an economy.

Equal treatment principle   a principle of trade guaranteeing that countries treat imported goods in the same way as domestically produced goods. Also called national treatment.

Euro the common currency of twelve of the fifteen countries comprising the European Union. The euro replaced the national currencies of these twelve countries in 2002.

European Free Trade Association (EFTA)   a regional trade organization that comprises four countries: Iceland, Liechtenstein, Norway, and Switzerland.

European Monetary Union (EMU)   refers to the twelve European Union countries that have adopted the euro as their common currency. The EMU is sometimes called the euro-zone.

European Union (EU)   the largest regional trade organization in the world comprising fifteen western European countries: Austria, Belgium, Denmark, Finland, France, Germany, Greece, Ireland, Italy, Luxembourg, the Netherlands, Portugal, Spain, Sweden, and the United Kingdom.

Exchange rate   a precise statement of the value of one currency relative to a second currency.

Exports   the goods or services that are sold to other nations.

Expropriation   occurs when a government takes ownership or control of a private company without compensating the previous owner.

Financial contagion   the rapid spread of a financial crisis from one country or region to other countries or regions. During the late 1990s, the effects of financial contagion were felt most keenly in East Asia, eastern Europe, central Asia, and South America.

Fixed exchange rate system   a system of converting nations' currencies at a rate that is tied to gold or to the U.S. dollar. The fixed exchange rate system was in place from the mid-1940s to 1973.

Flexible exchange rate system   a system of converting nations' currencies that relies on the forces of supply and demand to determine the value of each currency.

Foreign aid   the cross-border transfer of money, capital equipment, goods or services, information, technology, or advisors to help the recipient country.

Foreign direct investment (FDI)   cross-border investments made mainly by multinational corporations. FDI involves greenfield investments (the building of new production facilities) as well as mergers and acquisitions of existing firms.

Foreign exchange markets   a network of international financial institutions, such as commercial banks and investment banks, that facilitate international trade by converting currencies. Today, most of the business of foreign exchange markets involves the buying and selling of nations' currencies for profit.

Foreign exchange trading   the buying and selling of currencies in foreign exchange markets. Foreign exchange trading is the major business activity conducted in foreign exchange markets.

Freedom House   a nonprofit organization that is dedicated to promoting democracy and freedom worldwide. Publishes the annual *Freedom in the World* to record global progress toward democracy and freedom.

Free trade area   a type of regional trade bloc that reduces or eliminates trade restrictions among member nations, but permits member nations to negotiate other trade arrangements with nonmembers. Examples include the North American Free Trade Agreement and the Association of Southeast Asian Nations.

Free Trade Area of the Americas (FTAA)   the planned regional trade bloc for the thirty-four democracies of the Western Hemisphere.

Gangster economy   an economy run by organized crime. The term gangster economy has been used to describe the Russian economy in recent years.

General Agreement on Tariffs and Trade (GATT)   an international agreement designed to promote freer and fairer trade in the global economy from 1947 to 1994. The GATT was replaced by the World Trade Organization in 1995.

Global Compact a United Nations document, approved in 1999, that was designed to advance corporate responsibility in the global economy.

Global consumer boycott a campaign to discourage the purchase of products made by a company until the company changes its business practices. Global consumer boycotts were staged against Nike and Carnation in recent years.

Global economy the international web of individuals, firms, multilateral organizations, and governments that make production and consumption decisions.

Global financial architecture refers to the institutions and the practices of governments, businesses, and individuals when they engage in financial activities in the global economy.

Globalization the process by which local economies, political systems, and cultures are integrated with those of the larger global community.

The Global Sullivan Principles of Corporate Social Responsibility a document authored by the Reverend Leon H. Sullivan to encourage responsible business behaviors by companies in the global economy.

Global warming the gradual warming of global surface temperatures over time due mainly to the greenhouse effect.

Good governance refers to the manner in which the government discharges its responsibilities. Qualities of good governance includes the government's success in stopping crime and corruption, openness in the political system, and the rule of law in a country.

Greenfield investments a type of foreign direct investment that involves the construction of entirely new production facilities such as manufacturing plants, oil refineries and pipelines, and farms or plantations.

Greenhouse effect the result of gases trapped in the earth's atmosphere, such as carbon dioxide and chlorofluorocarbons, which holds in some of the heat that normally would have radiated back into space. The greenhouse effect is thought to be responsible for global warming.

Green revolution employs mechanization, hybrid seeds, pesticides and fertilizers, and scientific planting methods to expand crop yields.

Gross domestic product (GDP) the value of all newly produced goods and services, made by foreign and domestic businesses within a country, in a given year. The per capita GDP is GDP per person. The real per capita GDP is the GDP per person adjusted for inflation. The nominal GDP is the GDP not adjusted for inflation.

Gross national product (GNP) the value of all newly produced goods and services, made by a country's firms within the country's borders and in other countries, in a given year. The per capita GNP is GNP per person. The real per capita GNP is the GNP per person adjusted for inflation. The nominal GNP is the GNP not adjusted for inflation.

Group of Seven (G-7)   an organization of the world's seven most advanced economies including Canada, France, Germany, Italy, Japan, the United Kingdom, and the United States. The Group of Eight includes the G-7 plus Russia.

Group of Twenty (G-20)   an organization of nations founded in 1999 to promote dialogue and cooperation among the most powerful economies from the developed and developing world. Originally comprised of the G-7 countries plus eleven others, the G-20 will eventually expand to twenty member countries.

Herd mentality   the rush to buy or sell securities, or to make other types of investments, based on the buy or sell actions of other investors. The herd mentality sometimes results in panic selling of securities or other investments and contributes to financial contagion in the highly integrated global economy.

High-income country   a country with a per capita gross national product of $9,266 or more (in 1999).

Human capital   another name for labor. The term "human capital" is often used to highlight the fact that workers' native abilities are enhanced by knowledge and skills that they acquire through education or training.

Human development   a measurement of well being based on the protection of people's human rights, the eradication of poverty, the reduction of gross income inequalities, and the preservation of the natural environment.

Import quota   a trade barrier that sets a specific limit on the amount of an imported good.

Imports   the goods or services that are purchased from other nations.

International Center for Settlement of Investment Disputes (ICSID)   one of five institutions that make up the World Bank Group. The ICSID mediates financial disputes between foreign investors and host countries.

International Development Association (IDA)   one of five institutions that make up the World Bank Group. The IDA extends development loans, called credits, to the world's poorest and least creditworthy countries.

International Finance Corporation (IFC)   one of five institutions that make up the World Bank Group. The IFC extends loans to private firms in developing countries.

International financial institutions (IFIs)   refer to financial institutions responsible for supervising and regulating the conduct of countries and businesses in the global economy. Examples include the International Monetary Fund and World Bank.

International Labor Organization (ILO)   the most widely recognized labor organization in the world. Since 1946 it has been a part of the United Nations system and currently comprises 175 member countries.

International Monetary Fund (IMF)   a multilateral organization designed to stabilize the global economy and promote economic development through surveillance and technical and financial assistance.

International trade   occurs when individuals, firms, or governments import or export goods or services.

Internet   an international web of computer networks that connect business, educational, and government computer networks.

Lower-middle income country   a country with a per capita gross national product of between $756 and $2,995.

Low-income country   a country with a per capita gross national product of $755 or less (in 1999).

Managed exchange rate system   a system of converting nations' currencies whereby a government may buy or sell its own currency to stabilize its value. Many governments today will prevent rapid appreciation or depreciation of their currencies in this manner.

Maquiladoras   duty-free assembly plants typically operating in developing countries. Mexican maquiladoras have become increasingly important in Mexico's industrial sector in recent years.

Merchandise trade deficit   occurs when the value of a country's merchandise imports is greater than the value of its merchandise exports.

Merchandise trade surplus   occurs when the value of a country's merchandise exports is greater than the value of its merchandise imports.

MERCOSUR   a regional trade organization comprising four countries (Argentina, Brazil, Paraguay, and Uruguay) and two associate members (Bolivia and Chile). Also called the Common Market of the South.

Mergers and acquisitions (M&As)   occur when two existing companies are legally joined under single ownership. M&As account for the great majority of foreign direct investment.

Middle-income country   a country with a per capita gross national product (GNP) of between $756 and $9,265 (in 1999). This classification is sometimes subdivided into lower-middle-income countries (per capita GNP of $756 to $2,995) and upper-middle-income countries (per capita GNP of $2,996 to $9,265).

Millennium round (of the WTO)   the unofficial name for the stalled first round of trade negotiations among the World Trade Organization

(WTO) member nations. The unsuccessful WTO ministerial conference in Seattle in 1999 was supposed to have jump-started the Millennium round.

Ministry of Economy, Trade and Industry (METI)   the reorganized Japanese ministry designed to promote economic growth and trade that replaced the Ministry of International Trade and Industry in 2001.

Ministry of International Trade and Industry (MITI)   a quasi-public institution in Japan designed to support export industries through a variety of incentives such as tax breaks, low-interest loans, and grants for research and development.

Most-favored-nation (MFN) status   a principle of international trade by which any trade concession granted to one country would automatically apply to all countries holding MFN status. MFN status was automatically extended to all General Agreement on Tariffs and Trade member countries and the to World Trade Organization member countries.

Multilateral environmental agreements (MEAs)   agreements among nations designed to deal with environmental problems such as global warming, biodiversity, and ozone depletion. Examples include the Montreal Protocol and the Kyoto Protocol.

Multilateral Investment Guarantee Agency (MIGA)   one of five institutions of the World Bank Group. The MIGA encourages foreign investment in the developing world through insurance against noncommercial losses (war, civil unrest, nationalization, and so on).

Multilateral organizations   formal groups composed of representatives of more than one country. Examples include the World Trade Organization, the World Bank, and the International Monetary Fund.

Multinational corporations (MNCs)   companies that are based in one country, but own or control other companies—called affiliates—in one or more additional countries. Also called transnational corporations and multinationals.

Nationalization occurs when the government takes ownership or control of a private company, but compensates the previous owner.

Newly industrialized economies   the four Asian economies that have become industrialized and are considered developed economies. These economies are often referred to as the Asian tigers, and include Hong Kong SAR, Singapore, South Korea, and Taiwan.

New protectionism   supports greater government control on trade and foreign investment and a greater role for local peoples in making the economic decisions that affect their lives.

Nongovernmental organizations (NGOs)   organizations designed to share information about issues and to instigate reforms by governments, businesses, or international organizations. NGOs have become important organizations in global decision making.

North (the) an economic designation to describe the developed countries, many of which are located in the Northern Hemisphere.

North American Free Trade Agreement (NAFTA) a regional trade organization that comprises Canada, Mexico, and the United States.

Official development assistance (ODA) a type of foreign aid that targets economic development in developing and transition countries. ODA is granted by twenty-two richer nations that comprise the Development Assistance Committee—a subgroup of the Organization for Economic Cooperation and Development.

Offshore financial centers (OFCs) refers to many types of financial institutions such as banks, insurance companies, securities firms, and others that are unregulated, unsupervised, and prone to illegal business activity.

Organization for Economic Cooperation and Development (OECD) a regional organization of thirty countries designed to promote sustainable economic development for member and nonmember nations and global economic security.

Organization of Petroleum Exporting Countries (OPEC) a producer cartel that comprises eleven major oil producing nations from Africa, Asia, the Middle East, and South America.

Ozone depletion the weakening or destruction of the protective ozone layer in the earth's atmosphere due to releases of harmful chemicals such as chlorofluorocarbons into the atmosphere.

Principle of mutual benefit a principle of trade, domestic or international, that states that both parties can benefit from the exchange of goods or services.

Privatization the converting of state-owned enterprises into privately held businesses. Privatization is a cornerstone of market reforms in the transition countries.

Production sharing occurs when different components of a good are produced and assembled in stages in plants in different countries.

Protectionism the government's use of trade barriers or other restrictions to limit imports. These restrictions are designed to protect domestic firms and jobs. People who favor the use of trade barriers to help the domestic economy are sometimes called protectionists.

Purchasing power parity (PPP) makes adjustments in foreign exchange rates to account for differences in the cost of living in different countries. PPP can be used to adjust the gross national product (GNP), per capita GNP, wages, or other financial data.

Quality of life the overall conditions under which people live including people's access to a variety of consumer goods and services, health care, education, clean water, food, sanitation, energy, transportation and communications, and so on.

Race to the bottom a phrase commonly used to describe the exploitation of human and natural resources by companies, especially multinational corporations in the developing world.

Real capital refers to the factories, office buildings, farms, machines, and tools that people use to produce other goods and services. Real capital is a factor of production.

Regional development bank a multilateral institution designed to support sustainable economic development in a specific region of the world. Examples include the African Development Bank Group, the Asian Development ment Bank, and the Inter-American Development Bank.

Regional trade agreements (RTAs) trade agreements negotiated by countries to reduce trade barriers, mainly in a geographic region. RTAs are controversial because some believe they violate the World Trade Organizations most-favored-nation status.

Regional trade organization an economic alliance that promotes freer trade among member nations and other types of economic or political integration. The European Union is the world's largest and most integrated regional trade organization.

Relocalization a movement that supports small-scale community-oriented production and greater restrictions on foreign investment and foreign trade.

Rio Earth Summit a United Nations–sponsored meeting in 1992 that created guidelines for sustainable economic development on a global basis. *Agenda 21* was adopted at this summit.

Rule of law describes a condition in which all participants in an economy are subject to a fair and uniform set of laws and regulations.

Smoot-Hawley Tariff (of 1930) a severe U.S. tax on imports that touched off a trade war with America's trading partners and increased the severity of the global depression (called the Great Depression in the United States).

Social auditing independent monitoring of a company's operation, including working conditions, wage rates, compliance with health and safety regulations, and so on. Social auditing is a way in to ensure that companies are living up to their corporate code of conduct or other measure of corporate social responsibility.

Social capital refers to capital that the government provides, including roads, sewage systems, schools, courts and prisons, and other elements of the infrastructure.

South (the)   an economic designation to describe the developing countries, many of which are located in the Southern Hemisphere.

Subcontracting   a practice by which one company hires a second company (the subcontractor) to produce a good.

Subcontractor   a company that is contracted to produce a good for another company.

Sustainable economic development   the overall advancement of a country's economy, and improvement in the people's quality of life, over time.

Sweatshop   a manufacturing plant marked by unpleasant and dangerous working conditions, abusive bosses, low pay, and no labor power.

Tariff   a federal tax on an imported good. Tariffs can be designed to raise revenue for the government or to discourage imports. A tariff is a type of trade barrier.

Technology transfer   occurs when a multinational corporation's advanced research, production techniques, real capital, or other innovations are infused into the economy of a host country.

Terrorism   any act of terror or threat used to gain political advantage.

Trade barriers   government restrictions on imports including tariffs, import quotas, voluntary restrictions, embargoes, or other nontariff restrictions. Also called barriers to trade.

Trade deficit in services   occurs when the value of commercial services imported into a country are greater than the value of commercial services that are exported.

Trade liberalization   government policies that result in freer trade, such as the reduction or removal of trade barriers (tariffs, import quotas, and so on).

Trade-Related Aspects of Intellectual Property (TRIPS)   an agreement negotiated during the Uruguay Round of the General Agreement on Tariffs and Trade that set uniform, global standards to protect intellectual properties such as computer software, medicines, music, books, and other processes and products.

Trade surplus in services   occurs when the value of commercial services exported from a country are greater than the value of commercial services that are imported.

Transition country   a country that is transforming its economy from communism to capitalism. There are twenty-eight transition countries in eastern and central Europe and central Asia.

Transparency   refers to an openness, or free flow of information, to the public. Reforms to improve transparency apply to governments, multinational corporations, international organizations, and others.

Unsustainable debt   a country's foreign debt that is so large it cannot be repaid without devastating consequences for the country.

Upper-middle-income country   a country with a per capita gross national product between $2,996 and $9,265.

Venture capital   money that is invested in new businesses, but not money invested in mergers or acquisitions of exiting facilities. Also called risk capital.

Virtual firm   a company that conducts its business over the Internet.

Virtuous cycle   occurs when the development of new technologies and new products spawn an explosion of new business activity.

Voluntary restriction   a type of trade barrier that informally agrees to limit the amount of an imported good (a voluntary restraint agreement) or to boost exports to another country (voluntary export expansion).

World Bank (IBRD)   one of five institutions in the World Bank Group. The World Bank provides loans for development projects throughout the world.

World Bank Group   refers to five interrelated institutions that promote economic development, mainly in the developing world, including the World Bank, the International Development Association, the International Finance Corporation, the Multilateral Investment Guarantee Agency, and the International Center for Settlement of Investment Disputes.

World Trade Organization (WTO)   a multilateral organization designed to promote freer and fairer international trade. The WTO replaced the General Agreement on Tariffs and Trade in 1995, and was given greater authority to rule on trade disputes between nations.

Annotated Resource Guide

BOOKS

Anderson, Sarah, John Cavanagh, Thea Lee, and Barbara Ehrenreich. *Field Guide to the Global Economy.* New York: New Press, 2000. Examines mainly the negative aspects of globalization, a process that is driven by multinationals' relentless quest for profits at the expense of the majority of the world's people.

Bales, Kevin. *Disposable People: New Slavery in the Global Economy.* Berkeley: University of California Press, 2000. Examines the impact of globalization on workers, especially in the developing world.

Benyon, John, *Globalization: The Reader.* New York: Routledge, 2001. Addresses global issues such as new applications of technology, cultural homogenization, and the impact of the media on societies.

Berners-Lee, Tim, Mark Fischetti, and Michael L. Dertouzos. *Weaving the Web: The Original Design and Ultimate Destiny of the World Wide Web.* New York: HarperBusiness, 2000. Discusses how Tim Berners-Lee invented the World Wide Web, critical issues such as censorship and privacy, and the World Wide Web as a force for global change.

Brown, Lester R., et al. *State of the World 2000: A Worldwatch Institute Report on Progress toward a Sustainable Society.* New York: Norton, 2000. Monitors the world's resource base and current challenges to the environment. Advocates for sustainable economic development through wise uses of resources and population stability.

Burras, Bill, Jonathan Davidson, and Maeve O'Beirne. *The European Union: A Guide for Americans, 2000.* Washington, DC: Delegation of the

European Commission in the United States, 1999. Recounts the history, structure, operation, and future directions of the European Union.

Economic Report of the President: 2000. Washington, DC: U.S. Government Printing Office, 2000. Describes the government's position on key domestic and international economic issues. Extensive statistical data is updated annually.

Freedom House. *Freedom in the World: The Annual Survey of Political Rights and Civil Liberties, 2000–2001.* New York: Freedom House, 2000. An annual publication that ranks countries by level of political freedom and links political freedom to economic freedom and global prosperity.

French, Hillary. *Vanishing Borders: Protecting the Planet in the Age of Globalization.* New York: Norton and the Worldwatch Institute, 2000. Assesses current environmental problems and offers a plan of action to bring environmental security to the planet.

Friedman, Milton, and Rose Friedman. *Free to Choose: A Personal Statement.* New York: Avon, 1979. Advocates the benefits of free markets as the surest path to prosperity.

Friedman, Thomas L. *The Lexus and the Olive Tree: Understanding Globalization.* Rev. edition. New York: Anchor, 2000. Examines globalization, its potential to improve people's well being, and the conflicts with traditional cultures and ways of thinking.

Giddens, Anthony. *Runaway World: How Globalization Is Reshaping Our Lives.* New York: Routledge, 2000. Discusses the impact of globalization on people's traditions and on institutions such as the family and democracy.

Gilpin, Robert. *The Challenge of Global Capitalism: The World Economy in the 21st Century.* Princeton, NJ: Princeton University Press, 2000. Focuses on the impact of changing political events and technology on globalization and the strengths and weaknesses of the global economy.

Gregory, Paul R. *Comparative Economic Systems.* 6th ed. New York: Houghton Mifflin College, 1998. Compares and contrasts the types of economic systems since the fall of communism in the early 1990s while exploring current issues such as income distribution, economic growth, and market reforms. Designed for advanced students.

Hahnel, Robin. *Panic Rules: Everything You Need to Know about the Global Economy.* Cambridge, MA: South End, 1999. Outlines the weaknesses of the global economy and recommendations for addressing these problems.

Hutton, Will, and Anthony Giddens, eds. *Global Capitalism.* New York: New Press, 2000. Collection of essays dealing with globalization, information technology, global financial architecture, global culture, and economic inequalities.

International Monetary Fund. *World Economic Outlook: 1999.* Washington, DC: IMF Publications, 1999. Analyzes current economic trends of nations and world regions. Extensive annually updated statistical data.

———. *World Economic Outlook: 2000/2001.* Washington, DC: IMF Publications, 2000. Comprehensive analysis of annual performance of the world's economies. Extensive annually updated statistical data.

Longworth, Richard C. *The Global Squeeze: The Coming Crisis for First World Nations.* Chicago: Contemporary Books, 1998. Comments on the challenges inherent in creating a more integrated and interdependent global economy.

Luttwak, Edward. *Turbo Capitalism: Winners and Losers in the Global Economy.* New York: HarperCollins, 1999. Examines the impacts of unregulated capitalism surging through the global economy and the inequalities that have resulted.

Madeley, John. *Big Business, Poor Peoples: The Impact of Transnational Corporations on the World's Poor.* New York: Zed, 1999. Examines multinational corporations and the need to regulate their business behaviors.

Mander, Jerry, and Edward Goldsmith, eds. *The Case against the Global Economy: And for a Turn toward the Local.* San Francisco, CA: Sierra Club, 1997. Collection of essays dealing with the negative impacts of globalization on the environment, local economies, democratic institutions, and more.

Markley, Oliver W., and Walter R. McCuan. *America beyond 2001: Opposing Viewpoints.* San Diego, CA: Greenhaven, 1996. Debates controversial topics such as information technologies, the global economy, and alternative fuels.

Micklethwait, John, and Adrian Wooldridge. *A Future Perfect: The Challenge and Hidden Promise of Globalization.* New York: Times, 2000. Comprehensive examination of globalization and its mostly beneficial impact on peoples' economic lives and political freedoms.

Moran, Edward, ed. *The Global Ecology.* The Reference Shelf. Vol. 71. No. 4. New York: Wilson, 1999. A collection of current news articles that examines major ecological topics, issues, and problems.

Mutti, John H. *Nafta: The Economic Consequences for Mexico and the United States.* Washington, DC: Economic Strategy Institute, 2000. Examines how regional economic integration in North America is affecting the economies of the United States and Mexico.

Nye, Joseph S., and John D. Donahue, eds. *Governance in a Globalizing World.* Washington, DC: Brookings Institution, 2000. Examines the challenges in governance as peoples' cultures, economies, and environments are altered by globalization, and ponders the question of how globalization itself might be governed.

O'Rourke, Kevin H., and Jeffrey G. Williamson. *Globalization and History: The Evolution of a Nineteenth-Century Atlantic Economy.* Cambridge: MIT Press, 2001. Discusses the first great era of globalization during the 1800s, the technology that supported it, and the international flows of goods and capital that defined it.

Rajaee, Farhang. *Globalization on Trial: The Human Condition and the Information Civilization.* West Hartford, CT: Kumarian, 2000. Explores globalization with an emphasis on the present and future impacts of technology on humanity.

Reddaway, Peter, and Dmitri Glinski. *The Tragedy of Russia's Reforms.* Herndon, VA: U.S. Institute of Peace Press, 2001. Analyzes Russia's progress toward market capitalism and democracy during the Boris Yeltsin years.

Rowntree, Les, Martin Lewis, Marie Price, and William Wyckoff. *Diversity Amid Globalization: World Regions, Environment, Development.* Upper Saddle River, NJ: Prentice Hall, 2000. Comprehensive analysis of how different peoples and regions of the world have responded to the challenges of globalization.

Schwartz, Peter, and Blair Gibb. *When Good Companies Do Bad Things: Responsibility and Risk in an Age of Globalization.* New York: Wiley, 1999. Describes the importance of corporate social responsibility in the global marketplace and the negative consequences for businesses that stray from responsible behaviors.

Sjursen, Katrin, ed. *Globalization.* The Reference Shelf. Vol. 72. No. 5. New York: Wilson, 2000. A collection of current news articles about the impact of globalization on the global economy, world cultures, etc.

Smith, Adam. *An Inquiry into the Nature and Causes of the Wealth of Nations.* Chicago: Henry Regnery, 1953. A classic examination of the power of free enterprise in creating individual and national prosperity.

Smith, Dan. *The State of the World Atlas.* 6th ed. New York: Penguin, 1999. Examines multiple topics related to the global economy. Heavy use of maps to illustrate economic, political, and cultural topics.

Turner, Barry, ed. *The Stateman's Yearbook: 2000–2001.* 137th ed. New York: St. Martin's, 2000. Details recent economic, political, and other information for each country of the world. Data is updated annually.

United Nations. *Basic Facts about the United Nations.* Rev. ed. New York: United Nations Publications, 1998. Summarizes historical and contemporary efforts of the UN system in the areas of peacekeeping, economic and social development, human rights, decolonization, and other areas.

United Nations Conference on Trade and Development (UNCTAD). *The Least Developed Countries 2000 Report.* New York: United Nations Publications, 2000. Analyzes the economic performance of the least developed countries in the context of the global economy. Includes timely statistical data.

———. *Trade and Development Report, 2000.* New York: United Nations Publications, 2000. Focuses on trends in international trade and the role of trade in promoting economic development. Includes timely statistical data.

———. *World Investment Report 1999: Foreign Direct Investment and the Challenge of Development.* New York: United Nations Publications, 1999. Examines the role of FDI in economic development in the global economy. Includes annually updated statistical data.

———. *World Investment Report 2000: Cross-border Mergers and Acquisitions and Development.* New York: United Nations Publications, 2000. Analyzes trends in investments, especially foreign direct investment, by multinational corporations. Includes annually updated statistical data.

United Nations Development Program (UNDP). *Human Development Report: 1999.* New York: Oxford University Press, 1999. Analyzes human development with a focus on the globalization process and the growing disparities in technology and wealth between the developed and developing countries. Extensive statistical data in tabular form.

———. *Human Development Report: 2000.* New York: United Nations Publications, 2000. Analyzes human development with a focus human rights. Extensive statistical data in tabular form.

———. *Human Development Report: 2001.* New York: Oxford University Press, 2001. Analyzes human development with a focus on how the new technologies of the global economy can improve people's quality of life. Extensive statistical data in tabular form.

United Nations Educational, Scientific, and Cultural Organization (UNESCO). *World Education Report 2000.* New York: United Nations Publications, 2000. Analyzes progress made by the international community in the realm of education. Includes timely data on the key aspects of education for 180 countries.

U.S. Department of Commerce, Bureau of Economic Analysis, and Economics and Statistics Administration. *Survey of Current Business.* Washington, DC: U.S. Government Printing Office, September 2000. Monthly compilation of economic data dealing with topics such as international trade, FDI, and economic growth.

World Almanac and Book of Facts: 2000. Mahwah, NJ: World Almanac Books, 1999. Detailed comparisons of the countries of the world, including economic data on gross domestic product, labor force, trade, and so on.

World Bank. *Entering the 21st Century: World Development Report 1999/2000.* New York: Oxford University Press, 2000. Comprehensive examination of topics, issues, and problems related to global economic development. Extensive annually updated statistical data.

———. *The World Bank Atlas 2000.* Rev. ed. Washington, DC: World Bank, 2000. Assesses world economic and social conditions for 210 countries. Annually updated statistical data on many topics related to economic development.

———. *World Development Indicators: 2000.* New York: Oxford University Press, 2000. Statistical overview of economic conditions in different nations and regions of the world.

———. *World Development Report 2000/2001: Attacking Poverty.* Washington, DC: Published by the Oxford University Press for the World Bank, 2000. Detailed analysis of economic and other factors that influence economic development and poverty in the global economy. Extensive annually updated statistical data.

World Economic Forum. *The Global Competitiveness Report: 2000.* New York: Oxford University Press, 2000. Analyzes the economic conditions in countries and ranks the competitiveness of each using a number of indices.

World Resources Institute. *World Resources 2000–2001, People and Ecosystems: The Fraying Web of Life.* Washington, DC: World Resources Institute, United Nations Development Program, United Nations Environment Program, and the World Bank, 2000. Comprehensive exploration of ecosystems, the damage that has been done to ecosystems, and a course of action to repair damaged ecosystems.

World Trade Organization. *Trading into the Future: Introduction to the WTO.* 2nd ed. Geneva: World Trade Organization, 2000. Overview of the structure, purposes, and issues related international trade and the World Trade Organization.

FILMS AND VIDEOS

After the Warming. Ambrose Video, 1991. 2 videotapes, 55 minutes each (color). Discusses ways that people could respond to environmental crises, with a focus on the greenhouse effect and global warming.

Amazonia (Series). Library Video Company, 1996. 3 videotapes, 40 minutes each. Shows the conflict between economic development and environmental protection in Brazil.

Asian Values Devalued. Films for the Humanities & Sciences, 1998. 40 minutes (color). Exposes some of the policy errors and structural weakness of Asian economies in the wake of the Asian financial crisis of 1997–1998, and the enormous costs in money and human misery.

Born under the Red Flag: 1976–1997 (China: A Century of Revolution Series). PBS. 3 videotapes, 120 minutes each (color). Chronicles the evolution of a hybrid economic system in China, part centrally planned and part market oriented, during the final quarter of the twentieth century.

Business Ethics: A Twenty-first-Century Perspective. A Meridian Production. Films for the Humanities & Sciences, 1994. 19 minutes (color). Discusses the gray areas of business ethics in the global economy and the need for multinational corporations to agree on a core set of business values.

Chinese Capitalism: Moving the Mountain. BBC Production. Films for the Humanities & Sciences, 1994. 50 minutes (color). Examines the unique blend of communism and capitalism that constitutes China's economy and the unique economic challenges facing the world's most populous country.

Crisis: Planet Earth. Teacher's Video Company, 1991. 30 minutes (color). Discusses the greenhouse effect and global warming through the eyes of top NASA scientists.

Dodging Doomsday: Life beyond Malthus. BBC Production. 50 minutes (color). Discusses the earth's capacity to sustain its growing population.

Earth at Risk (Series). Schlessinger Media, 1992. 10 videos, 30 minutes each (color). Defines environmental problems and issues related to acid rain, clean air, clean water, degradation of the land, extinction, global warming, nuclear power, ozone depletion, the rain forests, and recycling.

Economic Recovery in Africa: The Role of the IMF (Series). Films for the Humanities & Sciences, 1996, 1998. 2 videotapes, 30–46 minutes each (color). Discuss the current market-oriented reforms in East Africa (Zambia, Tanzania, and Uganda) and West Africa (Côte d'Ivoire, Cameroon, and Mali), and the assistance they receive from the International Monetary Fund.

Emerging Powers: Bx4 (Wall Street Journal Video Series). Wall Street Journal, 1996. 4 videotapes, 50 minutes each (color). Documents the growth and challenges of four major economies that are destined to become major players in the global economy: Brazil, China, India, and Mexico.

European Union Educational Videos 2000. European Union. 9 titles on a single videotape, 70 minutes (color). Explores the origins and structure of the European Union, current issues involving the euro, and continued progress toward economic integration.

Expanding Europe: Round Five of the E.U. Buildout (Series). Films for the Humanities & Sciences, 1999. 7 videotapes, 25 minutes each (color). Introduces the coming enlargement of the European Union

(EU), and devotes a separate video to each of the following candidates for EU membership: Estonia, Poland, the Czech Republic, Hungary, Slovenia, and Cyprus.

The Fall of Communism. ABC News, 1991. 80 minutes (color). Examines the pivotal years from 1989–1990 when communism faltered, independence movements were strengthened, and the Soviet Union itself showed signs of collapse.

Fast Forward: Life inside Our Ever-Shrinking World (People's Century: Age of Hope Series). PBS, 1999. 60 minutes (color). Examines the impacts of globalization, technology, and other forces that tie the world together on the lives of people.

A Feast Amid Famine: The World Food Paradox. Guidance Associates. 60 minutes (color). Discusses the global problem of hunger and why hunger and famine exist in a prosperous global economy.

Free Market Economies: The Commanding Heights. Films for the Humanities & Sciences. 26 minutes (color). Discusses the successes of market-oriented reforms since the 1970s and the demise of communist and socialist economic systems.

Free Trade (Introductory Economics Series). Films for the Humanities & Sciences. 1993. 28 minutes (color). Examines the benefits of free trade and the need for adjustment assistance for displaced workers.

Free Trade Slaves. Films for the Humanities & Sciences, 1999. 57 minutes (color). Examines the impact of free trade zones in selected developing countries, emphasizing the exploitation of workers and costs to local economies.

Global Business: New Ways to Improve the Bottom Line (Series). Films for the Humanities & Sciences, 2000. 10 videotapes, 30 minutes each (color). Examines the process of business planning in the new global economy, exploring topics such as global marketing strategies, applications of new technologies to business, tapping employee knowledge, and considering the impact of business decisions on the environment.

Global Capitalism and the Moral Imperative. Films for the Humanities & Sciences, 1998. 30 minutes (color). Discusses the growing rich-poor gap resulting from globalization and how the international community should respond to the needs of the poor.

Global Economics (Series). Clearview. 5 videotapes, 10 minutes each (color). Explores regional economic unions, production relocation, the euro, Europe's unemployment crisis, and the world's great harbors.

Globalization: Winners and Losers. Films for the Humanities & Sciences, 2000. 40 minutes (color). Explores the costs and benefits of globalization, with an emphasis on globalization's impact on the developing world.

The History of the European Monetary Union. A Deutsche Welle Production. 20 minutes (color). Examines the evolution of the European Monetary Union, its institutions, and the adoption of the euro as its common currency.

The Home Planet (The Miracle Planet Series). PBS. Examines the ability of our planet to support growing human populations in the future.

The International Monetary Fund: Financial Cure or Catastrophe? Films for the Humanities & Sciences, 1998. 35 minutes (color). Analyzes weaknesses in the International Monetary Fund's approach to stabilizing the global economy during the Asian financial crisis.

The Internet: Portal to Everywhere. Films for the Humanities & Sciences, 2000. 45 minutes (color). Explores Internet business applications and illustrates how the Internet is dissolving past limits based on distance and time.

Is America Number One? Understanding the Economics of Success. Films for the Humanities & Sciences. 46 minutes (color). Contrasts the successful American economy with the economies of developing countries such as India.

Marx and Rockefeller on Capitalism. Britannica. 26 minutes (color). Presents a mock debate between Karl Marx and John D. Rockefeller on the theory and practice of both communism and capitalism.

Millennium: The IMF in the New Century (Series). Films for the Humanities & Sciences, 2000. 4 videotapes, 16–19 minutes each (color). Traces the role of the International Monetary Fund from its founding to the present in promoting global economic prosperity, while exploring its work in some depth in Argentina and in Korea.

The New Global Economics: A Real-World Guide (Series). Films for the Humanities & Sciences, 1999. 10 videotapes, 30 minutes each (color). Explores a variety of topics connected with the global economy, including how market-oriented economies function, the role of investment and financial systems in promoting economic growth, international trade, the European Union, and more.

New Worlds (The Living Planet Series). BBC and Time-Life Videos. 60 minutes (color). Describes the positive and negative impacts of humans on ecosystems.

The People Bomb. CNN, 1992. 105 minutes (color). Overview of the population explosion, efforts to curb the growing world population, and the stresses that overpopulation has on limited natural resources and fragile ecosystems.

People Power: The End of Soviet-Style Communism (People's Century: Communism—the Promise and the Reality Series). PBS, 1999. 60 minutes (color). Chronicles the collapse of the Soviet Union, investigates the major personalities of the era such as Mikhail Gorbachev and Boris Yeltsin, and more.

Planet Earth: Fate of the Earth (Planet Earth BX7). Teacher's Video Company, 1986. 57 minutes (color). Examines the conflict between preserving the natural environment and racing toward economic development in the global economy.

Population 2000 Series. Library Video Company, 1998. 2 videotapes, 11–13 minutes each (color). Examines why people continue to migrate to the world's urban centers and how the cities deal with rapid growth and overpopulation.

Russia in Ruins–Can the Nation Survive? Knowledge Unlimited, 1998. 18 minutes (color). Examines Russia's transition from communism to capitalism, the obstacles to this transition, and why Russia's success is important to the global economy.

Taking Care of Business: The Information Revolution. Films for the Humanities & Sciences. 58 minutes (color). Examines how advances in computer science, telecommunications, robotics, and other changes are revolutionizing the local workplace and the global marketplace.

Three Dynamic Economies (Series). Films for the Humanities & Sciences, 1997, 1998. 3 videotapes, 30 minutes each (color). Explores the unique economic challenges faced by China, Mauritius, and Peru as they enter the global economy.

Triumph of the Nerds (Series). PBS, 1996. 3 videotapes, 60 minutes each (color). Discusses the rise of the computer and its applications in contemporary society, and introduces some of the key players in this technological revolution, such as Steven Jobs and Bill Gates.

2000: Amazing Moments in Time. National Geographic, 1999. 60 minutes (color). Explores the advancement of life on Earth, the rise of civilizations, and the environmental challenges that exist today due to overpopulation.

Understanding Free Market Economics: Lessons Learned in the Former Soviet Union (Series). Films for the Humanities & Sciences, 1994, 1995. 6 videotapes, 30 minutes each (color). Discusses the International Monetary Fund and its role in applying free-market principles to the transition economies of Russia and eastern Europe. Successes and failures in the market transition are analyzed.

United Nations: It's More than You Think. Cambridge Research Group. 30 minutes (color). Discusses the many functions of the United Nations in the global age.

Women in the Struggle against Poverty: A Case Study. A Deutsche Welle Production. Films for the Humanities & Sciences. 30 minutes (color). Explores the struggles of women in Bangladesh to become entrepreneurs and financial contributors to their families and communities.

The Women's Bank of Bangladesh. Films for the Humanities & Sciences. 47 minutes (color). Examines the Grameen Bank and the use of microloans to jump-start the country's economy.

The World Bank: The Great Experiment. Films for the Humanities & Sciences, 1997. 2 parts, 50 minutes each (color). Develops a case study using Uganda as its focus to explore how the World Bank operates and what happens when the World Bank and host country come into conflict.

WEB SITES

African Development Bank (*www.afdb.org*). Provides timely data on the loans for development projects and other programs to promote economic stability in Africa, and general information about the ADB Group, its mission, its resources, and so on.

Amnesty International (*www.web.amnesty.org*). Provides information on the state of human rights around the world, dealing with racism, torture, political prisoners, and so on. Amnesty's documents and other publications are also listed.

Asian Development Bank (*www.adb.org*). Provides timely data on the loans for development and other projects that promote economic growth and development in Asia and general information about the ADB.

Asia-Pacific Economic Cooperation Group (*www.apecsec.org.sq*). Provides information on APEC, a regional trade organization, and its work to reduce trade barriers among member countries

Association of Southeast Asian Nations (*www.asean.or.id*). Provides information on ASEAN, a regional trade organization, and its work to reduce trade barriers among member countries.

Bureau of Economic Analysis (*www.bea.gov*). A U.S. government Web site that provides extensive data on the state of the American economy and on international comparisons on selected themes.

Development Assistance Committee (*www.dac.org*). DAC, a subgroup within the Organization for Economic Cooperation and Development, is the main provider of foreign aid in the world. DAC foreign aid data is tracked over time, by donor nation, and by recipients (nations and world regions).

Energy Information Administration (*www.eia.doe.gov*). A U.S. Department of Energy Web site that provides extensive past, present, and future data about energy consumption and production in the United States and around the world.

European Bank for Reconstruction and Development (*www.ebrd.com*). Provides information in the form of data and national case studies of development projects and other programs to assist the transition from communism to market-oriented economies. The focus is for assistance is eastern and central Europe, and central Asia.

European Commission to the U.S. (*www.eurunion.org*). Provides timely information about the structure, policies, and programs of the European Union including the regularly updated pamphlet *The European Union: A Guide for Americans.*

European Free Trade Association (*www.efta.int*). Provides information on EFTA, a regional trade organization, its policies to reduce trade barriers among member nations, and its connections with the larger European Union.

Freedom House (*www.freedomhouse.org*). Provides information on the state of freedom, including the rise of democratic governments, in annual publications that rank countries in these areas. The Freedom House also draws connections between basic freedoms and liberties and the prospects for economic development.

Global Policy Forum (*www.globalpolicy.org*). Provides information on global social and economic policies with a focus on the role of the United Nations, and the Three Sisters (International Monetary Fund, World Bank, and World Trade Organization) in the global economy.

Greenpeace (*www.greenpeace.org*). Provides information on a variety of environmental issues, such as protection of forests, genetic engineering of crops, and so on. The policies and activities of Greenpeace are also explained.

Inter-American Development Bank (*www.iadb.org*). Provides information on the structure and mission of the IDB, its loan policies, and current news related to the work of this regional development bank.

International Development Association (*www.ida.org*). Provides information about the IDA and the relationship between the IDA and the other main parts of the World Bank Group. Data tracing IDA loans over time is available.

International Finance Corporation (*www.ifc.org*). Provides information about the IFC and the relationship between the IFC and the other main parts of the World Bank Group. This site also contrasts IFC loans with those of the International Development Association and the World Bank.

International Labor Organization (*www.us.ilo.org*). Provides a wide variety of information about the mission and accomplishments of the ILO over time, especially the results of its conventions and recommendations, which have influenced global perceptions of workers' rights, child labor, social safety nets, and other important labor issues.

International Monetary Fund (*www.imf.org*). Provides volumes of statistical and narrative information on the state of the world's economy, past and present, with some commentary on prospects for growth and development for nations and regions. The IMF publishes the *World Economic Outlook.*

International Trade Administration (*www.ita.doc.gov*). A U.S. government Web site that provides data on international trade. Also provides information useful to businesses wishing to increase their exports or form other business relationships with companies in different countries.

Organization for Economic Cooperation and Development (*www.oecd.org*). Provides information on policies, programs, and foreign aid of the OECD member countries. Policies and programs vary widely and include topics such as economic development in the global economy, environmental protection, good governance, international crime, and so on.

Organization of Petroleum Exporting Countries (*www.opec.org*). Provides information about the OPEC oil cartel and about the global energy picture. Includes statistical data about world oil production and pricing and projections for future energy production and consumption on a global basis.

Oxfam International (*www.oxfaminternational.org*). Provides information about the organization, the mission, and the work of Oxfam in fighting poverty and injustice in the world. Includes recent information in its *Strategic Plan 2001–2004.*

Partnerships in Statistics for Development in the 21st Century (*www. paris21.org*). Since 1999, the Paris 21 Consortium has worked to improve statistical capabilities, especially in the developing world. Organized by international groups such as the United Nations, the Organization for Economic Cooperation and Development, the World Bank, and the International Monetary Fund, Paris21 has also established a series of development goals in its landmark "A Better World for All" publication.

Patent and Trademark Office (*www.uspto.gov*). A U.S. government Web site that provides statistical and other information policies and procedures for patent and trademark use in the United States and global economy. An in-depth treatment of international intellectual property is included.

Peace Corps (*www.peacecorps.gov*). A U.S. government Web site that outlines the mission and the work of the Peace Corps. Current events, case studies, and real stories of Peace Corps volunteers are included.

Population Reference Bureau (*www.prb.org*). Provides statistical data and timely articles related to population trends in the United States and world. The PRB also has related Web sites designed for educators, writers, students, and others. Some data from the U.S. Census 2000 is available.

United Nations (*www.un.org*). Provides general background on the UN system and on its structure and mission. Additional connections with the specialized agencies and programs of the UN are possible.

United Nations Children's Fund (*www.unicef.org*). Provides information about the work of UNICEF in different nations and regions worldwide, including current news stories. Publications about UNICEF and its work, mainly in the developing world, are also included.

United Nations Conference on Trade and Development (*www.unctad.org*). Provides a wide variety of statistical data dealing broadly with the topics of international trade and global economic development.

United Nations Development Program (*www.undp.org*). Provides a wide variety of information, in statistical and narrative forms, on the topic of economic development around the world. UNDP publishes the annual *Human Development Report*, with useful essays and data on the state of the global economy.

United Nations Educational, Scientific, and Cultural Organization (*www.unesco.org*). Provides information on a variety of social, cultural, economic, and political issues and topics in the global economy.

United Nations Environmental Program (*www.unep.org*). As the leading authority on the global environment within the United Nations system, the UNEP provides a wealth of information on the state of the world's environment and on policies and programs geared to protecting global ecosystems.

United Nations Population Fund (*www.unfpa.org*). Provides information in statistical and narrative form related to trends in global population growth and a host of other topics including health and health care, global crises, and so on.

World Bank (*www.worldbank.org*). Provides statistical and narrative information on countries and regions in the global economy. The World Bank publishes the *World Development Report* annually to summarize the state of the global economy.

World Economic Forum (*www.weforum.org*). Provides information to the public on the global economy, some of which is generated from its regional and annual meetings. A special section of the Web site is devoted to students, elementary through college, and teachers.

World Health Organization (*www.who.org*). Provides information about the state of health and health care systems in the world, progress toward the elimination of diseases, and challenges facing the global community—including the resurgence of tuberculosis and the HIV/AIDS epidemic.

World Intellectual Property Organization (*www.wipo.int*). Provides information about the WIPO and its work in defining legal protections for intellectual property in the fast changing global economy. Includes current events and topics and a new link to a virtual tour of intellectual property in everyday life.

World Resources Institute (*www.wri.org*). Provides information on the natural environment, the status on renewable and nonrenewable resources on the planet, and the relationship between humans and the environment.

World Trade Organization (*www.wto.org*). Provides a wide variety of information related to international trade and the benefits of freer trade in global markets. Provides free of charge a number of pamphlets and fact sheets on the topic of trade and trade policy.

Worldwatch Institute (*www.worldwatch.org*). Provides information mainly on the topic of environmentally sustainable development, with a focus on global environmental issues and concerns. Publishes books and reports and offers *WWNews* for current events on the topic.

World Wide Web Consortium (*www.w3.org/consortium*). Provides information on the background of the World Wide Web and information on current topics, including news releases. The W3C is widely recognized as a leading force in the technical evolution on the Web.

Index

Absolute advantage, 30–31
Acquired Immune Deficiency Syndrome (AIDS): cycle of poverty and, 170; the Free Trade Area of the Americas (FTAA) and, 48; quality of life and, 88–89; the World Health Organization (WHO) and, 98, 164–165
Advanced countries and economies. *See* Developed countries
African Development Bank Group, 97, 127
Agenda 21, 98, 118; *The Global Compact* and, 160, 171
Agreement on a Global System of Trade Preferences, 99
Aluminum Company of America (Alcoa), 14; monopoly and, 65
Annan, Kofi A., 22, 70–71, 145, 155; *The Global Compact* and, 158–161
Asian Development Bank, 25, 97, 127
Asia-Pacific Economic Cooperation (APEC) group, 32

Association of Southeast Asian Nations (ASEAN), 13, 32; free trade area and, 49
Australia-New Zealand Closer Economic Relations Agreement, 33

Banana war, 13–14, 36
Barriers to trade. *See* Trade barriers
Bell, Alexander Graham, 8, 16
Benz, Karl, 16
Berners-Lee, Tim, the World Wide Web and, 17
Bilateral investment treaties (BITS), 5; business climate and, 63; growth of, 64–65
Bill and Melinda Gates Foundation, 166
Brain drain, human capital and, 102
Bretton Woods Conference, 10–11; fixed exchange rate system and, 43, 161
Bush, George W., Kyoto Protocol and, 118
Business climate: foreign direct investment and, 62–63; foreign di-

rect investment (FDI) in the United States and, 65; Multilateral Investment Guarantee Agency (MIGA) and, 95, 103, 105

Capital, 77, 102–103
Capital deepening: savings and investment and, 103–104; the virtuous cycle and, 102–104
Capital flight, 104
Capital markets, 5
Capital stock, 60–61, 77, 102
Capitalism, 5; anti-capitalist sentiments and, 140–142; democracy and, 18–19, 105–106; resource use and, 100, 132
Cartel: oil reserves and, 52; Organization of Petroleum Exporting Countries (OPEC) and, 50–51
Chernobyl, 68, 119
China, 33; cultural homogenization and, 182–184; economy in transition, 87; energy and, 122–123; exchange rates and, 45; foreign aid and, 99; globalization and, 109, 114; GNP and purchasing power parity of, 93–94; growth goals and, 166; human rights and, 50; population and, 123, 179–180, 151; trade liberalization and, 154; U.S. trade with, 40–41
Civil society, 146 148
Code of conduct for multinationals, 69–72. See also Corporate social responsibility
Commission on Sustainable Development (CSD), 118, 171–172
Common Market for Eastern and Southern Africa (COMESA), 32
Common Market of the South (MERCOSUR), 13, 32

Commonwealth of Independent States (CIS), 87
Communism: trade and, 33, 100; weaknesses of, 18
Comparative advantage, 30–31, 75, 79. See also Specialization
Competitiveness, countries, rankings of, 106–109
Comprehensive Development Framework (World Bank), 166
Computers, 16–17; digital divide and, 76–77. See also Information and communications technologies (ICTs); Internet
Conglomerate, 56–57; IT&T and, 65–66
Cooke, William F., 8
Corn Laws, 7
Corporate code of conduct, 69
Corporate social responsibility: criticisms of MNCs and, 72– 75; The Global Compact and, 157–161; The Global Sullivan Principles and, 71–72; the International Labor Organization (ILO) and, 156–157; labor and, 68–71; multinational corporations (MNCs) and, 67–68
Council for Mutual Economic Assistance (COMECON), 33
Crime, international: corruption in Russia and, 149; economic freedom as deterrent to, 151; the European Union (EU) and, 47; the FTAA and, 48; the gangster economy (Russia) and, 105; global financial architecture and, 128; the OECD and, 99; offshore financial centers (OFCs) and, 38
Cuban Liberty and Democratic Solidarity Act, 50
Cultural homogenization, 3, 6, 131; Americanization and,

132–133; cultural identity and, 175; globalization and, 181–184; resistance to, 133–134

Customs union, 49

D'Abbans, Claude Jouffroy, 8

Daimler, Gottlieb, 16

DaimlerChrysler: Daimler-Benz and, 58; GNPs and MNC revenues, comparison of, 57; megamerger, costs of, 75; merger of, 61, 71

DeBeers, 14

Declaration on Fundmental Principles and Rights at Work, 69–70

Deforestation, United Nations Development Program and, 98, 115

Democracy: Freedom House and, 150–152; the global economy and, 18–19; multilateral organizations, anti-democratic forces and, 146–147; nongovernmental organizations (NGOs) and, 22, 26; the OECD and, 99–100; the virtuous cycle and, 105–106

Depression, defined, 9

Desertification, 114–115

Developed countries: competitiveness and, 106–109; energy production and consumption, 119–122; FDI inflows, 63–64; foreign assistance and, 99; foreign direct investment (FDI), impact on, 60–61; mergers and acquisitions (M&As) and, 59; population growth and, 178–179; quality of life and, 87–91; quality of life and purchasing power parity (PPP), 91–94; sustainable economic development and, 83–86; the virtuous cycle and, 100–106. See also High-income countries

Developing countries: competitiveness and, 106–109; criticisms and MNCs and, 72–75; the cycle of poverty and, 122–126; economic freedom, growth and, 150–152; energy production and consumption, 119–122; environmental stresses on, 114–115; FDI, impact on, 60–61; FDI inflows, 63–64; globalization and, 140–142; human development and, 163–164; M&As and, 59; MIGA and, 95; official development assistance (ODA) and, 99; population explosion in, 102, 178–181; quality of life and, 87–91; quality of life and PPP, 91–94; "Rio Declaration on Environment and Development" and, 171–176; sustainable economic development and, 83–84, 86, trade and, 153 155; the virtuous cycle and, 100–106; World Bank development strategies and, 148–150

Development Assistance Committee (DAC), ODA and, 99

Digital divide: global North and South and, 129–131; human development and, 165; narrowing of, 76–77

Dispute Settlement Body (of the WTO), 35–36

Dumping, defined, 50

Early Childhood Care and Development (ECD), 169–171

East Asian crisis, financial contagion and, 22–25, 42, 126

Economic Community of West African States (ECOWAS), 13, 32

Economic freedom, 18–20, 105–106; countries, ranking of,

21; economic growth and, 150–152; globalization and, 141–142, 144. *See also* Democracy

Economic Freedom of the World: 2001 Annual Report, 20

Economic globalization. *See* Globalization

Economic growth, 83–84; the digital divide and, 129–131; discrimination, negative impact on, 159–160; economic development and, 83–87; freedom and, 150–152; global institutions and, 94–100; GNP and PPP and, 91–94; human development and, 164–165; international comparisons of, 106–109; overpopulation and, 122–126; quality of life and, 87–91; terrorism and, 134–136; trade and, 153–155; the virtuous cycle and, 100–106

Economic sanctions: the UN and, 52, 170; the United States and, 50; the WTO and, 36

Ecosystems: defined, 114; the ecosystem approach to managing the world's resources, 176–178; multilateral environmental agreements (MEAs) and, 117–118; the "Rio Declaration on Environment and Development" and, 171–176; stresses on, 114–117; the UN and, 118–119

Electronic Numerical Integrator and Calculator (ENIAC), 16

Embargo: defined, 49; OPEC embargo on the United States, 51; U.S. embargo on Cuba, 50

Energy: global production and consumption, 119–122; OPEC and, 50–52; primary energy sources

and, 121–122. *See also* Organization of Petroleum Exporting Countries (OPEC)

Entrepreneurship: microloans and, 129; regional development banks and, 97; the virtuous cycle and, 104

Environment: Chad pipeline project and, 77–78; corporate blunders and, 68; the ecosystem approach to managing the world's resources, 176–178; 50 Years Is Enough and, 162; *The Global Compact* and, 70–71, 160; MEAs and, 117–119; MNCs, impact on, 72–75; "Rio Declaration on Environment and Development" and, 171–176; stresses on, 114–117; the UN and, 97–98, 118–119; weak regulations, impact on, 15

Environmentally sound technologies (EST), 160

Euro, 44, 47. *See also* European Union (EU)

European Atomic Energy Community (Euratom), 46

European Bank for Reconstruction and Development (EBRD), 97

European Central Bank (ECB), 46

European Coal and Steel Community (ECSC), 46

European Economic Community (EEC), 46

European Monetary Union (EMU), the euro-zone and, 47

European Union (EU), 5, 13–14, 25; regional integration and, 46–47, 129; trade disputes and, 36– 37; trade liberalization and, 32

Exchange rate: foreign exchange markets and, 42–44; PPP and, 91–94; trade and, 44–46

Exports, 12; categories of, 31; exchanges rates and, 44–46; foreign exchange markets and, 43; global expansion of, 31–34; by income level of country, 32; U.S. trade imbalances and, 39–42. *See also* International trade

Exxon Mobil: Chad oil pipeline and, 77–78; Exxon (1998) and, 58; merger between, 60, 66; rankings and, 55–57

Exxon Valdez, 68

Facsimile (fax) machine, 16

Fiber optics, 16

50 Years Is Enough Network: economic justice and, 161–63; marginalized peoples and, 128

financial architecture, global: defined, 126; 50 Years Is Enough Network and, 161–163; regulatory reforms and, 26, 64–65; weaknesses and reform of, 126–129. *See also* International Monetary Fund (IMF); World Bank Group; World Trade Organization (WTO)

Financial contagion, in East Asia, 22–25, 126, 128

Fitch, John, 8

Fixed exchange rate system, 43

Flexible exchange rate system, 43. *See also* Foreign exchange; Foreign exchange markets

Ford, Henry, 16

Ford Motor Company, 16; FDI in Brazil, 63, 65, 66, 71; GNPs and MNC revenues, comparisons of, 57; ranking by assets, 58; ranking of, 56

Foreign aid, 99, 129, 166

Foreign debt: cycle of poverty and, 170; debt relief and, 96, 162–163, 165

Foreign direct investment (FDI), 4, 5; BITS and, 64–65; China and, 33; criticisms of, 72–75; democracy, support for, 18; the digital divide and, 130; foreign affiliates, growth of, 62; global benefits of, 75–79; globalization and growth of, 62–64; growth of (U.S.), 66; the International Finance Corporation (IFC) and, 95; the MIGA and, 95; MNCs and, 59–62; profits and, 14–15; regional trade organizations, support for, 25; regulations, reductions in, 76; relocalization and, 50; terrorism and, 134–135; the United States and, 65–67

Foreign exchange, 44–46

Foreign exchange markets, 42–44; foreign exchange rates and, 44–46

Foreign exchange trading, 43–44

Foreign sales corporations (FSCs), 36–37

Fossil fuels: global warming and, 116; nonrenewable energy resources and, 119–120; oil, coal, natural gas, and, 121

Framework Convention on Climate Change, 118

Free trade area, 49

Free Trade Area of the Americas (FTAA), 47–48

Freedom House, 19–20, 106, 150–152. *See also* Democracy; Economic freedom

Freedom in the World: The Annual Survey of Political Rights and Civil Liberties 2000–2001, 19–20, 106

Friedman, Milton, economic freedom and, 19

Friedman, Thomas L., 26

Fulton, Robert, 8

Gates, Bill, Microsoft and, 16
General Agreement on Tariffs and Trade (GATT), 11–12; replacement by the WTO, 34; Trade-Related Aspects of Intellectual Property (TRIPS) and, 35–36, 144
General Electric: ranking by assets (1998), 58; ranking by revenues (2000), 56; tax havens and, 37; world's most admired companies and, 76
General Motors: expanding global markets and, 15; FDI in Brazil, 63, 65, 66, 71; GNPs and MNC revenues, comparisons of, 57; greenfield investment in Poland, 61, 78–79; ranking by assets (1998), 58; ranking by revenues (2000), 56
Generalize System of Preferences (GSP), 99; the United States and, 129
Gilpin, Robert, 24
The Global Compact, 70–71; the Nine Principles and, 157–161
The Global Competitiveness Report 2000, 107
Global economy: Bretton Woods and, 10–11; challenges facing, 113–136; components of, 3–5; defined, 3; democracy and capitalism and, 18–19; disruptions to (1914–1945), 9; early technologies of, 7–9; financial contagion and, 22–25; freedom and, 19–20; GATT and the WTO and, 11–12; globalization and, 5–7, 25–26; institutions, support for, 25–26; MNCs and, 14–15; new technologies of, 15–18; resistance to globalization and, 20–22; trade and, 12–14. See also Developed countries; Developing countries; Foreign direct investment (FDI); Globalization; International trade
Global Entrepreneurship Monitor 2000, 104
Global financial architecture: defined, 126; 50 Years Is Enough Network and, 161–163; regulatory reforms and, 26, 64–65; weaknesses and reform of, 126–129. See also International Monetary Fund (IMF); World Bank Group; World Trade Organization (WTO)
Global 5 Hundred: most admired companies and, 76; the world's largest corporations and, 55–57
"The Global Sullivan Principles of Corporate Social Responsibility," 71–72
Global trading system: GATT and the WTO and, 11–12, 34–37; issues and challenges, 49–52; poverty reduction and, 152–155; production sharing and, 79; regional trade organizations and, 13–14; specialization and, 12–13; UNCTAD and, 98–99, 128; the United States and, 38–40; U.S. trade imbalances and, 40–42. See also International trade
Global warming, 116–117; MEAs and, 118
Globalization: benefits of, 139–142; cultural homogenization and, 131–134, 181–184; defined, 5–6; the digital divide, impact on, 129–131; financial contagion and, 22–25; global financial architecture and, 126–129; human development

and, 164–166; institutions, support for, 25–26; NGOs and, 145–148; opportunities and challenges, 142–145; resistance to, 20–22; terrorism and, 134–136; trade and poverty reduction and, 152–155. *See also* Global economy

Good governance: Russia, failure of, 149, 167; the virtuous cycle and, 105

Government corporations, 56

Great Britain. *See* United Kingdom

Great Depression, in United States, 9

Green revolution, 101

Greenfield investments, 59–62; BITS and, 64–65; business climate and, 62–64; global benefits and, 75–79; the United States and, 65–67

Greenhouse effect, 116–117; MEAs and, 118

Greenspan, response to terrorism and, 134, 136

Gross domestic product (GDP), 9; comparisons, by countries' income status, 103; economic freedom, impact on, 150–152; U.S. nominal GDP, 38

Gross national product (GNP): comparison, level of development, 106–109; comparison of GNP, with MNCs' revenues, 56; defined, 83; global institutions, impact on, 94–100; measurement, using PPP, 91–94; mobilizing society's resources and, 100–106; quality of life and, 87–91; sustainable economic development and, 83–87

Group of Eight (G-8) countries, 127–129

Group of Seven (G-7) countries: defined and listed, 85–86; international crime and, 38

Group of Twenty (G-20) countries, 128

Heavily Indebted Poor Countries (HIPC) Initiative, 96, 167

Helms-Burton Act, 50

Herd mentality, East Asian financial crisis and, 23–24, 128

High-income countries: compared with low-income and middle-income countries, 84–86; ODA and, 99; quality of life and, 87–91; trade and, 31–32

Hong Kong SAR, British colony of Hong Kong, 7; newly industrialized economies and, 108–109; saving and investment of, 104; Special Administrative Region (SAR) of China and, 21, 86

Human capital: *The Global Compact* and, 159–160; investments in, 165; the virtuous cycle and, 101–102

Human development, 90–91; fragile progress of, 163–167; the human development index rankings and, 91

Human rights: China and, 50–51, 67; economic sanctions and, 50; EU membership and, 47; FTAA and, 48; *The Global Compact* and, 157–158; "The Global Sullivan Principles" and, 71–72; globalization and, 133; human development and, 90–91; MNCs' violations and, 73; NGOs and, 21–22, 25; Western values and, 132. *See also* Nongovernmental organizations (NGOs)

Import quota, defined, 49

Imports, 12; categories of, 31; exchange rates and, 44–46; foreign exchange markets and, 43; global expansion of, 31–34; U.S. trade imbalances and, 39– 42. *See also* International trade

Information and communications technologies (ICTs), 3–4, 16–17; digital divide and, 76–77, 129–131; trade and, 33–34; U.S. investment in, 103

Information Society Index, 131

Inter-American Development Bank Group, 97, 127, 129

International Bank for Reconstruction and Development (IBRD), 10, 95. *See also* World Bank Group

International Center for Settlement of Investment Disputes (ICSID), 95. *See also* World Bank Group

International Conference on Population and Development (ICPD), 125–126. *See also* Overpopulation; Population explosion

International Development Association (IDA), 10, 95. *See also* World Bank Group

International Finance Corporation (IFC), 10–11, 95. *See also* World Bank Group

International financial institutions (IFIs), 126–128, 131. *See also* International Monetary Fund (IMF); Regional development banks; World Bank; World Trade Organization (WTO)

International Institute for Management Development (IMD), 107–108

International Labor Organization (ILO): terms and conditions of work, listed, 156–157; workers' rights and, 69–71. *See also* Workers

International Monetary Fund (IMF), 4, 10; criticisms of, 21–22, 96–97, 133, 161–163; East Asian crisis, assistance, 24–25; economic development and, 94–97; global financial architecture and, 126–128

International Telephone and Telegraph (IT&T), 65

International trade: benefits of, 29–31; defined, 12; democracy, support for, 18; expanding volume of, 31–34; foreign exchange markets and foreign exchange rates, 42–46; the global marketplace and, 12–13; human progress and, 143–145; liberalization of, 5; pillars of the global economy and, 29–52; poverty reduction and, 152–155; terrorism and, 134–135; the United States in the global trading system, 38–40; U.S. trade imbalances and, 40–42; the WTO and, 34–37

International Trade Organization (ITO), 11

Internet, 4–5, 16–17; digital divide and, 130–132; history of, 17, 101

Japan: comparative GDP data and PPP, 93–94; East Asian financial crisis and, 23; exchange rates (the yen) and, 45; G-7 and, 38; high tech exports, rank of, 39; investments in the United States and, 65; Ministry of International Trade and Industry

(MITI), Ministry of Economy, Trade and Industry (METI), 42; recession in, 42; trade disputes, the WTO and, 35; U.S. FDI and, 66, 84; U.S. trade deficit with, 41

Keynes, John Maynard, 143–144
Kyoto Protocol, 118

League of Nations, collapse of, 9
Least developed countries (LDCs): population growth in, 123; quality of life in, 125, 129; Western culture and, 133
Longworth, Richard C., 6
Low-income countries: compared with high-income and middle-income countries, 85–86; GNP data and PPP, 91–94; ODA and, 99; quality of life in, 87–91; trade and, 31–32. *See also* Developing countries
Luttwak, Edward, 6

Managed exchange rate system, 44
Maquiladoras, 15; criticism of MNCs and, 73–74; the North American Free Trade Agreement (NAFTA) debate and, 48; production sharing and, 63
Marconi, Guglielmo, 8–9
Marx, Karl, 182. *See also* Communism
McDonald's Corporation: expanding global markets and, 15, 132–133; global culture and, 182–183
Merchandise trade deficit, the United States and, 40–41
MERCSUR, 13; trade liberalization and, 32
Mergers and acquisitions (M&As), 59–62; BITS and, 64–65; business climate and, 62–64; DaimlerChrysler and, 75; global benefits of FDI and, 75–79; megamergers, 59–60; the United States and, 65–67. *See also* Foreign direct investment (FDI); Multinational corporations (MNC)
Microinstrumentation and Telemetry Systems, 16
Microloans, 129
Microsoft, 16; world's most admired companies, 76
MicroStart Program, 129
Middle-income countries: compared with high-income and low-income countries, 85–86; development institutions and, 94–100; GNP data and PPP, 91–94; ODA and 99; quality of life in, 87–91; trade and, 31–32. *See also* Developing countries
Millennium Round, stalled WTO negotiations and, 21, 34, 36
Ministry of Economy, Trade and Industry (METI), 42
Ministry of International Trade and Industry (MITI), 42
Modems, 16
Montreal Protocol, 118
Moore, Mike, 35; poverty reduction through trade and, 152–155
Moral hazard, 128
Morse, Samuel F. B., Morse code and, 8
Most admired companies, Global 5 Hundred ranking (2000), 76
Most-favored-nation status: GATT and, 11; the WTO and, 34
Muckrakers, 67–68
Multilateral environmental agreements (MEAs), 117–118

Multilateral Investment Guarantee Agency (MIGA), 11, 95

Multinational corporation (MNC): BITS and, 64–65; criticisms of, 72–75; FDI and, 59–62; global benefits of, 75–79; global corporate responsibility and, 67–68, 71–72; global economy and, 3–4, 25; global rankings of, 55–59; growth of, 62–64; most admired companies and, 76; profits and, 14–15; the United States and, 65–67; workers' rights and, 68–71, 156–157

Nairobi Declaration, 118–119

National treatment of products: BITS and, 64; GATT and equal treatment, 11; the WTO and, 34

Nestlé, 15; consumer boycott and, 74. *See also* Corporate social responsibility

New protectionism, 50

New York Stock Exchange (NYSE): East Asian financial crisis and, 24; September 11 (2001) terrorist attacks and, 135

Newly industrialized countries, 63; developed countries and, 85–86; globalization and, 108–109, 130; savings and investing and, 103–104

Nike, 14; code of conduct and, 69; subcontracting and, 63; sweatshop working conditions and, 73, 132. *See also* Corporate social responsibility

Nongovernmental organizations (NGOs), 4; corporate social responsibility and, 67–68, 69, 74, 89, 128; 50 Years Is Enough Network and, 161–163, 165, 171; mission and tactics of, 145–148; resistance to globalization, 20–22, 26, 36

Nonrenewable resources, 119–121

North, global, 85; digital divide and, 129–131; energy consumption and, 120; globalization and, 141–142. *See also* Developed countries

North American Free Trade Agreement (NAFTA), 5, 13; free trade area and, 49, 63; maquiladoras and, 15, 48, 63, 73–74; regional integration and, 47–49; trade liberalization and, 32

Oceans, ecological stresses on, 117

Official development assistance (ODA): human development and, 164, 166; trend in, 99, 129

Offshore financial centers (OFCs), 37–38, 127

Organization for Economic Cooperation and Development (OECD): economic development and, 94, 99–100; energy production and, 120, 127; labor rights and, 70

Organization of Petroleum Exporting Countries (OPEC): the global trading system and, 50–51; oil reserves and, 52, 119

Otto, Nikolaus, 16

Overpopulation: global population growth and, 122–124; impact on, 102; labor force, most populous countries, 124; population control and, 125–126; population explosion and, 178–181

Oxfam, 165

Ozone depletion, 115–116; Montreal Protocol and, 118

Peace Corps, 130–131

Per capita GNP, 83; international comparisons of, 84–87; quality of life and PPP measurement of, 88–89. *See also* Gross national product (GNP)

Population: growth from 1950 to 2050, 123; world's largest countries (2000 and 2050), 124. *See also* Overpopulation; Population explosion

Population explosion, 178–181. *See also* Overpopulation

Population Reference Bureau (PRB), 123–124, 178; population explosion and, 178–181

Poverty: the cycle of poverty, 167–171; globalization and, 139–142, 152–155; human development and, 163–164; measuring with GNP and per capita GNP data, 91–94; population pressures and, 102, 122–126, 178–181; poverty reduction initiatives, 96, 167; quality of life, comparisons, 87–91; social and economic indicators, 90; terrorism and, 134; the UN and, 97–99; the World Bank and, 148–150. *See also* Developing countries; Foreign debt

Poverty Reduction and Growth Facility (PRGF), 96

Principle of mutual benefit, 29

Privatization, 62–63, 76; the IFC and, 95; the IMF and, 96, 149

Procter & Gamble, 56–57, 71

Production sharing, 63, 79. *See also* Maquiladoras

Protectionism, 49–50; the new protectionism, 50, 135, 144, 152–153. *See also* Trade barriers

Putin, Vladimir, 105

Quality of life: children and the cycle of poverty, 167–171; *The Global Compact* and, 157–161; global disparities in, 87–91; "The Global Sullivan Principles" and, 72; human development and, 163–167; least developed countries and, 125; measurement of, PPP and, 91–94; Quota, import quota defined, 49; sustainable economic development and, 83–84. *See also* Trade barriers

Real capital, 77

Regional development banks, economic development and, 94, 96–97, 127

Regional trade agreements (RTAs), growth of, 33

Regional trade organizations, 13–14, 26; the EU and, 46–47; NAFTA and, 47–49; trade liberalization and, 32–33. *See also* European Union (EU); North American Free Trade Agreement (NAFTA)

Relocalization, 50, 133–134

Renewable energy resources, 119–122

"Rio Declaration on Environment and Development," 171–176

Rio Earth Summit, 98; *Agenda 21* and, 118, 145, 162, 171–176

Rule of law, 20; IMF and, 96, 105, 167. *See also* Business climate

Russia: capital flight and, 104; development strategy and, 149; financial contagion and, 22, 42, 99; the gangster economy and, 105. *See also* Transition countries and economies; Union of Soviet Socialist Republics (USSR)

Sanctions, economic: the UN and,
52; the United States and, 50;
and the WTO, 36

Savings: East Asia and, 148; economic development, investment
and, 103–104; in the United
States, 103

Smith, Adam, *An Inquiry into the
Nature and Causes of the Wealth
of Nations,* 29

Smoot-Hawley Tariff, 9. *See also*
Protectionism; Trade barriers

Social auditing, 73

Social capital, 103

Social responsibility. *See* Corporate
social responsibility

South: digital divide and, 129–131;
energy consumption and, 120;
50 Years Is Enough Network
and, 161–163; global, 86; globalization and, 141–142. *See also*
Developing countries

Special Drawing Rights (SDR), 96

Specialization: protectionism and,
50, 155; trade and, 12–13,
30–31, 79, 145. *See also* Comparative advantage

Stephenson, George, 8

Strong currency, 43, 44–46

Structural Adjustment Programs
(SAPs), 10; criticisms of, 96,
133, 161–162

Subcontracting, 63; Nike subcontractors and, 14, 73

Sullivan, Rev. Leon H., 71; "The
Global Sullivan Principles of
Corporation Social Responsibil-
ity," 71–72

Sustainable economic development,
72; the ecosystem approach to
managing the world's resources
and, 176–178; defined, 83; 50
Years Is Enough Network and,
161–162; *The Global Compact*
and, 157–161; global
institutions and, 94–100; human
development and, 165–167; PPP
measurement of GNP and per
capita GNP, 91–94; quality of
life and, 87–91; richer and
poorer countries and, 106–109;
"Rio Declaration on Environment and Development" and,
171–176; uneven economic development and, 83–87; the virtuous cycle and, 100–106. *See
also* Developing countries; Environment; Poverty; Workers

Tariff: defined, 49; Smoot-Hawley
Tariff, 9. *See also* Trade barriers

Technology, 3–4; cultural homogenization and, 132; democracy
and, 22; digital divide and,
129–131; early technologies of
the global economy, 7–9; financial contagion, impact of, 24;
globalization and, 26, 141,
143–144; production and, 63;
"Rio Declaration on Environment and Development" and,
173; technologies of the new
global economy, 15–17; technology transfer and, 76–77; trade
and, 33–34; TRIPS and, 35–36;
virtuous cycle and, 101. *See also*
Information and communications technologies

Telstar, 16

Terrorism: defined, 134;
ecoterrorism, 52; the global
economy and, 134–136; the
World Trade Center (2001) and,
52, 134

Trade barriers, 5, 9; customs unions
and free trade areas and, 49; the
EU and, 46–47; the FTAA and,
48; GATT and the WTO, impact

on, 11–12; harmful effects of, 141–142; MNCs, circumvention of, 15, 20; NAFTA and, 47–48; protectionism and, 49–50; regional trade organizations and, 13–14; trade disputes and, 36–37; trade liberalization and, 31–33, 144–145, 152–155; the WTO and, 34

Trade deficit: causes of, 42; exchange rates and, 45–46; the NAFTA debate and, 48; U.S. merchandise and, 40–41

Trade liberalization: GATT and the WTO, impact on, 11–12; global benefits of, 141–142, 144–145, 152–155; global institutions, support for, 31–33; protectionism and, 49–50; WTO and, 34. *See also* International trade; World Trade Organization (WTO)

Trade surplus: China and, 33; U.S. services and, 41–42

Trade war, 9–10; banana war and, 13–14, 36

Transition countries and economies, 18; the brain drain and, 102; competitiveness and, 106–109; countries, list of, 87; development strategy and, 148–149; EBRD and, 97; FDI and, 62–64; M&As and, 59; MIGA and, 95; quality of life in, 89–90; quality of life, PPP measurement of, 91–93; sustainable economic development and, 83–84, 87; trade liberalization and, 33. *See also* Russia

Transnational corporations. *See* Multinational corporations (MNC)

Transnational organizations, global economy and, 4–5. *See also* International Monetary Fund (IMF); Regional development banks; World Bank Group; World Trade Organization (WTO)

Transportation: early technologies and, 7–8; the global economy and, 4; new technologies and, 15–16

Union Carbide, Bhopal tragedy and, 68

Union of Soviet Socialist Republics (USSR), 18; Chernobyl nuclear meltdown and, 68; collapse of, 87; trade and, 33. *See also* Russia; Transition countries and economies

United Kingdom, 10; economic freedom, ranking of, 21; GNP data and PPP measurements, 93–94, 100; high tech exports, rank of, 39; U.S. FDI and, 66, 84

United Nations (UN), economic development and, 94, 97–99; environmental protection and, 118–119; *The Global Compact* and, 157–161; global financial architecture and, 126–127; population growth and, 125–126; the "Rio Declaration" and, 171–176. *See also the specialized agencies and programs of the UN*

United Nations Children's Fund (UNICEF), 74; state of the world's children and, 167–171

United Nations Conference on Environment and Development. *See* Rio Earth Summit

United Nations Conference on Trade and Development (UNCTAD), 4; FDI, regulations and, 76; MNCs, rankings of, 58;

the UN system and, 98–99;
workers' rights and, 69–71
United Nations Development Program (UNDP): human development and, 90–91; opportunity, inequality of, 73; sustainable economic development and, 98
United Nations Economic and Social Council, 130
United Nations Educational, Scientific, and Cultural Organization (UNESCO), 98
United Nations Environmental Program (UNEP), 98; MEAs and, 118–119
United Nations Population Fund (UNFPA), 123–125
United States: advanced economies and, 84–86; Americanization, global culture and, 132; Bretton Woods Conference and, 10–11; early technologies and, 8–9; East Asian crisis, impact on, 23–24, 42; economic freedom and, 20–21; entrepreneurship and innovation and, 104; FDI and, 65–67; GATT and, 11; global competitiveness and, 108; the global trading system and, 38–40; Great Depression and, 9; high tech exports, rank of, 39; most admired companies and, 76; new technologies and, 15–17; OECD and, 99–100; top trading partners, rank of, 40; trade imbalances and, 40–42; U.S. GDP and PPP measurements of, 91–94; U.S. MNCs, rankings of, 55–59; the WTO and, 35–37
Unsustainable (foreign) debt, 96; debt relief and, 96, 162, 167
U.S. Department of Energy (DOE), 120–121; *International Energy Outlook 2000* and, 121–122

Venture capital, 104
Virtual firm, 101
Virtuous cycle: capital deepening and, 102–104; defined, 100; democracy and, 105–106; entrepreneurship and, 104; good governance and, 105; human capital and, 101–102; technology and, 101
Voluntary restrictions (on trade), defined, 49

Wal-Mart Stores: corporation social responsibility and, 73; global ranking, by revenues and employees, 56; GNPs and MNC revenues, comparison of, 57
Watt, James, 7
Weak currency, 43, 44–46
Wheatstone, Charles, 8
Wilkinson, John, 7
Women: cycle and poverty and, 168–171; East Asia, education and, 149; entrepreneurship and, 104; family planning and, 102, 125; fertility rates, global comparison of, 90, 123, 125; *The Global Sullivan Principles* and, 71–72; ILO "core conventions" and, 69–70; the International Conference on Population and Development and, 125; population growth rates and, 179–180; the "Rio Declaration on Environment and Development" and, 175; UNDP and, 98
Workers: *Agenda 21* and, 118; employment by sector, developed versus developing countries, 85–86; *The Global Compact* and, 159–160; "The Global Sullivan

Principles" and, 71–72; ILO, terms and conditions of work and, 156–157; MNCs, exploitation by, 72–75; MNCs, job creation and, 62, 78; rights of, 68–72. *See also* Nongovernmental organizations (NGOs)

World Bank, 4, 10; Chad Pipeline project and, 77–78; criticisms of, 20–22, 96, 133, 161–163; IBRD, within the World Bank Group, 95. *See also* World Bank Group

World Bank Group, 10–11; East Asia and eastern Europe, development lessons from, 148–150; economic development and, 94–95; global financial architecture and, 126–127; human development and, 163–167. *See also the five institutions that comprise the World Bank Group*

World Competitiveness Yearbook 2000, 107–108

World Economic Forum (WEF), 107, 133

World Health Organization (WHO), 74, 98

World Resources Institute (WRI), 114; the ecosystem approach and, 176–178; global resource depletion and, 117

World Trade Center, terrorist attack and, 52, 134

World Trade Organization (WTO), 5; the case for globalization and, 144, 152–155; expanded volume of trade and, 32–34; GATT and, 11–12; the global financial architecture and, 126–128, 144; NGOs' resistance to, 20–22, 25; principles and operation of, 34–37, 65, 94

World War I and World War II, the global economy, disruption of, 9

World Wide Web, 17

About the Author

DAVID E. O'CONNOR is a nationally recognized economics teacher, author, and consultant. He has taught economics at the Edwin O. Smith High School in Storrs, Connecticut, since 1975. He has served as a College Board Economics consultant and as president of the Connecticut Council for the Social Studies. He is the author of a number of books and teacher's guides in the fields of economics, ethnic history, and world history including *Economics: Free Enterprise in Action* (1988), *The Global Economy: A Resource Guide for Teachers* (2000), and *Basic Economic Principles: A Guide for Students* (Greenwood Press, 2000), and has contributed articles to historical and educational journals, including *Social Education*.

CRIME
MYSTERIES

ALSO BY BARBARA JOHNSTON ADAMS
THE PICTURE LIFE OF BILL COSBY

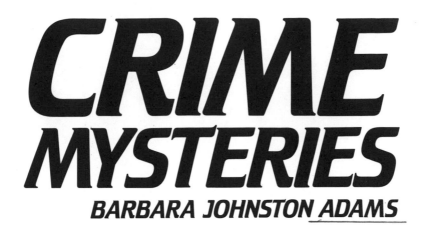

CRIME MYSTERIES

BARBARA JOHNSTON ADAMS

FRANKLIN WATTS
NEW YORK/LONDON/TORONTO/SYDNEY/1988

R0065436583

Photographs courtesy of:
AP/Wide World Photos: pp. 11, 14, 40,
43, 48 (bottom), 51 (top), 53, 58, 69, 75;
Sygma: p. 17 (Lassier-Hamelin);
UPI/Bettmann Newsphotos: pp. 23, 26, 30,
35, 36, 48 (top), 51 (bottom), 62, 67;
The Bettmann Archive: pp. 80, 82, 85, 86.

Library of Congress Cataloging-in-Publication Data

Adams, Barbara Johnston.
Crime mysteries.

Bibliography: p.
Includes index.
Summary: Retells the stories of five famous crimes,
including a kidnapping, a double murder, a series of
bombings, a bank robbery, and a disappearance, all of
which remain mysterious.
1. Crime and criminals—Case studies—Juvenile
literature. [1. Crime and criminals] I. Title.
HV6025.A27 1988   364.1   87-27423
ISBN 0-531-10517-2

Copyright © 1988 by Barbara Johnston Adams
All rights reserved
Printed in the United States of America
6 5 4 3 2 1

CONTENTS

A Note to the Reader 7

1 The Sewer Rats' Robbery 9

2 The Disappearing Judge 21

3 Kidnapped 38

4 The Mad Bomber 56

5 The Fall River Murders 73

Source Notes 90

For Further Reading 92

Index 93

To R. A., supersleuth

A NOTE TO THE READER

Crime Mysteries tells the stories of five famous cases: a double murder, a series of bombings, a kidnapping, a bank robbery, and a disappearance. All made newspaper headlines when they occurred, and all continue to fascinate. Each of these crimes, in its own way, has become a part of modern-day history. And each has about it a special mystery that sets it apart from other crimes.

THE SEWER RATS' 1 ROBBERY

It's 10:00 A.M. on a hot Monday morning in July 1976. A customer tries to enter the Société Générale bank building in Nice in southern France. She wants to put some jewelry in her safe deposit box in the bank's vault. The bank is closed, however, even though it's past time for it to open for business. The line of people outside the bank grows. "What's going on?" the customer asks.[1] But no one knows.

Inside the bank, everyone is asking questions. The most important one is being asked by the manager of the bank, Jacques Guenet: "Why won't the door [to the bank's vault] open?"[2] The door, made of steel three feet thick, usually swings wide with no more than a gentle push after bank officials have used two keys to unlock it. This morning, though officials have tried many times, the door refuses to budge.

Monsieur Guenet waits for the locksmiths in the cool, high-ceilinged main hall of the bank. He isn't worried. In the fifty years that the same door has protected the vault, it has become stuck once before and needed repair. But nothing has ever happened to the money, the bars of gold, or the other valuables in the vault.

When the locksmiths arrive, they insert the keys in the vault's doors. Carefully, in complete silence, they listen as the lock does exactly what it's supposed to do. However, the door still sticks. "There's nothing wrong with the lock," the locksmiths tell the bank officials.[3] Since the locksmiths are experts from Fichet-Bauche, a well-known company, they must be right. "Something on the other side is keeping the door from opening," they suggest. "That's impossible!" bank officials exclaim.[4]

Faced with the closed door and the impatient customers outside, the bank officials have no choice but to have a hole drilled in the vault's wall next to the door. The drilling takes several hours. Finally, there is a hole large enough for someone to look through. The next words spoken are the worst a bank manager can hear. "You've been robbed!" Guenet is told. "It's not true!" he replies.[5] "You must call the police," the locksmiths tell him.[6]

The inside of the vault is a mess. The floor is covered with papers, cash, jewelry, and even bowls and cups of gold and silver. Later it's learned that the value of the items on the floor comes to almost $2 million.

When the police arrive, they find that many of the safe deposit boxes have been opened. The robbers had left behind their tools: blowtorches, hammers, and drills. The reason the vault door wouldn't open was because it had been welded shut.

At first glance, the police are as puzzled as the bank officials. How did the robbers get into the vault? The door, it was thought, was so well built that a modern alarm system was believed to be unnecessary. Soon the police have the answer. Behind one of the safes in the vault is a hole leading to what looks like a long tunnel. "They must have used the sewers!" exclaims the first detective on the scene.[7]

The sewer system in Nice is a maze of pipes and tunnels. Some are small, but others are large enough for a per-

*The Société Générale bank building,
following the discovery that robbers
had broken into the bank*

son to walk through. A truck can even be driven along an underground road. Anyone can go to City Hall and get a diagram that shows every twist and turn of the sewers.

After the first shock had worn off, the investigation went into high gear. Newspapers all over the world carried headlines calling the robbery the biggest of the century. Many wealthy people live in Nice, some of whom had left their money in the bank vault. The value of the cash, gold, jewelry, and other stolen items was thought to be between $10 million and $15 million.

Customers at the bank didn't have to keep a list of what was in their safe deposit boxes, so it was impossible to total the exact amount taken. Before leaving for summer vacation, some people had put more valuables than usual into their boxes to avoid theft from their own homes. The police also knew that some bank customers hid cash and other valuables in their boxes so they wouldn't have to pay taxes on these items.

The more the police learned, the more they had to admit that an enormous amount of effort and hard work had gone into planning the robbery. For months beforehand, the thieves had tunneled toward the vault from the city's sewers. Although a police station was only a few blocks away from the bank, no one had seen or heard anything suspicious.

The police knew that the amount of work involved meant that a gang of robbers, not just one or two individuals, had entered the vault. As shown from the leftover food and bottles, the gang must have been in the vault for several days. Since the robbery was discovered on a Monday morning, the gang could have had all weekend—from July 16 to July 19—to open the safe deposit boxes if they'd begun late on Friday. (The bank was closed on that summer weekend.)

Once they had broken through the vault's wall, the robbers were quite comfortable. They had hooked a long electric cable to a socket in an underground parking garage, so they had light and power for their tools. Smoke and other odors went out through air vents.

As investigators put together the pieces of the crime, they realized that the gang's leader had to have been very clever. Tools were carried a long distance from the point where the robbers entered the sewer system to the pipe closest to the vault.

After getting close to the vault, the thieves then had to dig a twenty-foot-long tunnel that was high enough for them and for their equipment. Investigators found that the tunnel was kept from collapsing by propping up the ceiling and cementing the walls. The earth had to be taken away so no one would notice. The robbers hid their ongoing work by making it look as though it was part of the job of regular city sewer employees.

In addition to being clever, the gang's leader and his men were determined. While underground, they had to put up with the terrible smell of the sewer waste and with the big rats that lived in the pipes.

The Nice investigators spent weeks following every clue. They dusted for fingerprints—there were no useful ones, for the gang had worn gloves. They checked the background of the bank's customers and employees. They traced the tools the robbers had left behind. They talked to their contacts among the city's network of criminals.

Eventually, all their work paid off. Some names began to appear on a "wanted" list. Before the robbery, local police in a village outside of Nice had questioned five men after receiving a phone call. Asked why they were gathered at a house that didn't belong to them, the men said that the owner had let them use it for a while. After the discovery of the crime, Nice police went back to the house. The men were gone. The police found, along with other evidence, a flashlight covered with what the crime lab found to be sewer mud. The house had, for a time, been the hideout for the "Sewer Rat" gang. (This was the nickname given to the robbers by the French press.)

An artist's drawing showing the manhole located in a nearby parking area through which burglars attained access to the bank's vault

As more names were added to the police list, the investigators feared that the criminals would find out how close the police were, and leave the city or even the country. The authorities decided it was time to act.

After one hundred days of investigation, twenty-seven people were taken into police custody in Nice and in other French cities. All but seven were released. Six were put in jail for taking part in the bank robbery. The seventh person was also jailed, but for unrelated charges.

Only a small amount of the stolen goods had been

found so far. It was clear that the leader of the Sewer Rats—the mastermind who had planned the crime—was still at large.

The police checked the gang leaders they knew, especially those in the city of Marseilles, a center for organized crime in France. But none, they believed, had the ability to be the mastermind of the robbery. Then, acting on a tip, the police arrested a man named Albert Spaggiari, known to his friends as Bert. The police had been told that he was the leader they sought.

Who was Albert Spaggiari? He was a man who could easily charm others. An adventurer, he had been in many countries and many prisons. He was well known in his Nice neighborhood, where he ran a photography store. But he was a mysterious man, and continues to remain one to this day.

Spaggiari was born in a mountain village in the French Alps early in the 1930s. Although he was smart and loved to read, Spaggiari had done only average work in school. He sometimes got into trouble. Through his reading, he became interested in a famous bandit who lived in Sicily. At seventeen, he ran away from home to try to meet this outlaw. Italian police found him, put him in jail for a few days for entering the country illegally, and then sent him home.

When he became an adult, Spaggiari repeated this pattern—having illegal adventures, getting caught, spending time in jail, and returning home.

Spaggiari volunteered to be a paratrooper in Indochina. During the fighting there, he was jailed for stealing. He later joined the Secret Army Organization in Algeria, a group that tried to keep the territory French when President Charles de Gaulle was moving toward giving it independence. According to Spaggiari's own account, he twice joined in attempts on de Gaulle's life. He received another prison term.

After his arrest for the Société Générale bank robbery,

Spaggiari was questioned steadily for more than a day. Spaggiari's trouble with the law in the past had been on political and military matters, so the police weren't completely sure they had the right man. But eventually he broke down and confessed to being the robbers' leader. Spaggiari revealed details of the robbery to the police and later in a book he wrote.

The robbery had been planned with the precision of a military campaign. Spaggiari had gathered his Sewer Rats from among criminals in Marseilles and from contacts who had become his buddies over the years. For over four months, the gang had made their preparations. Members of the gang had rented an apartment in Nice and used it while they worked in the sewers. Dressed in workmen's uniforms, the gang used underground roads to bring in their materials.

Some heavy equipment was lowered through a manhole in a street near a pedestrian crosswalk. The men worked at night, starting at about 10:00 P.M., and slept during the day. Because they had been used to swift, dangerous jobs, the men frequently got into fights with one another as the days of digging and drilling stretched into weeks.

Finally, in late May, they reached the bank's foundation. Next they had to break through the bank's wall and then through the wall of the vault. Pneumatic jacks and electric drills helped to do the job. As the men went back and forth through the sewers each day, the rats that scampered past became bolder. Once a gang member even found one in his pocket. Most of the men hated the rodents, but one treated them as pets.

Spaggiari revealed that just before the gang was ready to begin the robbery, they learned that the president of France at that time, Giscard d'Estaing, was due to visit Nice. Knowing that security forces would check the sewers, they had to delay the date of the robbery. But the gang had done such a good job of disguising their work that the inspectors didn't uncover anything.

Before entering the vault, the gang decided not to take

*Albert Spaggiari, self-confessed
ringleader of the gang*

any guns with them. If they were surprised by guards, they planned to use tear gas to give themselves time to get away.

As the robbers finally crawled into the vault, they began, Spaggiari said, to grin and slap each other on the back. It was, he pointed out, like stepping into the cave of Ali Baba: there were riches beyond belief. The vault was made up of three separate rooms, and the robbers broke into each one.

Spaggiari also told the police that an unlooked-for bonus had come their way. Department stores and other businesses had dropped their weekend money into a night deposit slot at the bank. The robbers kept hearing more loot fall into the vault.

In spite of the enormous amount the gang made off with, Spaggiari said he was upset because they opened only several hundred out of a possible four thousand safe deposit boxes. Some of the boxes were difficult to break into, and the gang ran out of time.

According to Spaggiari, he "donated" part of his portion of the haul to a secret international organization made up of so-called soldiers of fortune. This organization's members held strong political views. What the other gang members did with their share, he said, was up to them.

Just before leaving the vault, the Sewer Rat gang wrote on a wall the slogan: *"Sans armes, sans haine, et sans violence,"*[8] meaning "Without guns, hatred, or violence." For this crime at least, they had been "gentlemen robbers," with no desire to do physical injury to anyone.

Spaggiari said that their escape had almost been their undoing. During the night, a heavy rain had fallen, and they were nearly swept away by the dangerously rising water in the sewers.

After his arrest, Spaggiari was put in jail. As in other important criminal cases in France, he could not be released on bail while awaiting trial. Facing the possibility of a long prison term if he was found guilty, he realized that he might be an old man by the time he was free again. But Spaggiari was never one to sit back. He liked to be in control.

Every Thursday, Spaggiari was taken from the jail to a Nice courthouse to see Judge Richard Bouazis. The judge questioned him about the details of the robbery. Four months after his arrest, the judge wanted to know still more about the way the gang had managed to get into the bank. Spaggiari promised to draw a map of the sewers.

The questioning on March 10, 1977, went on for several hours as Spaggiari smoked his favorite cigars. He wasn't handcuffed; his guards were stationed outside the door. Only his lawyer, Jacques Peyat, the judge, and a court typist were in the room.

"Did you bring the map?" the judge asked.[9]

Spaggiari took a folded piece of paper from his jacket pocket.

"I've got something here that may interest you," he replied.[10] The lawyer handed the map to the judge.

The judge looked puzzled. Spaggiari hadn't drawn it very clearly.

"Want me to show you?" Spaggiari asked.[11]

He walked slowly to the judge's desk as if to point to something on the map. Then, moving quickly to a window near the desk, he flung it open and jumped out. The judge and lawyer rushed to the window.

Spaggiari leapt to a ledge overhanging the building, then to the roof of a parked car and, rolling off, landed on his feet in the street. A motorcycle was waiting next to the car, its rider racing the engine. Spaggiari jumped onto the motorcycle and was soon out of sight.

The escape took just seconds. No one had time to react. Only a shout hung in the air: *"Arretez-le! Arretez-le!"* ("Stop him!")[12]

Policemen gave chase, but the motorcycle had a head start and was soon lost in city traffic. Roadblocks were set up and border guards alerted. A manhunt got underway. But Spaggiari had disappeared. He hasn't been seen since.

It was an embarrassing situation for the investigators, and it didn't help that, at the time, elections were coming up. The people of France followed the story on television and in the newspapers. The press called Spaggiari "France's favorite crook."

Two years passed. The trial of the six robbers who were picked up before Spaggiari finally ended. Three were acquitted. The other three were sentenced to prison terms. Spaggiari was sentenced to life in prison—if he is ever caught. Only a portion of what was stolen from the bank was recovered.

Some people believe Spaggiari is hiding in South America. But to this day, he remains a man of mystery.

A DISAPPEARING
2 JUDGE

It's so hot on this August night in New York City that the heat lifts in waves off the sidewalk. The tall, elegant man in a brown business suit waves good-bye to two people as he gets into a taxi in front of a restaurant on West 45th Street. They see him settle back in his seat as the taxi pulls out into traffic. With that simple act, Judge Joseph Force Crater, the man in the brown suit, began a mystery that continues to this day. For wherever that taxi took him, Judge Crater has never been seen again.

The disappearance of Judge Crater in 1930 remains one of the most tantalizing mysteries of this century. It has never been proved that a crime was committed in connection with what happened that summer night, but it seems likely that one did occur. The question: Who arranged for the exit of this well-known man? Is it possible that Crater planned his own disappearance?

Joe Crater had a lot to live for. He was viewed as an intelligent and skillful lawyer who had quickly become successful in the exciting, rough-and-tumble times of the 1920s.

For just over three months before his disappearance, he had been a justice of the New York Supreme Court. According to rumor at the time, the Supreme Court of the United States in Washington, D.C., was a possibility in the judge's future.[1]

When Crater disappeared, he was forty-one years old, about six feet tall, and weighed 185 pounds. His hair was dark, mixed with gray. His description, however, doesn't reveal what an unusual-looking man he was. Judge Crater, it must be admitted, looked a little like a turtle.

Most people noticed that for so tall and broad-shouldered a man, he had a narrow neck and a small head. He walked with short steps, although his legs were long. Aware that his neck wasn't his best feature, Crater wore high starched collars that belonged to an earlier age of men's fashions. Everyone who knew the judge said that he was very particular about the way he dressed. These details became important the moment he stepped into the taxi. How could such a man—one who didn't blend in with the crowd on a city street—vanish completely?

At first, no one believed that Joe Crater *had* vanished. Together with his wife, Stella, he had been vacationing at their summer home in Belgrade Lakes, Maine. The court was on its summer break, and the judge enjoyed relaxing in Maine, after his hard work at court. Crater's appointment as justice was only temporary. He was taking the place of a judge who was retiring. Within a few months, he'd have to win his place on the court in his own right.

As Crater stretched out to sunbathe on the dock next to the lake, he had many reasons to feel satisfied with his life. Born in Pennsylvania in 1889, he had two brothers and a sister. His strong arms and wide shoulders, he proudly told people, came from the long hours he had spent loading

Judge Joseph Crater

fresh fruit and vegetables for his father's business. Crater had graduated from Lafayette College and earned a law degree from Columbia University.

Stella and Joe Crater were married in 1917. The people Crater met through his work and the couple's friends believed that theirs was a happy marriage. They had no children. During the winter months when they couldn't stay in Maine, they lived in their Manhattan apartment.

The year Crater disappeared marked the end of ten years of good times for America. By the day Crater vanished—August 6—the United States and many other countries had been in what became known as the Great Depression.

Joe Crater was a careful man. He had invested only a small amount of money in the stock market. When the Depression came, it didn't hurt him. But what happened to him may well have had roots in what was happening in America.

Attitudes were not the same as they once had been. As long as things were fine, people had been willing to ignore the not-so-honest dealings of some businessmen and politicians. But, when times got rough, these same people began to examine practices they'd once been willing to overlook.

Crater was not only a lawyer, but he also taught law at two universities. Most important, he had become involved in politics. Politics and politicians—especially in New York City—were suddenly getting a lot of attention. Some of Crater's friends were making newspaper headlines.

George F. Ewald was one of these people. Just a few months earlier, Ewald had been charged with buying his position as magistrate in a New York City court. The buying of offices was not uncommon. Reporters often noted that one year's salary was the price some judges paid. People remembered that shortly after Ewald had become magistrate, Crater had been the main speaker at a banquet given in Ewald's honor.

Crater himself already had political power. Undoubtedly, he intended to seek more. He was president of a famous political group in the city, the Cayuga Democratic Club. This club was an important headquarters for Tammany Hall, the name by which the Democratic party in power in New York City was then known. The Seabury investigations, about to get underway, revealed corruption throughout the Tammany Hall administration. Every city service could be bought for a price. In fact, the mayor of the city, Jimmy Walker, was eventually forced to resign.

In the months before Crater disappeared, the Seabury investigations were like a thunderstorm about to break loose. It was never proved, however, that Crater had anything to do with the Ewald case. Nor was it shown that he had done anything wrong in connection with another headline-making story. This was a real estate deal involving the multimillion-dollar sale of a New York hotel and its land. Though Crater had withdrawn thousands of dollars from bank accounts in the spring of 1930, no one ever found out where that money went.

These were some of the relevant events around the time that Joe Crater left with his wife to vacation in Maine.

In mid-July, Crater returned to New York City to attend to some business. In a book Stella Crater later wrote, she noted many times that her husband usually did not share the details of his work with her. So she didn't know why he had left for the city.

During this period, Crater had also made a trip from New York to Atlantic City, New Jersey. It was later reported in newspaper and magazine articles that Crater was something of a ladies' man. On this Atlantic City trip, for instance, accounts in the press said that Crater and one or two friends had been at a party with some women.

Although his wife later said she didn't believe these reports, those who knew Crater in New York said he was often seen entertaining show girls. The judge loved going to Broadway plays and musicals, and often went to restau-

rants and clubs afterward. Here he had ample opportunity to meet attractive women. These personal details weren't important before August 6, but, since one of the last people to see him *was* a show girl, they later became pieces of the unsolved puzzle.

After taking care of whatever business he'd had, Crater returned to Maine. But he didn't stay long. Sometime during August 2 or 3, he received a message that put him back on a train for New York in a hurry.

Now the real mystery began to unfold. Crater told his wife he had to go to New York for only a few days. "I've got to straighten those fellows out," he said.[2] The meaning of this remark has never been explained. On August 3, Crater kissed Stella good-bye and was driven to the train station by the couple's chauffeur, Fred Kahler. Before he left, he promised he'd be back in Belgrade Lakes in time to celebrate his wife's birthday on August 9. But Stella never saw Joe again.

What Crater did after arriving in Manhattan was pieced together later. In the city on August 4, he went to his and Stella's apartment at 40 Fifth Avenue. There he told the couple's live-in maid that she could take time off until the end of the week, when she could return and clean the apartment. Crater then visited his doctor, Augustus Rizzi, perhaps for treatment of a finger he'd accidentally hurt in closing a car door. Rizzi invited Crater to dinner the next night.

On August 5, the day before he disappeared, the judge was seen in his offices at the courthouse. He greeted Fred-

Stella Crater, wife of the missing judge. She eventually reopened the probe into her husband's disappearance by charging he was murdered for political reasons.

erick Johnson, his legal secretary, and Joseph Mara, an assistant. Crater was seen at lunch and then, as planned, had dinner with Dr. Rizzi. He stayed at the doctor's home until after midnight.

Wednesday, August 6, was sunny. For many days, it had been above ninety degrees. Crater went to his office at the usual time. After that, however, he didn't follow his usual workday. Crater gave Mara two checks to cash. They totaled $5,150. Mara returned with two envelopes. Without bothering to count the money, which was very unlike the judge, Crater stuffed the envelopes into his coat pocket.

He spent most of the rest of the morning in his office with the door closed. It turned out that he was sorting papers and putting them into two briefcases and five cardboard containers. A short while later, Crater called Mara into his office and had him tie up the containers. Mara later said he couldn't see what was in them. Then, after telling Frederick Johnson to lock up the office when he left work, Crater had Mara help him take the two briefcases and the containers by taxi to Crater's apartment.

Mara placed the bundles where Crater asked him to. "You may go now," the judge told Mara. "I'm going up to Westchester for a swim this afternoon. I'll see you tomorrow."[3] Crater, however, didn't go to his office the next day.

Westchester County is just north of New York City, a short train ride away if Crater wished to get there quickly. There's no record, however, of whether or not Crater went there. In fact, no one found out what he did on the afternoon of August 6. And no one ever again saw the papers that Mara helped carry to the apartment. They vanished as completely as the judge.

At about 7:00 P.M., Crater went to a ticket agency to ask for one ticket to a Broadway show for that night. The show was called *Dancing Partner*, a hit comedy. The ticket agent, a man who knew Crater, told him the show was so popular it might be hard to buy even a single seat. However, the agent said he'd try to find a ticket and would leave it at the theater box office for Crater to pick up later.

The judge then entered the Billy Haas restaurant at 332 West 45th Street. No sooner had he given his hat to the woman in the checkroom than he saw a friend, William Klein. Klein, a lawyer for theater producers, had a dinner companion. She was Sally Ritz, a show girl. Klein invited Crater to join them for dinner. Crater accepted, for he loved to talk about show business.

Klein told the police later that it was easy to see that Crater had enjoyed the food and the conversation. He looked relaxed. Klein remembered that the judge said he'd be going back to Maine in a day or two. He planned to stay there, he went on, for several weeks, until the court began its new term on August 25.

The dinner was long. It was past curtain time when, about 9:15, the two men and Sally Ritz left the restaurant. Yet Crater didn't seem to be in a hurry to pick up the ticket the theater agent had promised to leave for him. The three talked briefly on the sidewalk. Then Crater hailed a taxi, got in, and . . . vanished forever. Someone did pick up the theater ticket, but the man at the box office couldn't remember what the person looked like.

It was not until a month later that the disappearance began to make headlines. This "lost" month probably wiped out any chance the police had to learn what really happened.

In Belgrade Lakes, Stella Crater at first did not become alarmed. Since there was no phone in the house, Joe often showed up unexpectedly. When her birthday on August 9 came and went, however, she did become anxious. It was unlike her husband not to get in touch with her and let her know he'd been delayed. Then there was the red canoe that was delivered to her doorstep by a local storekeeper. He told Stella that the judge had ordered it as a birthday present before leaving Maine. Surely Crater must have planned on sharing his wife's pleasure in this gift.

But Stella had lived in what she herself called a cocoon. She didn't know much about her husband's business dealings. So she guessed he'd be along soon, joking with her about her concern.

After more days passed, however, Stella became more worried. She phoned Simon Rifkind, a lawyer friend. Rifkind worked for Senator Robert Wagner in a position Crater had once held. Wagner, whose son later became mayor of New York City, was in Europe. He'd been very helpful to Crater's career. Rifkind told Stella not to worry. He offered to see what he could find out.

More time passed with only silence for an answer. Stella sent the chauffeur, Fred Kahler, to New York to check the Fifth Avenue apartment. After arriving, Kahler wrote Stella a note telling her that the apartment was all right, but that there was no sign of the judge. Kahler said that the maid told him the bed had been slept in, but she couldn't tell on which night. Fred Kahler also told Stella that, when he started phoning Crater's friends in New York, they warned him about making too much of a fuss. They thought that if the newspapers got word of Crater's absence, it might hurt his chances of running for his court position in the fall. His friends were sure he would show up.

By August 25, the day that Crater was due back in court after summer break, there was no longer any way to hide the fact that something was wrong. When another supreme court justice reached Stella in Maine to ask where Crater was, she packed and left for the city.

Joe Crater's political friends continued to advise Stella not to make too much of a fuss because it could damage her husband's career. A private search had already begun, they

Sally Ritz, one of the people Judge Crater had dined with on the night he vanished

-31

told her. A city detective, Leo Lowenthal, had checked the apartment. He'd found the vest to the suit Crater had worn in the Billy Haas restaurant. But, since it had been so hot, Lowenthal said that the judge could simply have left it behind. Following the advice of Crater's friends, Stella returned to Maine. Too worried to sleep or eat properly, she was close to collapse.

On September 3, Rifkind finally phoned Police Commissioner Edward Mulrooney to report Crater's disappearance.

WIDE HUNT IS BEGUN
FOR JUSTICE CRATER

read the headline in New York newspapers. A larger headline, however, carried news that French and German airmen were celebrating nonstop flights across the Atlantic. Lindbergh, the American who had been first to achieve this honor, met the fliers while New Yorkers cheered.

But Judge Crater's name was to be remembered in America long after the French and German flights had been forgotten. The Bureau of Missing Persons of the New York Police Department opened File 13595—a number that would become famous. Once started, publicity about the Crater case continued beyond the next fifty years.

The Missing Persons Bureau put out a poster with a photograph and a description of Crater. It was sent to police and sheriffs across the United States. Law officials around the world would eventually look for the missing judge. The poster offered a $5,000 reward for information resulting in locating Crater. In 1930, that was a large amount when a newspaper cost only 2¢, a man's business suit could be bought for $35, and a new Dodge car was $895.

The description of Joe Crater was very detailed. It mentioned that he had false teeth and an injured right index finger. Even his watch and reading glasses were described.

In the course of their investigation, the police carefully searched the Crater apartment. Nothing unusual was found.

A check of the judge's safe deposit box showed that it was empty. The police did learn of several women who said they knew the judge. One had dropped out of sight. But she soon returned saying that she'd just wanted to get away from reporters.

A lawyer came forward and told of a woman who had come to him wishing to file a suit against Crater. But she must have used a false name since no such woman could now be located. No suit was ever filed.

It was more difficult to learn about some of Crater's other activities. Fred Kahler said that Crater often didn't give him an exact address to drive to. Instead, the judge frequently got out of the car at a corner and told the chauffeur to pick him up at that same place or at another corner at a later time.

Forty days after her husband vanished, Stella received a ransom letter. But the police decided that it was a fake. In the fall, a grand jury investigation was ordered. Stella refused to go to New York from Maine. She was too ill to travel, she said. Detectives went to Belgrade Lakes and gave her a list of written questions, which she did answer.

After several months and almost one thousand pages of testimony, the grand jury ended its investigation. The taxi driver, the last person to have seen Crater, never made himself known, although many appeals were made. And, while the court papers Crater had left in his office were in order, the contents of the papers he took to his apartment the day he vanished were never explained.

The Missing Persons Bureau followed up every clue. As Crater's photograph was seen by more people, reports poured in that he'd been found. He was thought to be a passenger on a ship sailing for Europe, the driver of a car in Canada, a monk in Mexico, a prospector looking for gold in California, an accident victim in a Mississippi hospital. Occasionally he was reported to be in two places at the same time. But all of these leads proved false.

The case took yet another strange turn in January 1931

when the judge had been gone for five months. Stella returned to the Fifth Avenue apartment again. This time, in a drawer that had been empty when the police had searched it, she found several large envelopes. They held over $6,000 in cash, three checks, stocks and bonds, Crater's will leaving his estate to her, and his insurance policies. But, most surprising of all, one envelope held a note to Stella in the judge's own handwriting.

This note, not dated, listed the names of people Joe said owed him money. He suggested that Stella contact them and collect. At the end of the note, which looked as if it had been hastily written, Joe had scribbled, "I am very weary, Love Joe."

Stella's discovery caused an uproar. She hadn't seen the envelopes, she said, when she'd come to the apartment late in the summer. Why hadn't the police found this material before? Had someone—possibly Crater himself—gotten into the apartment and put the material in the drawer? If so, how had he or she gotten past the police guard? Once again, there were no answers.

As months went by, it became less likely that Crater would be found. The judge was such a well-known figure it seemed impossible that he could be walking around, perhaps a victim of memory loss, and not be recognized. Even his friends now believed that murder was more and more a possibility.

In 1939, Crater was declared legally dead. On the advice of her lawyer, Stella tried to collect on her husband's three insurance policies. However, to get what is known as double indemnity—twice the face value of the policies—it had to be shown that death had resulted from accidental or violent means. Without a corpse, this was difficult to prove; the attempt failed. Stella received only the face value of the policies, about $20,500.

Interest in the case of the missing judge refused to die. In 1959, an article in *Life* magazine told of how "a huge hole" had been dug in a Yonkers, New York, backyard in

Marie Eisenmenger identifies a picture of the missing jurist as the man who entered her store in a town in California in May of 1936. There were many reports of people seeing the missing judge.

Lucky Blackeit, a desert prospector, claimed to have encountered Judge Crater in the desert in August 1936.

a search for Crater's body. A butcher had once owned a house in Yonkers, and before his death he told a detective friend that he believed Crater had been murdered there. The butcher saw blood splattered all over the kitchen. Tammany Hall friends, the butcher said, sometimes used the house for parties. The *Life* article, with two pages of photographs, pointed out that nothing was found in the backyard hole.

Stella Crater looked for and found a job when she was in her sixties. She died in 1969 in a nursing home in Mount Vernon, New York, where she had lived for six years. "They never let me forget," she once said of all the years of press coverage.[4] Most of the other people connected with the case have also died.

It's been a long time now since Joseph Crater vanished. Babe Ruth, who was hitting home runs when Crater disappeared, has been dead for forty years. The Empire State Building, not yet open to the public when the judge dropped out of sight, has been dwarfed by taller skyscrapers. And more than skylines have changed in America. The judge, if he chose to take on a new identity in some remote part of the world, would be about one hundred years old. What reason would he have had to keep silent as he became an old man?

It seems likely that the case of Judge Crater will never be solved. In keeping with his love of Broadway plays, the judge certainly left the last act of his life a mystery. Crater may have been blackmailed, as Stella's lawyer believed. Or a criminal he'd sent to jail might have decided to take revenge. Or Crater may not have agreed to some plan proposed by Tammany leaders.

Every person who learns the details of Crater's story has an idea of where he went on that hot night of August 6, 1930. What do you think happened?

3 KIDNAPPED

A college student named Barbara is led from a motel room into the night by a man and his smaller companion. They put her into a waiting car. With the man driving, the car speeds off. The smaller person, a woman, holds Barbara down in the backseat.

For a while, the car continues to move, then goes over some bumps and stops. Barbara shivers, for she's wearing only nightclothes. The man tells her that this is a kidnapping and that she must cooperate. Her father will be asked to pay a large sum of money and, when the kidnappers collect, she will be freed. In the meantime, she will be put underground, but she will be safe if she obeys instructions.

The place the kidnappers plan to put her has water, food, a battery, air vents, a light, a water pump, and other supplies. The man repeats many times that he and his companion do not want to hurt her, but the young woman is terrified.

The woman gives Barbara an injection to sedate her. By this time, her hands and feet are tied. After carrying her a short distance away from the car, the man puts her on the ground. He places a sign under her chin and takes two photographs. (She later learns that the sign says "kidnapped.")

In spite of the injection, Barbara is awake when she's lowered into a large box buried in the woods. She tries to persuade the kidnappers not to bury her, but they persist. The man tells her they will be back later to check on her. As Barbara lies in the box, its top is closed and screwed tight. She hears dirt being thrown on it. After a few more muffled words, she's left alone. Silence surrounds her.

It was a couple of weeks before Christmas 1968, when this strange story began, a story that put one American family through a terrible ordeal. While some people were in the holiday spirit, a great many others—all across the country—were suffering from the flu. Barbara Mackle was one of those on the sick list at Emory University in Atlanta, Georgia. To make matters worse, she was in the middle of final exams for the fall quarter of her junior year. When she called home to Miami, Florida, her mother, Jane, decided to come and care for her. Remaining in Miami was Barbara's father, Robert, a millionaire real estate executive. Her brother, Bobby, was in Philadelphia, where he was a graduate student.

As soon as Mrs. Mackle reached Atlanta, she checked into a motel near the campus. It was Friday, December 13. Barbara joined her there, staying for the weekend and on into the following week. It was a quiet few days. Barbara tried to study for her exams. At 3:00 A.M. on Tuesday, December 17, Barbara was still bothered by the flu, but she was asleep. Suddenly, there was a knock on the door of the motel room. Mrs. Mackle went to the door and was told by a man outside that a friend of Barbara's had been in an accident and was in the hospital. Mrs. Mackle believed the friend to be Stewart Woodward, a young man who had

The motel near Emory University in Atlanta from which Barbara Jane Mackle was kidnapped

known Barbara for several years. She unlocked the door, and the man forced his way into the room. He was carrying a gun. A shorter, slightly built person followed him.

Just then, Barbara woke up. At first, she didn't know what was happening. She saw two strangers in the room. Mrs. Mackle assumed the pair were robbers and hoped that they would just take their money and jewelry and then leave. But the two intruders weren't thieves—they were there to kidnap Barbara.

While she struggled, Mrs. Mackle was forced down on one of the beds, a cloth held to her face. The cloth was soaked in a drug to make her sleepy. She was also tied up, and her mouth was loosely taped. Barbara Mackle was then taken from the room and put in the kidnappers' car.

After some time, Mrs. Mackle succeeded in freeing herself and called the police. She also called Barbara's friend, Stewart Woodward. She realized that the kidnappers had made up the story about Stewart's accident to get into the room. Stewart, also a student at Emory, immediately came to the motel. When he arrived, Mrs. Mackle asked him to call her husband in Miami.

Robert Mackle, used to making important business decisions quickly, took action right away. He called the FBI. The entire Mackle family started to gather in Atlanta. But then a new development switched the action to Miami.

A phone call from the male kidnapper to the Mackle's Miami home gave instructions to dig under a rock near some plants in the yard. FBI agents found a ransom note in a bottle. The note was detailed. It told the Mackles that Barbara was alive, had been kidnapped, and was buried somewhere. The note spelled out exactly what the family had to do to get her back. If the family paid $500,000, she would be rescued. If a doublecross or other tricks were attempted, she might never be found.

The Mackles were told to place an advertisement in Miami area newspapers saying, "Loved one, please come home. We will pay all expenses and meet you anywhere at any time. Your Family."[1] When the kidnappers read this signal, they would know that the demands of the ransom note had been met. Then the Mackles would receive a phone call telling Robert where to drop off the ransom money.

The FBI was convinced that all contact with the kidnappers would take place in Miami, so family members decided to return to Florida from Georgia. No one had any way of knowing that out in the woods, about twenty miles northeast of Atlanta, Barbara lay cold and terrified in the buried box.

Newspapers learned of the kidnapping and reported it, but no news of the kidnappers' ransom note or the fact that Barbara was buried, or of the $500,000 demand was printed or broadcast. The Mackles were a prominent family, and the press believed the kidnapping to be a top story. But the FBI knew that the less publicity, the better were Barbara's chances of being rescued.

Gathering the money together—it had to be in unmarked $20 bills—took a while. The First National Bank of Miami cooperated wholeheartedly. Bank officials, however, had to copy down the serial numbers of the bills so they could be traced. Then the money had to be packed into a certain size suitcase.

In addition to getting the ransom ready, the FBI made other preparations. A special radio and microphone were installed in Robert Mackle's car so he could talk with the FBI when he delivered the ransom. Incoming calls were monitored. Stationed in cars all around Miami, FBI agents were on the alert. J. Edgar Hoover, the FBI director at the time, personally assigned the man in charge. The FBI's rule for kidnap cases was to recover the victim safely, then to catch the kidnappers.

Finally, all was ready. The advertisement in the newspapers appeared on December 18. The kidnappers' call came next. The instructions given over the phone to Robert Mackle were complicated. He had trouble finding the ransom

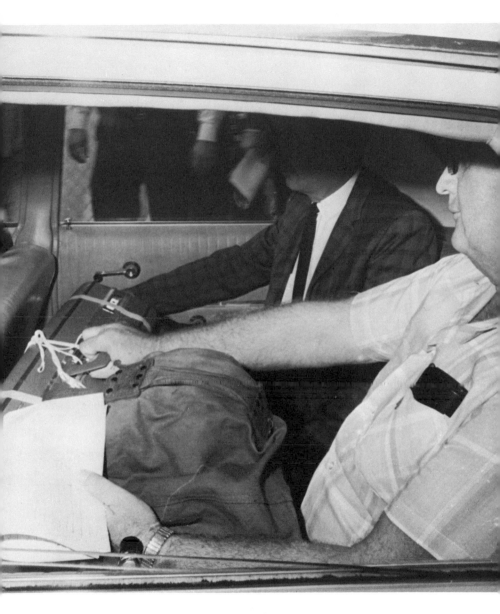

*An estimated $500,000 in ransom money
leaves the Miami Police Department.*

drop-off point. Eventually, however, Barbara's father put the ransom where he was told to.

The local police, however, knew only that Barbara had been kidnapped in Atlanta. Nothing about the Miami operation had been relayed to them. The police saw a man run away from them when they stopped to investigate a parked car with out-of-state license plates. Thinking it was a burglar, they chased the running figure, and he dropped the suitcase with the ransom in it. Then he escaped. Unknowingly, the police had put Barbara in more danger by breaking up the ransom delivery.

When Robert Mackle learned what had happened, he was extremely upset. Who could tell whether he'd ever hear from the kidnappers again? If the ransom wasn't picked up successfully, why would the kidnappers live up to their side of the bargain and reveal Barbara's whereabouts?

One good thing did happen when the police accidentally stopped the ransom drop. The male kidnapper left his car behind and ran away. This 1966 Volvo proved to be a treasure trove of information. A photograph of Barbara in the car showed positively the link with the crime. With what they found, FBI agents soon identified the kidnappers.

The male kidnapper had recently been known as George Deacon, but this turned out to be an alias for Gary Steven Krist, an escaped convict. The woman was identified as Ruth Eisemann Schier. A room key found in the car revealed that the couple had stayed in the same motel near Emory University as Barbara and her mother had.

As the FBI traced Krist's background, it was learned that he had been a thief from an early age and had been in trouble with the law all his life. The authorities also found out that he had scored very high on intelligence tests, putting him in the "genius" class.

However, Krist could be dangerous. He'd been in more than one institution and, in 1966, he'd escaped from prison in California by climbing over its high walls.

Twenty-three-year-old Krist was a master at changing

identities, often talking his way out of tight places and telling whatever story happened to suit his purpose at a particular time. His companion for Barbara Mackle's kidnapping was a twenty-six-year-old woman born in Honduras in Central America. Ruth Eisemann Schier was well educated and—until she had fallen in love with Krist—not a criminal.

Krist and Eisemann Schier were responsible for one of the most sensational kidnappings in American history. The FBI had reason to be concerned. As evidence continued to mount, agents learned that Krist had planned this crime down to the last detail. At the Miami Institute for Marine Sciences, where Krist had worked, the FBI found an outline in glue of a coffin-shaped box on the floor of his workshop. A mechanic there remembered telling Krist how to power a fan with a battery. Since employees often built boxes to hold fish and other ocean creatures, Krist's work hadn't aroused suspicion.

Knowing all this, the Mackles and the FBI believed that the kidnappers had really been telling the truth in their ransom note about Barbara being buried alive in some sort of container. But where was it?

On Thursday, December 19, the Mackles received an envelope from the kidnappers. It contained the photograph Krist had taken of Barbara with the sign saying "kidnapped." Also in the envelope was a ring taken from Barbara to prove her identity.

The FBI continued to put together more pieces of the puzzle. Agents learned that Krist had rented a car after the police had found his. He'd been treated at a local hospital for some injuries he'd gotten when the police chased him at the ransom drop. Krist was easy to trace because he loved to talk.

While the FBI had a great deal of information on Krist and Eisemann Schier, agents didn't know the answers to two questions that really mattered: Where were the kidnappers now? Was Barbara Mackle all right? Hours passed with no word. Finally, what they hoped for happened. Krist made contact again.

Newspapers as well as television and radio broadcasts had provided a message from Robert Mackle saying he wasn't responsible for what had happened at the first ransom drop-off. Barbara's father pleaded for a second chance to save her. Krist believed him and gave him that chance.

This time Krist made contact through a Catholic priest. They had spoken earlier in the kidnapping when Krist wanted to urge Robert Mackle to follow the ransom note's directions. Now new directions were given by Krist to the priest. This time the arrangements worked. When the FBI checked, agents saw that the suitcase with the money was gone.

Krist had promised Robert Mackle that he'd free his daughter within twelve hours after receiving the ransom. The waiting began again. The FBI knew that the ransom was the second largest ever paid in an American kidnapping case as of 1968.

The Atlanta FBI office had been busy all this time, although the main operation for the Mackle case had shifted to Miami. Phone calls came in by the hundreds, and all leads had to be checked. Just before 1:00 P.M. on December 20, a switchboard operator in the Atlanta office answered the phone yet another time.

This conversation, however, was different: Krist was the caller. He told the operator he had information on how to locate Barbara Mackle. As instructed, the operator tried to transfer the call to an FBI agent, but Krist refused to let her do this. He insisted instead on giving *her* the directions. The operator took them down. As soon as she gave them to the agents in the office, FBI cars raced away. They headed for Norcross, a small town outside Atlanta.

The directions said to go a little more than three miles from a certain intersection. But which way? It wasn't clear. Cars raced along a number of roads looking for the small house mentioned by Krist.

Finally, the agents found a dirt road. It led into the

woods and ended near a place where people had thrown away parts of old cars and other junk. It was about 4 P.M., and, because of December's short days, the sky was darkening quickly. FBI men spread out through the area, searching through the dead leaves. One agent heard a noise underfoot. It sounded like several knocks. Pushing away the leaves, he saw fresh red Georgia dirt.

Agents started digging with their bare hands. No one had a shovel. They called to Barbara. They ran to the nearby junk piles and got tin cans and other objects to work with. At last, they saw ventilation tubes, then a large box that was screwed shut. Finally, they pried the box open. There, smiling up at them, was Barbara Mackle.

The agents gently helped her out of the box. Many of them had tears in their eyes. Barbara was the kind of person who thought of the feelings of others first, and even now she asked how her family was doing. Then she told the agents, "You are the handsomest men I've ever seen."[2] This made everyone smile. When J. Edgar Hoover himself phoned the Mackles to tell them that Barbara had been rescued and was fine, there was a lot of crying and smiling in Miami as well as in Atlanta. Barbara's father immediately left for Georgia to take her home.

For more than eighty hours, Barbara Mackle had been a captive underground. The box she had been sealed in was made of plywood and fiberglass. As Krist had said, an air system operated by a battery kept her from suffocating. Food, water, and other supplies had been put into the box for her. A list of directions on how to use the different items was also there. The tiny light, Barbara later said, had gone out a few hours after she was buried.

Alone and in the dark, she had kept her wits about her. Even though she was always cold and damp, she hadn't gotten sicker with the flu she'd had when Krist put her underground. Luck, hard work, and the cooperation of many people led to her rescue. But she had been extremely brave.

Now that Barbara had been rescued, the FBI could

concentrate on catching the kidnappers. Agents picked up Krist's trail quickly, but he used his head start to get across the entire state of Florida. As it turned out, Krist and Ruth Eisemann Schier were separated after the first ransom drop failed. The FBI would later learn what happened to her. For the time being, they went after Krist.

The hunt began in West Palm Beach, Florida, where, on Friday, December 20, Krist bought a boat for $2,300 and paid for it in $20 bills from the ransom. The man who sold him the boat became suspicious and called the FBI. Krist went north in the speedboat to Saint Lucie Inlet. From there, a canal forms a link between the Atlantic Ocean and the Gulf of Mexico. By using this route, Krist could cut west across Florida. But there were serious disadvantages to his choice.

Along the waterway, locks changed water levels so boats could pass in and out of Lake Okeechobee and, eventually, into the waters of the Gulf of Mexico. At each lock, every boat operator had to fill out a form. In addition, no one could go through a lock after 10:00 P.M. Because Krist had to follow these rules, he was delayed.

Even though the FBI caught on to what he was doing, Krist still managed to get all the way past Fort Myers and into the Gulf of Mexico before he was spotted. The FBI followed him by air, holding their fire so they could capture him alive. When one helicopter started hovering fifteen feet

Above: *this is a view of the gravelike hole in which Ms. Mackle was buried alive.* Below: *the coffinlike box in which Barbara Mackle was buried. Here it is being carried into the courthouse during the kidnapper's trial.*

above the water, Krist beached his boat on Hog Island. He ran into the island's thick mangrove swamp.

FBI men jumped from the helicopter into the water and started into the swamp. The mud stuck to their business suits. One agent reached Krist's abandoned boat. Most of the ransom money was in it. Krist had spent some and carried about $20,000 onto the island.

Local law officials as well as FBI men poured onto the island. Eventually, three hundred men joined in the search. Bloodhounds sniffed and men tripped in the sticky mud. Krist managed to stay hidden. Darkness came, and the main search in the tangled jungle came to a halt. The pursuers were certain they'd find Krist with the dawn.

Two men from the Charlotte County sheriff's office continued to patrol a section of the island. They heard something moving. Slowly, they waded into the water and stalked the sound. When they got close, their flashlight picked out Krist huddled in some mangrove roots. He surrendered without a fight.

It was just after midnight on Sunday, December 22. Krist had managed to elude his chasers on Hog Island for almost twelve hours. Exhausted, he was brought to the mainland and taken to a hospital. There, under strict guard, he was charged with the kidnapping.

Krist had been on the FBI's "Ten Most Wanted Fugitives" list. History was made when the FBI added Ruth Eisemann Schier's name. She was the first woman to be listed since the FBI began the tradition in 1950.

Eisemann Schier was more successful than Krist in eluding the law. For more than two months after the kidnapping, the FBI couldn't locate her. Agents checked with her family in Honduras, but she hadn't returned to her native country. If she hadn't been fingerprinted when she applied for a job, she might have remained free for a long time.

In February 1969, under a false name, Eisemann Schier applied for a position in a hospital in Norman, Oklahoma.

*Gary Steven Krist (right),
one of the kidnappers*

*Ruth Eisemann Schier (center),
the other kidnapper*

As a routine part of the job application process, she was fingerprinted. The fingerprints of applicants were then sent to the Oklahoma State Bureau of Investigation for checking against their records. On March 5, that bureau identified fingerprints from Norman as being the same as those of the only woman on the "Ten Most Wanted" list. Eisemann Schier was then arrested.

She had taken a bus out of Miami after leaving Krist at the first ransom drop. She'd worked briefly in Texas and then gone to Oklahoma. In Norman, she got a job as a waitress. Since Norman was where the University of Oklahoma was located and she looked like a student, Eisemann Schier managed not to be recognized.

Because the kidnappers hadn't taken Barbara Mackle across the Georgia state line, they couldn't be prosecuted under the so-called Lindbergh Law. This law had been passed following the 1932 kidnapping of the infant son of Charles Lindbergh, the famous aviator.

A few months before Krist and Eisemann Schier were captured, a portion of the Lindbergh Law had been changed. Because of this change, the death penalty was no longer a possibility for persons charged under this federal law. Under state laws in Georgia, however, ransom kidnappers could still receive the death penalty. Therefore, when Krist went on trial in Georgia for kidnapping for ransom, he faced a possible death sentence if found guilty. In a separate trial, Eisemann Schier pleaded guilty to the lesser crime of kidnapping.

On May 26, 1969, a jury found Krist guilty, but made a "recommendation of mercy."[3] Instead of the death penalty, he received a life sentence. In her trial, Eisemann Schier received a seven-year jail term.

Barbara Mackle and her father leaving the Decatur, Georgia, courthouse during Krist's trial

These trials were not the end of the story, however. Barbara Mackle wrote a book (with Gene Miller, a reporter) describing the kidnapping. Gary Steven Krist wrote a book about his life. In 1979, Krist was set free on the condition that he return to Alaska, where he was to help in his family's fishing business. The terms of Krist's parole prohibited him from returning to Georgia or from moving out of Alaska without permission of the Georgia parole board.

At the time, the *Atlanta Journal and Constitution* reported that the judge who had presided at Krist's trial, FBI agents, several attorneys, and others connected with the case believed it was a mistake to let Krist out of jail. On December 7, 1985, the same newspaper reported that Krist had falsely told his parole board he'd been accepted by a medical school in Mexico. The article went on to note that Krist had graduated from a Washington state college in 1984.

Ruth Eisemann Schier was also freed. In 1972, after three years in jail, she was granted a reprieve and deported to Honduras. She could not return to America for fifty years. According to the *Miami Herald*, she married and had children after inheriting a large sum of money when her mother died.

Barbara Mackle wanted nothing more than to forget about the kidnapping. After graduating from Emory University, she married Stewart Woodward, the same friend who had come to help her mother in the Georgia motel.

But, during the last days of December 1968, all of these events—from the kidnappers' trials to Barbara Mackle's marriage—were still in the future. After her rescue from the buried box, Barbara went home for a joyous reunion with her family.

Four days later, it was Christmas Eve. Three American astronauts were orbiting the moon—the first humans ever to do so. At 9:30 that night, they beamed a half-hour television show back to earth. The moon seemed lonely and barren in a black sky. Out of Apollo 8's window, the astronauts could see a green-and-blue vision. "A grand oasis in the big vastness of space," one astronaut called the earth.

In a special message at the end of their television show, the astronauts took turns reading from the Bible. Then the commander of the mission, Colonel Frank Borman, said, "Good-bye, good night. Merry Christmas. God bless all of you, all of you on the good earth." One family in Miami, Florida, knew exactly what he meant.

4 THE MAD BOMBER

New Year's Eve in New York City is a busy time for police. Celebrations bring people to restaurants, nightclubs, and private parties. On this chilly night, several hundred thousand people stand in Times Square to cheer and sing as midnight approaches. But the last few hours of 1956 give the police no reason to celebrate. Someone has been hiding bombs all over the city. Can they find the next one before it explodes?

The unknown bomber has been leaving bombs for sixteen years. Thirty-two have been planted in telephone booths, theaters, railroad stations, and other public places. The first few bombs are "duds"—they don't explode. In later years, however, some will go off. Others are located and taken apart by police before they can cause damage. All these bombs are made in a similar way by using gunpowder, a pipe, watch parts, and batteries.

During the 1956 holiday season, the bomber takes action again. The night before Christmas, an employee of the main branch of the New York Public Library enters a telephone booth. By accident, he drops a coin on the floor.

When he bends down to pick it up, he notices a homemade pipe bomb that he recognizes from pictures of similar bombs he's seen in newspapers. It's attached to the underside of the shelf below the phone.

The employee throws the explosive out of a window into a clump of ivy in a park behind the library. The police clear the park of people. For an hour and a half, all cars and pedestrians are kept away from 42nd Street between Fifth and Sixth Avenues while bomb squad detectives remove the device. No one is injured, but the police are still worried. They aren't any closer to identifying the person the press calls the "Mad Bomber."

The first of the bomber's devices was placed on a windowsill at the Consolidated Edison building at West 64th Street in New York City on November 18, 1940. (Consolidated Edison is a utility company supplying electricity to the city. New Yorkers call it by its nickname, "Con Ed.") Ten months later, a second bomb was picked up on a New York street about four blocks from another Consolidated Edison building. Neither bomb exploded. From the way the bombs were constructed, police believed that a man who had gone through military training was making them. Hand-printed notes to Consolidated Edison said that the bombs were being left because the bomber felt that the utility company had injured him in the past.

Next came a surprise. The bomber suddenly stopped leaving bombs. In December 1941, when the United States entered World War II, the bomber wrote another note explaining why he'd stopped. He told police that to show his support for his country, he would not place any more bombs for the rest of the war. The bomber signed the note with the initials "F.P." Police were only too glad to let the bomber's case rest. They filed away his notes and hoped they'd never hear from him again.

In 1951, however, the bomber again began leaving what he called his "units," and this time they were more dangerous. They were built so that they were much more likely to go off.

New York Police bomb squad detectives
carry a bomb that was planted by the "Mad
Bomber" in the New York Public Library.
They are at a disposal site in Queens,
New York. The bomb is enclosed in a steel
mesh envelope and the officers wear body
and face armor to protect them against
the possibility of a premature blast.

In March of that year, the first bomb exploded in Grand Central Terminal—the big, busy railroad station in the middle of Manhattan. The next month, the city's newspapers reported that a bomb had gone off in an empty telephone booth in the New York Public Library. This would turn out to be one of the bomber's favorite places. These bombs were small; they didn't do much damage, and no one was injured.

In August and September 1951, the bomber left two more bombs in telephone booths: one in Grand Central Terminal and one in a Consolidated Edison building. Both of these exploded, but fortunately there were no injuries. The one left at Con Ed went off at 6:15 A.M. when only the night watchman was in the building. The company also received a mail bomb sent from White Plains, New York, a city about a forty-five-minute drive from Manhattan. This bomb didn't go off.

Then, on October 22, 1951, the *New York Herald Tribune* received a special delivery letter printed in block letters. It said, "Bombs will continue until the Consolidated Edison Company is brought to justice for their dastardly acts against me. I have exhausted all other means." The note went on to say that bombs had been planted in a restroom of the Paramount Theater and in Pennsylvania Railroad Station on the west side of Manhattan.

When the police bomb squad arrived at the Paramount, they did find a four-inch-long bomb about a half inch in diameter. It contained a .25-caliber bullet, a small amount of smokeless powder, and a trigger mechanism that could set off the bomb if someone unknowingly disturbed it. Only a few of the people watching the midnight show were aware of the police search.

Police said that the Paramount Theater bomb couldn't have caused serious damage, but that flying fragments might have injured persons nearby if it had exploded. So far, no one had been injured in any of the bomber's blasts, but the letter the *Herald Tribune* had received also contained a more threatening sentence. The bomber wrote, "If I don't get justice, I will continue, but with bigger bombs."

The police didn't just look around New York City for explosives left by the Mad Bomber. They talked with mental health professionals, examined the bomber's handwriting, checked fingerprints, and worked with explosive engineers. But each clue proved to be a dead end.

Since the bomber kept mentioning Consolidated Edison, employee records for the company were examined. In November 1951, a former Con Ed worker was charged with sending the company a letter and a fake bomb filled with sugar. This man, however, was released and the charge against him dropped for lack of evidence. It later turned out that he was not the Mad Bomber.

With the seven bombs left in 1951, the bomber changed his method from the early 1940s. He no longer limited his bombings to Consolidated Edison buildings; he expanded his range. In the following six years, he continued to leave explosives in theaters, subway stations, a department store, and a bus station, as well as in railway terminals and telephone booths.

The first time a person was injured in one of the bomber's blasts was on December 8, 1952, when one of his so-called units exploded in the Lexington Theater at 50th Street and Lexington Avenue. In March 1954, a bomb went off in a men's restroom in Grand Central Terminal. Two people were hurt. Then in a blast that received a lot of publicity, a bomb exploded at famous Radio City Music Hall, injuring four people.

The fall of 1955 added a bombing in a theater, injuring one. In 1956, a men's restroom attendant was injured by an explosion in Pennsylvania Station, and six people were hurt when a bomb went off in the Brooklyn Paramount Theater. In the same year, a guard at the RCA building in Manhattan found a bomb but thought it was only a length of pipe. Wanting to use it in a plumbing project, he took it home, where it went off harmlessly when no one was nearby.

Although the bomber certainly was dangerous, he seemed to be purposely keeping his units small, and the injuries, with one exception, were minor. The attendant in the men's restroom in Pennsylvania Station had to spend two months in a hospital and, a year later, was still unable to return to work.

The bomber also often made phone calls warning police that a bomb had been placed. These calls cut down on the number of injuries. The newspapers called him the "*Mad Bomber*," and it was plain to see that the man did need help from mental health experts. But maybe this nickname, police reasoned, had a second meaning. Why was this man so angry? If they could figure out the answer, maybe they'd have the key to his identity.

In the meantime, New Yorkers were changing their habits because of the bombings. Attendance at theaters dropped off. People avoided public telephone booths, restrooms, and other places where bombs had been found.

Police figured out that about one-third of the Mad Bomber's explosives were placed on days or nights that fell within three days of a full moon. Since ancient times, people had noted that some criminals are more active near the time of a full moon. Reasons for this are still not understood. By the 1950s, criminals who took action at this time of the month had been given a name by crime investigators; they were called "mooners." Extra detectives were assigned to look for the Mad Bomber as the full moon shone, but with no results.

Police went to Dr. James Brussel for help. Dr. Brussel was a new kind of criminal detective. At the time, he was assistant commissioner of the New York State Department of Mental Hygiene. A psychiatrist, he was trained in the branch of medicine that deals with mental, emotional, or behavioral disorders. Dr. Brussel pioneered in using psychiatry to understand criminal behavior.

Gathering all the information they could, the police went to Dr. Brussel, hoping for insight. But instead of finding some overlooked clues, he gave them a complete

description of the man they hunted. He did it in such detail, too, that more than thirty years later what he said is remembered with amazement.

Dr. Brussel said the bomber was a bachelor between forty and fifty years old who spent a great deal of time thinking about himself. Such a man, the psychiatrist noted, would be very clean and neat and neither fat nor thin but of medium build. He probably lived alone or with female relatives, Dr. Brussel continued, and was religious and honest. The Mad Bomber would be cunning, have good mechanical skills, and have at least a high school education.

Dr. Brussel then put a finishing stroke to the word-picture he had created. "When you arrest the Mad Bomber," he predicted, "he'll be wearing a double-breasted suit, and it will be buttoned."[1]

Police, startled at the sharpness of Dr. Brussel's description, had it published on Christmas Day 1956 in the *New York Times*. Maybe, they thought, the portrait would remind someone of a neighbor or relative. But, as 1957 began, no one came forward with information.

The first day of the New Year saw New York City police frantically running down reports of bombs. By January 2, police estimated they had received 130 false bomb reports since Christmas Eve when the bomb had been discovered in the New York Public Library. In one day alone, thirty crank calls were received. In addition, false alarms were reported in Dallas, Texas; Kansas City, Missouri; Wichita, Kansas; Philadelphia, Pennsylvania; and other cit-

A New York City fireman holds pieces of a homemade bomb that exploded in Pennsylvania Station at the height of rush hour in January 1955.

ies. Publicity about the Mad Bomber was stirring things up across America.

Checking on these false alarms was time-consuming and costly, and blocked the search for the real bomber. People convicted of making false bomb calls were dealt with strictly by the justice system. A New Jersey man was sentenced to thirty days in jail. In Brooklyn, two high school girls paid $2,500 in bail and had to appear in court.

All the commotion did have a funny side. What was feared to be a bomb in a theater turned out to be a box of cookies. At the Museum of Natural History, a bomb scare turned up a harmless length of metal pipe in a fourth-floor dinosaur room.

Seven of the thirteen letters written by the bomber to newspapers, Consolidated Edison, and police were mailed from White Plains, New York. Police decided to use handwriting analysis to narrow their search. Believing that the bomber lived in Westchester County, where White Plains is located, Deputy Inspector Frederick Lussen, in charge of the case, made a request. He asked to look at the forms that people in Westchester fill out when they apply for automobile licenses. Several license forms were found on which the handwriting looked like that of the Mad Bomber, but these people proved innocent.

For the same reason, on Inspector Lussen's orders, county employees examined forms filled out by people who might serve on a jury. Hundreds of thousands of documents were checked, including court records and papers at the county clerk's office.

The way the bomber formed some of the letters of the alphabet gave experts hope that they could match the handwriting on a document with his. The bomber's printed letter "G," for instance, had a line drawn across the top in addition to the regular line across the middle of the letter. The bomber also formed the letter "H" in an unusual way, and his letter "R" had a little loop in the center.

On January 9, 1957, sixteen more detectives were added

to those already looking for the bomber. The force now had fifty detectives out of the Manhattan West headquarters in the West 54th Street station. "No break in the case is expected immediately," a spokesperson said.[2]

Meanwhile, false bomb threats, although fewer in number than over the New Year's holiday, were still coming in. After a phone tip was received, a plane leaving Miami, Florida, for New York City was delayed while it was searched. Nothing was found.

On January 10, a new development in the case occurred when the *New York Journal-American* made public a letter it had received from the bomber. The letter was in answer to an appeal published in that newspaper, offering to let the bomber use the pages of the paper to tell his story. For the first time, the bomber evidently believed a few people were interested in listening to him.

In the letter to the *Journal-American*, the bomber said, "Before I am finished, the Consolidated Edison Company will wish that they had brought to me in their teeth what they cheated me out of." According to this sentence and parts of his other letters, what the bomber wanted was becoming clearer. His main complaint was that he believed the company owed him money for health problems having to do with an injury he'd received as a Con Ed worker. Extra effort was now put into an ongoing day-and-night search of company records dating back twenty years.

On January 15, 1957, another letter arrived at the *Journal-American*. In this one, the bomber said, "I did not get a single penny for a lifetime of misery and suffering." He also said that because of his complaints against Con Ed, he did not consider himself "guilty." To encourage the public to help in the search for this dangerous man, a police association added $1,000 to reward money already offered for information leading to the arrest and conviction of the Mad Bomber. This brought the total reward offered to $26,000.

It was just before five o'clock in the afternoon when Alice Kelly, an office worker at Consolidated Edison for twenty-five years, found a particular file of papers. Kelly was one of the people going through old records to see if any claims made by Con Ed employees would give a clue to the bomber's identity. What caught her eye in the file were some of the same words the bomber had used in his *Journal-American* letters. After a closer look, she told her boss, "I think I have it."[3]

The file she had found told the history of a claim by a George Metesky of Waterbury, Connecticut. Metesky had asked for payment by Consolidated Edison for ill health he believed resulted from an injury suffered in 1931. Under the law, such a claim had to be made within a year. Since Metesky waited more than three years to file, his request was not considered by the company. Records showed that Metesky had received sick pay for half a year and an amount of money from his own insurance company.

Close to midnight on January 21, 1957, four New York detectives arrived at Metesky's house in a run-down section of Waterbury. With them was a captain in the Waterbury police force and three of his detectives. They brought a search warrant. Some of the men went around the back of the dark house, stepping through the weeds in the overgrown yard. The New York men went up on the porch and knocked on the door. Lights came on, and a man in pajamas opened the door a crack. "What's this all about?" he asked. Told of the search warrant, he stood quietly to one side and let the men in. After a few more remarks, he said, "I know why you fellows are here. You think I'm the Mad Bomber."[4]

While detectives questioned Metesky, his two sisters stood in the background. Gray-haired women who worked in two factories in Waterbury, they had no idea their brother had been planting bombs. For many years, they had been supporting him.

Told to put on street clothes, Metesky dressed in exactly the kind of double-breasted suit psychiatrist Brussel had predicted he'd wear. That wasn't all Dr. Brussel was

Accused "Mad Bomber" George Metesky being
booked in Waterbury, Connecticut, after
reportedly confessing that he was the bomber.

right about. Metesky was of medium build and kept himself clean and neat. His gold-rimmed glasses were always in place and his shoes shined. Metesky lived with female relatives, was good at mechanical jobs, attended church most Sundays, and had gone to high school for two years. Dr. Brussel had been close to or exactly on target about all these facts.

Taken to Waterbury police headquarters, Metesky willingly confessed to being the Mad Bomber. He told police that in 1931, there had been a strong gush of gas from a boiler at the New York Consolidated Edison building where he worked. The fumes choked him. Ever since then, he'd believed that the accident had caused him to have health problems. He'd had two diseases affecting his lungs—pneumonia first, then tuberculosis. In an attempt to cure his ills, he'd spent three years living in Arizona. But nothing worked. He returned to Connecticut but couldn't hold down a job.

When his attempts to get money from Con Ed failed, he said that he became more and more bitter. Nine years after the accident, he decided to start planting bombs to draw attention to his claim against the company. The bombs were a cry for help.

Years went by. Finally, when the *Journal-American* offered to listen to what he had to say, he welcomed the chance. Eventually, the information he gave to the newspaper led to his arrest. Why had he signed his letters "F.P."? detectives asked. The initials, he replied, stood for "fair play." Parts for making the type of explosive the Mad Bomber was known for were found at Metesky's home. The garage in back of his house had been his bomb workshop.

After being taken from Connecticut to New York, Metesky was put in Bellevue Hospital for examination by mental health experts. There he was held under guard. By January 25, James Murray was acting as Metesky's attorney.

In the weeks following his arrest, Metesky told police more about his life. He said he was one of four children of a Lithuanian immigrant father. His father had saved part of his salary from a job as a night watchman and bought a

These were some of the materials used to make bombs, found in Metesky's garage near his house in Waterbury. Materials included gunpowder, pipes, springs, plugs, batteries, rubber bands, watches, and red socks used to enclose the bombs.

house in Waterbury. Metesky was the youngest in his family and, after his mother had died, his sisters took over the running of the household. They worked all day in Waterbury factories and never married. His brother, the only one to leave home, had a wife and children in another city.

When Metesky was caught in the gush of gas while working at Consolidated Edison, his sisters nursed him before they left for work and when they returned at night. They knew he was bitter toward the company, but he never told them what he was planning.

After placing his first bombs at or near Con Ed buildings, Metesky decided he wasn't getting enough publicity. So he began to put them in public places. At the time of his arrest, he was making a bomb larger than he'd ever made before.

Metesky would drive from Connecticut to New York, he told police, while his sisters were at work. At first, he didn't put any powder in the bombs until he reached the city. He'd sit in his car, he said, load the powder, and then take the subway to where he wanted to leave the explosive.

Once he was nearly caught. He said that while sitting in his car in 1952 about to load the powder, a motorcycle policeman pulled alongside. But the policeman was just checking on other parked cars on the block. After that, Metesky loaded the bombs at home. To keep them from exploding, he cushioned them with rags and put them in one of his old socks.

Police asked Metesky why he'd stopped planting bombs during World War II. He answered that because he'd once been in the armed forces, he felt that, for the war years, he should put the good of his country ahead of his personal complaints.

During the months following his arrest, judges and doctors discussed and sometimes argued about what action they should take concerning Metesky. No one came forward for the $26,000 reward. Alice Kelly, the Con Ed employee who had found Metesky's file, said she wouldn't claim the money. A newspaper article reported that "the money might never be paid."[5]

While Metesky continued to be examined at Bellevue, a group appointed by the court listened to thirty-five witnesses about the bombings. Some of the witnesses were people injured by Metesky's bombs. Charges were then brought against Metesky. These included attempted murder, damaging buildings by using explosives, endangering lives, and carrying a dangerous weapon. Charges were limited to five years before Metesky's arrest as, by law, any other of his acts were too far in the past for charges to be brought against him.

In March 1957, Metesky was ordered to go on trial. Judge John Mullen gave the order in spite of objections raised by Metesky's lawyers and after hearing a report on

Metesky's mental health. The report was given by a psychiatrist at Bellevue, who said that although Metesky knew what he was doing when he placed his bombs, he did not know that his acts were against the best interest of society.[6]

At the end of March, Metesky's lawyer, James Murray, had an especially strong argument with Judge Mullen about legal steps taken in the case. At the center of their argument was a report from Bellevue that said Metesky was not able to understand the charges brought against him and thus should not be brought to trial. Judge Mullen insisted that Metesky should be tried for his bombings.

Metesky was in court from time to time during these days. Reporters said he appeared quiet and calm and was able to answer questions. Plans were made to choose a jury, but then Metesky, who had been unhealthy for years, became very ill.

His tuberculosis had been getting worse for some time. Now he had to be taken from Bellevue to another hospital for treatment. Since he couldn't go to court, the members of the court came twice to his hospital room. The first time, as Metesky lay in bed, a Bellevue psychiatrist said he was insane and couldn't be cured. The second time he was so ill he coughed and choked and had to be given oxygen. It was thought he had only a few months to live.

Finally, on April 18, Metesky was ordered to a hospital for the criminally insane. He was not brought to trial, and a connection was never proved between the gust of gas at Con Ed and his later ill health.

Awards were given to police officers who had worked on his case and to reporters who had written about it. The New York State Workmen's Compensation Board refused to consider an appeal made by Metesky for money he still felt he should have received for the Con Ed accident.

On September 10, 1957, an old unexploded bomb was found in a New York theater. Its design showed that it was Metesky's work. With the finding of this bomb, police said they were officially closing the Mad Bomber case.

But Metesky fooled everyone again. By November 1958, doctors reported that his health was improving. By 1972, he not only was still alive, but he was trying to have himself declared able to stand trial.

Then, in 1973, the U.S. Supreme Court ruled that persons accused of criminal acts could not be sent to a New York State mental hospital unless a jury had said they were dangerous. This ruling directly affected Metesky and several hundred other patients.

Late in 1973, Metesky appeared before a judge to hear the charges against him dismissed. Doctors determined he was now harmless and could live in Waterbury with his one surviving sister. By now Metesky was seventy years old and had spent seventeen years in state institutions. When he was released on December 13, he said he would never use violence again.

Metesky went home. He was alert and in good health. In fact, a few years later, he gave some advice to police. In a 1975 interview with a reporter, he suggested a way to catch the person who had just bombed New York's La Guardia Airport. Assuming there was one male bomber, Metesky said, "If you can get him to communicate, to give the reasons . . . you can take it from there."[7] Metesky must have been remembering his own series of letters to the *Journal-American* over the winter of 1956–57 when he'd finally found some people who would listen to his story.

In an unexpected way, the Metesky case has had an effect on the way today's crimes are solved. The FBI now has a National Center for the Analysis of Violent Crime. This center has a team of what is called criminal personality profilers—experts who receive the facts of a crime from local police. Given these facts, the team is able to send back to law officers a detailed description of the person or persons they should seek.

Each criminal mind has its own mysteries. In the more than thirty years since police had to look for the Mad Bomber, some of these mysteries have begun to be understood.

THE FALL RIVER
5 MURDERS

Lizzie Borden took an ax
And gave her mother forty whacks;
When she saw what she had done,
She gave her father forty-one![1]

A clock ticks in a narrow little house in Fall River, Massachusetts, on an August morning in 1892. Sweating workers in the city's mills and factories struggle through the worst heat wave to hit New England in years. The Bordens, the family living in the house, ordinarily might be thinking about their noontime meal. Two family members, however, will never enjoy another bite. During the morning, someone has brutally murdered Andrew and Abby Borden, husband and wife. Who committed the crimes?

Andrew Borden's ancestors were among the first settlers of Fall River. They wisely bought a great deal of land and became wealthy as Fall River prospered. By the late 1800s, the city was an important textile manufacturing center. Railroads and steamships connected it with Boston and New York.

Although all Bordens were considered leading citizens, some were better off than others. As a young man, Andrew Borden had to work hard as an undertaker. He used money he had inherited and the profits from his undertaking business to invest in farmland and buildings he could rent. Before too long, the only things left over from his days as an undertaker were the dark suits he continued to wear.

Money was important to Andrew Borden. By the time he was seventy, he had $500,000, a large sum in those days. He owned a bank, mills, houses, and farms. But he was regarded around Fall River as a man who watched every cent. Sometimes he could be seen carrying a basket of eggs from one of his farms to sell in the marketplace. "Generous" and "openhearted" weren't words used to describe him.

Andrew married Sarah Morse. They had two daughters, Emma and Alice. Alice died young. When Sarah learned she would have a third child, Andrew must have hoped for a boy. Another daughter was born in 1860. Andrew gave her his name for a middle name: Lizzie Andrew Borden.

Sarah died when Emma was twelve and Lizzie was two. Several years later, Andrew married thirty-year-old Abby Durfee Gray. Abby had not been married before. She was known as a pleasant, mild-mannered woman.

Even though the family had plenty of money and could have lived in the fashionable part of the city known as "The Hill," Andrew bought a small house in a neighborhood near the business district. Since other Borden relatives *did* live on The Hill, Andrew's family seemed by contrast to be poor relations. By 1892, Emma was forty-one and Lizzie, thirty-two. Both were unmarried and likely to remain so. They were completely dependent on their father for support.

On August 4, the day of the murders, the Borden family's maid, Bridget Sullivan, began her daily work. Her first job was to make breakfast for the household. Abby, Andrew, and Lizzie were at home. Emma was visiting a friend in the town of Fairhaven, about fifteen miles away.

A copy of an 1890 photo-
graph of Lizzie Borden

There was also a house guest, John Morse, Lizzie and Emma's uncle, who had stayed overnight with the Bordens.

Bridget wasn't feeling well that morning. She and Andrew and Abby had all been sick to their stomachs for the last two days. Lizzie hadn't been as sick but had mentioned feeling somewhat ill herself. A large roast had been part of several recent family meals. Meat and other foods often spoiled quickly during the summer months in those days before refrigeration.

In spite of her illness, Bridget made breakfast. Andrew, Abby, and Uncle John ate early. Lizzie didn't come down from her upstairs bedroom until just before 9 A.M. By that time, breakfast was over, and Uncle John had left for the day. Lizzie had a cup of coffee, while Andrew and Abby went about their regular morning routine.

The house had an old-fashioned floor plan. Originally a two-family home with an apartment on each floor, it had been changed only a little when the Bordens moved in. The apartment layout meant that there were no hallways on either of the two main levels. Thus it was necessary to walk through one or more rooms to reach the back of the house from the front. This fact was to be important in the murder investigation.

Another fact that was later to prove important was the Bordens' habit of locking doors. The two outside doors to the house each had locks. Every lock was used when the family went in and out. In addition, the inside bedroom doors also had been locked in recent years. A member of the family would unlock a bedroom door, enter the room, and then lock the door again. This strange habit was a reflection of the lack of trust in the household.

Distrust among the Bordens had come out into the open about five years earlier. Andrew had given Abby a house for the use of her sister. This had made Emma and Lizzie jealous, so Andrew then gave them a house they could own and rent to someone. Andrew had also sent Lizzie on a European trip. But the stage was set for bad feelings. Lizzie and Emma started eating their meals separately from their stepmother and father. In remarks to others, Lizzie, in particular, made it clear that she didn't like Abby.

The morning routine went on as usual on the day of the murders. Andrew went upstairs, got dressed, and left for the business section of the city just as he did every morning. Bridget, still feeling sick, went into the yard and vomited, but she remembered to lock the rear screen door when she returned. Abby, Lizzie, and Bridget were now alone in the house.

Abby made up the bed in the upstairs guest room where Uncle John had slept the night before and then went downstairs into the dining room to dust. She told Bridget to wash the first-floor windows and then mentioned that she was going back to the guest room to put fresh pillowcases on the pillows on Uncle John's bed. Bridget saw Abby go upstairs at about 9:30 A.M. She never came back down.

No one was ever able to say where Lizzie was between 9:00 and 9:30 that morning. Bridget later said Lizzie came to the rear screen door that led to the yard sometime during this half hour and gave her confusing instructions about locking or unlocking the door. As a result of this conversation, the door was left unlocked while Bridget washed the outside of the windows. She got water from the barn at the back of the house. During this same time, Bridget had a short talk with the next-door neighbor's maid. All this time, she saw no one inside the downstairs rooms of the house (she could look in as she washed the windows), or in the yard, or at the screen door. She then went back into the house and began washing the insides of the windows.

It was later proved by medical authorities that between 9:00 and 9:30 A.M., Abby Borden was killed in the upstairs guest bedroom. She was murdered by nineteen blows of an ax to her head and back. One blow went five inches into her skull. She fell to the floor between a bureau and the bed.

At 10:40 A.M., Mrs. Kelly, the next-door neighbor

whose maid had talked with Bridget, left her house for a dentist appointment. As she walked past the Borden house, she saw Andrew returning home. He was struggling to unlock his front door. Inside the house, Bridget heard Andrew using his keys and went to the door to help. While she struggled with the bolt on the inside of the door, she muttered something under her breath and heard Lizzie laugh somewhere behind her.

Bridget later said that Lizzie came downstairs in about five minutes and asked her father if he had any mail for her. Bridget also heard Lizzie tell Andrew that Abby had received a note and had gone out to help a sick friend.

As he often did near the middle of the day, Andrew decided to take a nap. Perhaps he still hadn't fully recovered from his upset stomach. He lay down on a couch in the downstairs sitting room. Bridget was finishing the windows in the dining room. Lizzie joined her there and ironed a few handkerchiefs.

The two women had a brief conversation. Lizzie encouraged Bridget to go to a sale at a downtown store. Bridget said she was interested but felt tired and still a little sick. With her job done, Bridget went upstairs to her third-floor attic bedroom to lie down for a rest.

Between 11:00 and 11:15 A.M., someone killed Andrew with eleven blows of an ax. He slipped from sleep to death while lying on the sitting room couch. Bridget heard nothing until Lizzie yelled to her, "Come down quick! Father's dead. Somebody came in and killed him!"[2]

Bridget ran downstairs to find Lizzie standing near the rear screen door. As Bridget started to go to where Andrew lay, Lizzie told her, "Don't go in there. Go over and get the doctor. Run!"[3] Bridget went to get the Bordens' physician, Dr. Bowen, who lived across the street. The doctor was out. Bridget ran back to Lizzie. She then asked Lizzie the question that would be repeated over and over in the days and months to come: "Where were you when this happened?" Lizzie answered, "I was in the yard and heard a groan, and came in and the screen door was wide open."[4] But she would vary this answer in the future.

Lizzie sent Bridget to find Alice Russell, a friend of Lizzie's and Emma's. In the meantime, Mrs. Churchill, the Borden's neighbor on the other side of the Kellys, noticed Lizzie standing by the rear door. The houses on the block were so close together that Mrs. Churchill could call across to ask if something was the matter. Told of Andrew's death, she hurried over to take charge. She had someone go to a nearby phone and call the police (the Borden home had no phone). Mrs. Churchill also asked Lizzie where she had been when Andrew was killed. This time Lizzie said she'd been in the barn behind the house.

When Dr. Bowen arrived at the Borden home, he examined Andrew's body. It was now 11:30 A.M., and Dr. Bowen believed that Andrew had been dead for no more than twenty minutes. Mrs. Churchill, Alice Russell, and Bridget clustered around Lizzie to comfort her. Dr. Bowen left briefly to send a telegram telling Emma to return home.

Lizzie seemed to be very much in control of herself. Bridget, however, was worried about Abby and said she wished she knew where to find her. Once Bridget mentioned her concern, Lizzie spoke up. She said she was almost sure she had heard her stepmother come in and go upstairs. Why didn't Bridget check? Lizzie suggested. Bridget refused to go upstairs alone, so Mrs. Churchill went with her. They found Abby dead, lying on the far side of the guest bedroom.

Dr. Bowen had returned to the Bordens after sending the telegram. He found Abby's body face down. Her skull had been battered, but the blood was congealed. Abby obviously had died before her husband. At this point, several police officers arrived. Then Uncle John returned from visiting relatives. These people later swore that John had been with them at the time of the killings. The peaceful home he had left in the morning was now a scene of murder and confusion.

THIRD ST.

SECOND

NORTH

VIEW OF THE VICINITY OF THE MURDERS.

I. Borden house.
II. Borden barn.
III. The well.
IV. Fence with barbed wire on top.
V. Side entrance.
VI. Churchill residence.

VII. Dr. Bowen's house.
VIII. Dr. Chagnon's house.
IX. Kelley house.
X. Yard from which officers watched the Borde
XI. Kelley's barn.
XII. Pear orchard.

*The neighborhood where
the murders took place*

Police questioned all the members of the household that day. By evening, all of Fall River had heard the horrifying news. Crowds began to gather in the street in front of the house. The next day, the story was on the front pages of newspapers. Because Andrew had been an important citizen in Fall River society, police felt they had to move carefully. This wasn't just any family—it was the Bordens.

By Saturday, when the double funeral was held, the police knew they had little choice but to arrest Lizzie. The city was in an uproar; people feared the ax murderer. Lizzie seemed to be the only person to have been in the right place at the right time. After the funeral, the mayor of Fall River, in answer to Lizzie's questions, told her that she was suspected of the crimes. This turned out to be a serious mistake on the mayor's part.

Lizzie was not arrested right away. Beginning on August 9, an inquest was held concerning the murders. The inquest took place in private before Judge Blaisdell, who had known Lizzie since she was a child.

Witnesses appeared and gave testimony, with Lizzie and Bridget undergoing the longest questioning. Bridget, an Irish immigrant, was a likely suspect, because servants were considered lower-class and ignorant in those days. What was more, servants had been known at times to take violent action against their employers. Yet no one was ever able to prove that Bridget had been on anything but good terms with the Bordens.

Just before as well as during the inquest, interesting new facts came to light—about the murder weapons, for instance. Policemen had found an ax head in a box of dusty tools in the Borden basement. It had been freshly rubbed in stove ashes, perhaps to make it look as though it had been in the box for a long time. Most important, its wooden handle—from which blood would have been hard to remove—had been broken off.

Another startling twist was the evidence given by two pharmacists from a Fall River drugstore. They testified that

Lizzie Borden as she appeared
when identified by the drug clerk

on the afternoon before the murders, Lizzie had come into their store asking for prussic acid, a poison. They said that she told them she wanted it to clean a fur cape. It was against the law to sell this poison without a prescription, so the pharmacists had refused Lizzie's request. When questioned, Lizzie said the pharmacists' story was untrue. She even said she didn't know where the drugstore was located. This was hard to believe, for the store was close to the house she had lived in for years.

The pharmacists' story was of particular interest because it turned out that Abby Borden had visited Dr. Bowen the day before she died and told him she thought she was being poisoned. The doctor had believed that Abby's upset stomach was the result of bad food, not poisoning, and had sent her back home. But the fact that Abby had told him about possible poisoning reveals how uneasy she must have been.

The district attorney, Hosea Knowlton, questioned Lizzie long and hard at the inquest. She kept changing her story. She would put herself at a certain place at a certain time on the fateful morning, and then she would suddenly remember that that wasn't right, she'd really been somewhere else. One time she was eating pears in the yard, another time she was in the loft of the barn looking for lead weights for a fishing rod. Since the heat on August 4 had been so intense, it was hard to believe that anyone would have willingly stayed in the loft for long. Yet Lizzie said she'd been there twenty minutes to a half hour. In addition, a police officer had examined the loft right after the crimes and had not noticed any footprints or other disturbance of the dust on the floor.

In 1892, modern detective techniques were just being developed. Fingerprinting as a means of criminal investigation would not be used in the United States until 1903. All that could be proved at the time, according to the best analysis available, was that the contents of the Bordens' stomachs contained nothing unusual.

Lizzie's own words at the inquest were the most damaging testimony given. Nevertheless, many people wanted to believe she was innocent. It was unthinkable that a dutiful daughter would kill her parents on a sunny summer morning. Well-bred American women were supposed to be frail and feminine, ideally suited to be wives and mothers. How could Lizzie have swung an ax so many times? It was hard to believe since Lizzie was active in several women's groups and in many church activities. She had even taught a Sunday school class.

In spite of public opinion in her favor, Judge Blaisdell ordered Lizzie's arrest at the end of the inquest. She went to jail in Taunton, Massachusetts, since no bail was allowed on a murder charge. But even jail wasn't too terrible a place for a Borden. Lizzie had her meals sent over from the best hotel, and she spent a great deal of time in a comfortable room made available for her use.

After the inquest, several hearings were held. Lizzie, who had a lawyer representing her from the start, eventually was represented by three attorneys. During the first hearing, Judge Blaisdell, who was again in charge, had Lizzie's damaging testimony from the inquest read aloud. At the close of this hearing, the judge said it was "more probable than not" that Lizzie had committed the murder of her father.[5] She was not yet charged with her stepmother's murder. The judge's statement meant that Lizzie would now go before a grand jury. (Twelve or more members hear evidence about an alleged crime to determine if there is enough evidence to warrant a trial.)

The most surprising event of the grand jury hearing happened at the very end. After testifying, one witness made a most unusual request. Alice Russell, the friend who had come to the Borden house, asked to return to court with more information. What Alice had to say didn't help Lizzie's case.

Alice told the grand jury that three days after the murders, she had seen Lizzie burn a dress in the kitchen stove. Lizzie had told her the dress was soiled with brown paint. It was quickly noted that dried blood might easily be the same color. The day after Alice's testimony, December 2, 1892, Lizzie was charged with the murders of her father and stepmother.

Lizzie Borden's trial began on June 5, 1893, after she had been in jail for ten months. The inquest and hearings had attracted a lot of attention, but the scene of the trial in New Bedford, Massachusetts, was like a carnival. Business in that part of the state stopped. Reporters came from all over the East Coast, and every hotel room for miles around was taken. Fences had to be put up around the courthouse to control the crowds.

Lizzie had good lawyers. Her leading lawyer was George Robinson. Robinson had recently been governor of Mas-

*Lizzie Borden (far left) and her friends
in court: Emma Borden, Rev. Mr. Buck,
Mrs. C. J. Holmes, and Mr. C. J. Holmes*

sachusetts. Hosea Knowlton, who had questioned Lizzie at
the inquest, was the leading lawyer presenting the case
against her. Three judges would hear her case; two of them
had daughters about Lizzie's age. One of the judges, Justin
Dewey, had been appointed to the state supreme court by
George Robinson.

The jury was chosen. With all the newspaper coverage,
everyone had heard of the murders, and many people had
formed their opinions about Lizzie's guilt or innocence. All
the court asked in selecting the jury was that the members
judge the evidence fairly. The twelve men selected were
from nearby communities. They were a mixture of businessmen, mechanics, and farmers. Nearly all were fifty
years old or older. No women were on Lizzie's jury. (At
this time women were not allowed to serve on murder juries.)

On the advice of her lawyers, Lizzie came to her trial
dressed in black, a sign of mourning for her parents. Her
red hair was carefully arranged, and the style of her clothes
was very fashionable. Her striking eyes, often mentioned
by the press, were an unusual shade of gray.

During the course of the trial, Lizzie never had to
testify. She remained calm and dignified. Only once or

twice, at particularly dramatic moments in the courtroom, did a purple-red flush come over her face.

The trial gave Americans a lot to talk about. Everything seemed to work in Lizzie's favor. Her damaging testimony at the earlier inquest was kept out of the trial on the grounds that she had been under arrest. It was possible for her lawyers to make this claim because the mayor had told Lizzie she was suspected of the crimes. The defense also succeeded in keeping out of the trial the two pharmacists' story about Lizzie's attempt to buy poison. The fact that these statements couldn't be used was a great handicap to the prosecution.

There was plenty of testimony in Lizzie's favor. The defense noted that there had been a robbery in the Borden house not too long before. Perhaps, Lizzie's lawyers observed, the same robbers had returned. It also was possible that someone who disliked Andrew's business dealings had killed the Bordens. To support this suggestion, it was reported that strangers had been seen in the neighborhood on the day of the murders. An ice cream peddler said he'd seen a woman who looked like Lizzie coming from the barn at about the time that Andrew was killed. This account supported Lizzie's claim that she had been in the barn when the second murder occurred. Neighbors and friends who had come into the Borden house immediately after the murders said there hadn't been a trace of blood on Lizzie's hands or dress.

The prosecution was able to make some points. A study of the Bordens' skulls revealed that the ax head found in the basement box fitted the wounds perfectly. In addition, experts testified that a woman of Lizzie's height and weight could have swung an ax with enough force to inflict the

Lizzie Borden and her lawyer,
ex-governor George Robinson

deadly wounds. It was noted that it was possible the blood could have splattered *away*, not *onto* her. As for the note Lizzie claimed had come for Abby from a sick friend, no such note was ever found. Nor did anyone come forward and say he'd delivered such a message.

The prosecution also pointed out that if a stranger had entered the Borden house, gone upstairs, and killed Abby, the murderer would then have had to hide for an hour and a half before killing Andrew (the time doctors said had passed between the murders). In a house with no hallways, where the doors between rooms were kept locked, this would not have been easy. Even if someone *had* managed to hide, what was the motive for the killings? Nothing was missing from the house.

It came time for the judge's final remarks or "charge" to the jury. Judge Dewey's words came close to asking the jury to find Lizzie not guilty, although he was not supposed to take sides. In fact, one of the newspapers covering the trial headlined its report: JUDGE'S CHARGE A PLEA FOR THE INNOCENT.[6]

The jurors who filed out of the courtroom to reach a verdict had many reasons to want to believe someone other than Lizzie was the murderer. If they found her guilty, they would, in a sense, find Fall River society guilty. As men, they had a stake in the belief then held by many: women were happiest at home where they could be taken care of by a father or a husband. If Lizzie—in the grip of unhappiness, jealousy, or other emotions—could kill her parents, then the New England world of the late 1800s would be turned upside down.

It took the jury only an hour to reach a verdict. Members later said they never reviewed any of the testimony or exhibits made available to them. Their vote was immediate and unanimous. Only for appearance's sake did they sit and wait for sixty minutes to pass. "Not guilty!" rang out in the courtroom. Lizzie began to cry as a cheer went up from the spectators.

The society that supported Lizzie during her trial backed

away from her quickly, however. It didn't look good when, soon after the trial, she and Emma used part of the money they'd inherited to buy a big house on The Hill. Lizzie even changed her first name to the more fashionable Lisbeth. Yet it's doubtful her new life satisfied her.

True, she went on trips to cities like Boston and New York. She owned a team of horses and a carriage and could go for drives in the country. But she wasn't a respected citizen. In Fall River, the name Borden now meant scandal.

Lizzie lived for thirty-five years after her parents' murders. Although for a time the sisters stayed together, Emma eventually moved out of the big house. Lizzie finally was truly alone. She died in June 1927 in Fall River. She'd never fully recovered from an operation the year before. Within ten days, Emma died in New Hampshire. Their deaths, however, didn't bring an end to the questions.

Many books and hundreds of articles have discussed the murders. Plays, a ballet, movies, and television productions went over and over the story. One author said that Lizzie had killed Andrew and Abby during a sick spell caused by a disease. Another suggested that Emma had somehow managed to sneak back home from her friend's house in Fairhaven and commit the murders. Still others were certain that Bridget was guilty. A researcher found that Andrew had been about to give Abby a farm; perhaps Lizzie had killed her parents in a rage over this gift. But no one could be completely sure that his or her story was the right one.

Before she died, Lizzie found company in her own backyard by feeding small animals and birds. When she drew up her will, she left a good deal of money to organizations that take care of lost or sick animals. She had been comforted by creatures that couldn't talk.

Maybe somewhere among the details surrounding the crimes, there are overlooked facts that would prove the murderer's identity without a doubt. Today, however, the verdict given at Lizzie's trial still stands. The killings of Andrew and Abby Borden are listed as unsolved.

SOURCE NOTES

Chapter 1
1. Follett, Ken and René Louis Maurice, *The Gentlemen of 16 July*, (New York, 1978), p. 4.
2. *Ibid.*, p. 8.
3. *Ibid.*, p. 7.
4. *Ibid.*, p. 8.
5. *Ibid.*, p. 9.
6. *Ibid.*, p. 10.
7. *Ibid.*, p. 12.
8. Robert Daley, "The Heist of the Century," *The New York Times Magazine*, (December 19, 1976), p. 93.
9. *Newsweek*, (March 21, 1977), p. 44.
10. Albert Spaggiari, *Fric-Frac*, (Boston, 1979), p. 252.
11. *Ibid.*, p. 254.
12. *Ibid.*, p. 256.

Chapter 2
1. Jay Robert Nash, *Among the Missing*, (New York, 1978), p. 174.
2. Gordon Manning, "The Most Tantalizing Disappearance of Our Time," *Colliers*, (July 29, 1950), p. 14.

3. Lee Churchill, *They Never Came Back*, (New York, 1960), p. 81.
4. Stella Crater with Oscar Fraley, *The Empty Robe*, (New York, 1961), p. 203.

Chapter 3
1. Gene Miller with Barbara Jane Mackle, *83 Hours Till Dawn*, (New York, 1971), p. 113.
2. Hank Messiek and Burt Goldblatt, *Kidnapping: The Illustrated History*, (New York, 1974), p. 139.
3. Miller, *83 Hours Till Dawn*, p. 394.

Chapter 4
1. *Crimes and Punishment*, vol. 8 (New York, 1985), p. 1260.
2. *The New York Times*, (January 10, 1957), p. 21.
3. *The New York Times*, (January 23, 1957), p. 18.
4. *Ibid.*
5. *The New York Times*, (February 16, 1957), p. 19.
6. *The New York Times*, (March 1, 1957), p. 46.
7. *The New York Times*, (January 9, 1976), p. 26.

Chapter 5
1. Popular rhyme revealing public opinion after Lizzie Borden's trial.
2. Joyce Williams, J. Eric Smithburn, Jeanne Peterson, eds., *Lizzie Borden: A Case Book of Family and Crime in the 1890s*, (Indiana, 1980), pp. 16–17.
3. Frank Spiering, *Lizzie*, (New York, 1984), p. 37.
4. Joyce Williams et al., *Lizzie Borden*, pp. 16–17.
5. Robert Sullivan, *Good-bye Lizzie Borden*, (Vermont, 1974), p. 51.
6. Ann Jones, *Women Who Kill*, (New York, 1980), p. 231.

FOR FURTHER READING

Crater, Stella with Fraley, Oscar. *The Empty Robe*. New York: Doubleday, 1961.

Follett, Ken and Maurice René Louis. *The Gentlemen of 16 July*. New York: Arbor House, 1978.

Green, Jonathan. *Greatest Criminals of All Time*. New York: Stein and Day, 1980.

Jeffers, H. Paul. *Wanted by the FBI*. New York: Hawthorn Books, 1972.

Lincoln, Victoria. *A Private Disgrace*. New York: G. P. Putnam's Sons, 1967.

Michaud, Stephen G. "The FBI's New Psyche Squad," *The New York Times Magazine*, October 26, 1986.

Miller, Gene with Mackle, Barbara Jane. *83 Hours Till Dawn*. New York: Doubleday, 1971.

Nash, Jay Robert. *Among the Missing*. New York: Simon and Schuster, 1978.

———. *Bloodletters and Badmen*. New York: Evans, 1973.

———. *Look for the Woman*. New York: Evans, 1981.

Sullivan, Robert. *Goodbye Lizzie Borden*. Brattleboro, Vermont: The Stephen Greene Press, 1974.

INDEX

Astronauts, 54–55
Atlanta Journal and Constitution, 54

Blackeit, Lucky, 36
Blaisdell, Judge, 81, 83, 84
Borden, Abby Durfee
    Gray, 73, 74, 76–78,
    82–84, 87–89
Borden, Alice, 74
Borden, Andrew, 73, 74,
    76–78, 81, 83, 84, 87–89
Borden, Emma, 74, 76, 77,
    79, 85, 89
Borden, Lizzie Andrew,
    74–79, 81–89
Borden, Sarah Morse, 74
Borman, Frank, 55
Bouazis, Richard, 19
Bowen, Doctor, 78, 79, 82

Brussel, James, 61, 63, 66,
    68
Buck, Reverend, 85

Churchill, Mrs., 79
Consolidated Edison, 57,
    59, 60, 65, 66, 68–71
Crater, Joseph Force, 21–
    29, 31–37
Crater, Stella, 22, 24–27,
    29, 31, 33, 34, 37
Criminal personality profi-
    lers, 72

de Gaulle, Charles, 15
Dewey, Justin, 85, 88

Eisemann Schier, Ruth,
    44, 45, 49–52, 54
Eisenmenger, Marie, 35

Ewald, George F., 24, 25

Fall River, Mass., 73–74,
  88, 89
Federal Bureau of Investigation (FBI), 41, 42, 44–
  47, 49, 50, 52, 54, 72

Giscard d'Estaing, Valéry,
  16
Grand Central Terminal,
  New York, 59, 60
Great Depression, 24
Guenet, Jacques, 9, 10

Holmes, C. J., 85
Holmes, Mrs. C. J., 85
Hoover, J. Edgar, 42, 47

Johnson, Frederick, 27–28

Kahler, Fred, 27, 31, 33
Kelly, Alice, 65–66, 70
Kelly, Mrs., 77–78
Klein, William, 29
Knowlton, Hosea, 83, 85
Krist, Gary Steven, 44–47,
  49–54

Life magazine, 34, 37
Lindbergh, Charles, 32, 52
Lindbergh Law, 52
Lowenthal, Leo, 32
Lussen, Frederick, 64

Mackle, Barbara Jane, 38–
  42, 44–48, 52–54

Mackle, Bobby, 39
Mackle, Jane, 39, 41, 54
Mackle, Robert, 39, 41, 42,
  44, 46, 47, 53
Mad Bomber, 56–72
Mara, Joseph, 28
Metesky, George, 56–72
Miami Herald, 54
Miller, Gene, 54
Missing Persons Bureau,
  New York, 32, 33
"Mooners," 61
Morse, John, 76, 79
Mullen, John, 70, 71
Mulrooney, Edward, 32
Murray, James, 68, 71

National Center for the
  Analysis of Violent
  Crime, 72
New York Herald Tribune,
  59
New York Journal-American,
  65, 68, 72
New York Public Library,
  56–59
Nice, France, 9–20

Paramount Theater, New
  York, 59
Pennsylvania Railroad Sta-
  tion, New York, 59–62
Peyat, Jacques, 19

Radio City Music Hall,
  New York, 60

RCA building, New York, 60

Rifkind, Simon, 31, 32

Ritz, Sally, 29, 30

Rizzi, Augustus, 27, 28

Robinson, George, 84–86

Russell, Alice, 79, 84

Ruth, Babe, 37

Seabury investigations, 25

Sewer Rats' Robbery, 9–20

Société Générale bank robbery, 9–20

Spaggiari, Albert, 15–20

Sullivan, Bridget, 74, 76–79, 81, 89

Tammany Hall, 25, 37

Wagner, Robert, 31

Walker, Jimmy, 25

Woodward, Stewart, 41, 54

ABOUT
THE AUTHOR

Barbara Johnston Adams' books for young people include *The Picture Life of Bill Cosby* and *Winners: Women and the Nobel Prize* (written under the pen name Barbara Shiels). Her articles have appeared in such magazines as *America* and *Topic* and in many newspapers, including *The Washington Post*.

A former editor of children's books in New York City, Ms. Adams now works as a freelance writer and consultant. She frequently is invited to talk about writing with students in public school classes. The idea for *Crime Mysteries* originated in these talks.